T&P BOOKS

THAI

VOCABULARY

FOR ENGLISH SPEAKERS

ENGLISH-
THAI

The most useful words
To expand your lexicon and sharpen
your language skills

9000 words

Thai vocabulary for English speakers - 9000 words

By Andrey Taranov

T&P Books vocabularies are intended for helping you learn, memorize and review foreign words. The dictionary is divided into themes, covering all major spheres of everyday activities, business, science, culture, etc.

The process of learning words using T&P Books' theme-based dictionaries gives you the following advantages:

- Correctly grouped source information predetermines success at subsequent stages of word memorization
- Availability of words derived from the same root allowing memorization of word units (rather than separate words)
- Small units of words facilitate the process of establishing associative links needed for consolidation of vocabulary
- Level of language knowledge can be estimated by the number of learned words

T&P Books Publishing
www.tpbooks.com

ISBN: 978-1-78767-229-1

This book is also available in E-book formats.
Please visit www.tpbooks.com or the major online bookstores.

THAI VOCABULARY
for English speakers

T&P Books vocabularies are intended to help you learn, memorize, and review foreign words. The vocabulary contains over 9000 commonly used words arranged thematically.

- Vocabulary contains the most commonly used words
- Recommended as an addition to any language course
- Meets the needs of beginners and advanced learners of foreign languages
- Convenient for daily use, revision sessions, and self-testing activities
- Allows you to assess your vocabulary

Special features of the vocabulary

- Words are organized according to their meaning, not alphabetically
- Words are presented in three columns to facilitate the reviewing and self-testing processes
- Words in groups are divided into small blocks to facilitate the learning process
- The vocabulary offers a convenient and simple transcription of each foreign word

The vocabulary has 256 topics including:

Basic Concepts, Numbers, Colors, Months, Seasons, Units of Measurement, Clothing & Accessories, Food & Nutrition, Restaurant, Family Members, Relatives, Character, Feelings, Emotions, Diseases, City, Town, Sightseeing, Shopping, Money, House, Home, Office, Working in the Office, Import & Export, Marketing, Job Search, Sports, Education, Computer, Internet, Tools, Nature, Countries, Nationalities and more ...

TABLE OF CONTENTS

Sports

Education

Arts

Rest. Entertainment. Travel

PRONUNCIATION GUIDE

T&P phonetic alphabet	Thai example	English example

Vowels

[a]	ห้า [hâ:] – hâa	shorter than in ask
[e]	เป็นลม [pen lom] – bpen lom	elm, medal
[i]	วินัย [wi? naj] – wí–nai	shorter than in feet
[o]	โกน [ko:n] – gohn	pod, John
[u]	ขุนเคือง [kʰùn kʰɯ:aŋ] – khùn kheuang	book
[aa]	ราคา [ra: kʰa:] – raa–khaa	calf, palm
[oo]	ภูมิใจ [pʰu:m tɕaj] – phoom jai	pool, room
[ee]	บัญชี [ban tɕʰi:] – ban–chee	feet, meter
[eu]	เดือน [dɯ:an] – deuan	similar to a longue schwa sound
[er]	เงิน [ŋɤn] – ngern	e in "the"
[ae]	แปล [plɛ:] – bplae	longer than bed, fell
[ay]	เลข [lê:k] – lâyk	longer than in bell
[ai]	ไปป์ [paj] – bpai	time, white
[oi]	โพย [pʰo:j] – phoi	oil, boy, point
[ya]	สัญญา [sǎn ja:] – sǎn–yaa	Kenya, piano
[oie]	อบเชย [ʔòp tɕʰɤ:j] – òp–choie	Combination [ə:i]
[ieo]	หน้าเขียว [nâ: si:aw] – nâa sieow	year, here

Initial consonant sounds

[b]	บาง [ba:ŋ] – baang	baby, book
[d]	สีแดง [sǐ: dɛ:ŋ] – sěe daeng	day, doctor
[f]	มันฝรั่ง [man fà ràŋ] – man fà–ràng	face, food
[h]	เฮลซิงกิ [he:n siŋ kì?] – hayn–sing–gì	home, have
[y]	ยี่สิบ [jî: sìp] – yêe sip	yes, New York
[g]	กรง [kroŋ] – grorng	game, gold
[kh]	เลขา [le: kʰǎ:] – lay–khǎa	work hard
[l]	เล็ก [lék] – lék	lace, people
[m]	เมลอน [me: lɔ:n] – may–lorn	magic, milk
[n]	หนัง [nǎŋ] – nǎng	name, normal
[ng]	เงือก [ŋɯ:ak] – ngêuak	English, ring
[bp]	เป็น [pen] – bpen	pencil, private
[ph]	เผา [pʰàw] – phào	top hat

T&P phonetic alphabet	Thai example	English example
[r]	เบอร์รี่ [bɤ: rîː] – ber–rêe	rice, radio
[s]	ซอน [sôn] – sôm	city, boss
[dt]	ดนตรี [don triː] – don–dtree	tourist, trip
[j]	ปั่นจั่น [pân tɕàn] – bpân jàn	cheer
[ch]	วิชา [wíʔ tɕʰaː] – wí–chaa	hitchhiker
[th]	แถว [tʰɛːw] – thăe	don't have
[w]	เคียว [kʰiːaw] – khieow	vase, winter

Final consonant sounds

[k]	แม่เหล็ก [mɛː lèk] – mâe lèk	clock, kiss
[m]	เพิ่ม [pʰɤːm] – phêrm	magic, milk
[n]	เนียน [niːan] – nian	name, normal
[ng]	เป็นห่วง [pen hùːaŋ] – bpen hùang	English, ring
[p]	ไม่ขยับ [mâj kʰà ja p] – mâi khà–yàp	pencil, private
[t]	ลูกเป็ด [lûːk pèt] – lôok bpèt	tourist, trip

Comments

Mid tone - [ā] การคูณ [gaan khon]
Low tone - [à] แจกจ่าย [jàek jàai]
Falling tone - [â] แต้ม [dtâem]
High tone - [á] แซ็กไซโฟน [sáek-soh-fohn]
Rising tone - [ǎ] เนินเขา [nern khǎo]

ABBREVIATIONS
used in the vocabulary

English abbreviations

ab.	-	about
adj	-	adjective
adv	-	adverb
anim.	-	animate
as adj	-	attributive noun used as adjective
e.g.	-	for example
etc.	-	et cetera
fam.	-	familiar
fem.	-	feminine
form.	-	formal
inanim.	-	inanimate
masc.	-	masculine
math	-	mathematics
mil.	-	military
n	-	noun
pl	-	plural
pron.	-	pronoun
sb	-	somebody
sing.	-	singular
sth	-	something
v aux	-	auxiliary verb
vi	-	intransitive verb
vi, vt	-	intransitive, transitive verb
vt	-	transitive verb

BASIC CONCEPTS

Basic concepts. Part 1

1. Pronouns

you	คุณ	khun
he	เขา	khăo
she	เธอ	ther
it	มัน	man
we	เรา	rao
you (to a group)	คุณทั้งหลาย	khun tháng lăai
you (polite, sing.)	คุณ	khun
you (polite, pl)	คุณทั้งหลาย	khun tháng lăai
they (masc.)	เขา	khăo
they (fem.)	เธอ	ther

2. Greetings. Salutations. Farewells

Hello! (fam.)	สวัสดี!	sà-wàt-dee
Hello! (form.)	สวัสดี ครับ/ค่ะ!	sà-wàt-dee khráp/khâ
Good morning!	อรุณสวัสดิ์!	a-run sà-wàt
Good afternoon!	สวัสดีตอนบ่าย	sà-wàt-dee dtorn-bàai
Good evening!	สวัสดีตอนค่ำ	sà-wàt-dee dtorn-khâm
to say hello	ทักทาย	thák thaai
Hi! (hello)	สวัสดี!	sà-wàt-dee
greeting (n)	คำทักทาย	kham thák thaai
to greet (vt)	ทักทาย	thák thaai
How are you? (form.)	คุณสบายดีไหม?	khun sà-baai dee măi
How are you? (fam.)	สบายดีไหม?	sà-baai dee măi
What's new?	มีอะไรใหม?	mee à-rai mài
Goodbye!	ลาก่อน!	laa gòrn
Bye!	บาย!	baai
See you soon!	พบกันใหม่	phóp gan mài
Farewell! (to a friend)	ลาก่อน!	laa gòrn
Farewell! (form.)	สวัสดี!	sà-wàt-dee
to say goodbye	บอกลา	bòrk laa
So long!	ลาก่อน!	laa gòrn
Thank you!	ขอบคุณ!	khòrp khun

Thank you very much!	ขอบคุณมาก!	khòrp khun mâak
You're welcome	ยินดีช่วย	yin dee chûay
Don't mention it!	ไม่เป็นไร	mâi bpen rai
It was nothing	ไม่เป็นไร	mâi bpen rai

Excuse me! (fam.)	ขอโทษที!	khŏr thôht thee
Excuse me! (form.)	ขอโทษ ครับ/คะ!	khŏr thôht khráp / khâ
to excuse (forgive)	ให้อภัย	hâi a-phai

to apologize (vi)	ขอโทษ	khŏr thôht
My apologies	ขอโทษ	khŏr thôht
I'm sorry!	ขอโทษ!	khŏr thôht
to forgive (vt)	อภัย	a-phai
It's okay! (that's all right)	ไม่เป็นไร!	mâi bpen rai
please (adv)	โปรด	bpròht

Don't forget!	อย่าลืม!	yàa leum
Certainly!	แน่นอน!	nâe norn
Of course not!	ไม่ใช่แน่!	mâi châi nâe
Okay! (I agree)	โอเค!	oh-khay
That's enough!	พอแล้ว	phor láew

3. How to address

Excuse me, ...	ขอโทษ	khŏr thôht
mister, sir	ทาน	thâan
ma'am	คุณ	khun
miss	คุณ	khun

young man	พ่อหนุ่ม	phôr nùm
young man (little boy, kid)	หนู	nŏo
miss (little girl)	หนู	nŏo

4. Cardinal numbers. Part 1

0 zero	ศูนย์	sŏon
1 one	หนึ่ง	nèung
2 two	สอง	sŏrng
3 three	สาม	săam

4 four	สี่	sèe
5 five	ห้า	hâa
6 six	หก	hòk

7 seven	เจ็ด	jèt
8 eight	แปด	bpàet
9 nine	เก้า	gâo

10 ten	สิบ	sìp
11 eleven	สิบเอ็ด	sìp èt
12 twelve	สิบสอง	sìp sŏrng
13 thirteen	สิบสาม	sìp săam
14 fourteen	สิบสี่	sìp sèe
15 fifteen	สิบห้า	sìp hâa
16 sixteen	สิบหก	sìp hòk
17 seventeen	สิบเจ็ด	sìp jèt
18 eighteen	สิบแปด	sìp bpàet
19 nineteen	สิบเกา	sìp gâo
20 twenty	ยี่สิบ	yêe sìp
21 twenty-one	ยี่สิบเอ็ด	yêe sìp èt
22 twenty-two	ยี่สิบสอง	yêe sìp sŏrng
23 twenty-three	ยี่สิบสาม	yêe sìp săam
30 thirty	สามสิบ	săam sìp
31 thirty-one	สามสิบเอ็ด	săam-sìp-èt
32 thirty-two	สามสิบสอง	săam-sìp-sŏrng
33 thirty-three	สามสิบสาม	săam-sìp-săam
40 forty	สี่สิบ	sèe sìp
41 forty-one	สี่สิบเอ็ด	sèe-sìp-èt
42 forty-two	สี่สิบสอง	sèe-sìp-sŏrng
43 forty-three	สี่สิบสาม	sèe-sìp-săam
50 fifty	ห้าสิบ	hâa sìp
51 fifty-one	ห้าสิบเอ็ด	hâa-sìp-èt
52 fifty-two	ห้าสิบสอง	hâa-sìp-sŏrng
53 fifty-three	หาสิบสาม	hâa-sìp-săam
60 sixty	หกสิบ	hòk sìp
61 sixty-one	หกสิบเอ็ด	hòk-sìp-èt
62 sixty-two	หกสิบสอง	hòk-sìp-sŏrng
63 sixty-three	หกสิบสาม	hòk-sìp-săam
70 seventy	เจ็ดสิบ	jèt sìp
71 seventy-one	เจ็ดสิบเอ็ด	jèt-sìp-èt
72 seventy-two	เจ็ดสิบสอง	jèt-sìp-sŏrng
73 seventy-three	เจ็ดสิบสาม	jèt-sìp-săam
80 eighty	แปดสิบ	bpàet sìp
81 eighty-one	แปดสิบเอ็ด	bpàet-sìp-èt
82 eighty-two	แปดสิบสอง	bpàet-sìp-sŏrng
83 eighty-three	แปดสิบสาม	bpàet-sìp-săam
90 ninety	เก้าสิบ	gâo sìp
91 ninety-one	เก้าสิบเอ็ด	gâo-sìp-èt
92 ninety-two	เก้าสิบสอง	gâo-sìp-sŏrng
93 ninety-three	เกาสิบสาม	gâo-sìp-săam

5. Cardinal numbers. Part 2

100 one hundred	หนึ่งร้อย	nèung rói
200 two hundred	สองร้อย	sŏrng rói
300 three hundred	สามร้อย	săam rói
400 four hundred	สี่ร้อย	sèe rói
500 five hundred	ห้าร้อย	hâa rói
600 six hundred	หกร้อย	hòk rói
700 seven hundred	เจ็ดร้อย	jèt rói
800 eight hundred	แปดร้อย	bpàet rói
900 nine hundred	เก้าร้อย	gâo rói
1000 one thousand	หนึ่งพัน	nèung phan
2000 two thousand	สองพัน	sŏrng phan
3000 three thousand	สามพัน	săam phan
10000 ten thousand	หนึ่งหมื่น	nèung mèun
one hundred thousand	หนึ่งแสน	nèung săen
million	ล้าน	láan
billion	พันล้าน	phan láan

6. Ordinal numbers

first (adj)	แรก	râek
second (adj)	ที่สอง	thêe sŏrng
third (adj)	ที่สาม	thêe săam
fourth (adj)	ที่สี่	thêe sèe
fifth (adj)	ที่ห้า	thêe hâa
sixth (adj)	ที่หก	thêe hòk
seventh (adj)	ที่เจ็ด	thêe jèt
eighth (adj)	ที่แปด	thêe bpàet
ninth (adj)	ที่เก้า	thêe gâo
tenth (adj)	ที่สิบ	thêe sìp

7. Numbers. Fractions

fraction	เศษส่วน	sàyt sùan
one half	หนึ่งส่วนสอง	nèung sùan sŏrng
one third	หนึ่งส่วนสาม	nèung sùan săam
one quarter	หนึ่งส่วนสี่	nèung sùan sèe
one eighth	หนึ่งส่วนแปด	nèung sùan bpàet
one tenth	หนึ่งส่วนสิบ	nèung sùan sìp
two thirds	สองส่วนสาม	sŏrng sùan săam
three quarters	สามส่วนสี่	săam sùan sèe

8. Numbers. Basic operations

subtraction	การลบ	gaan lóp
to subtract (vi, vt)	ลบ	lóp
division	การหาร	gaan hǎan
to divide (vt)	หาร	hǎan
addition	การบวก	gaan bùak
to add up (vt)	บวก	bùak
to add (vi, vt)	เพิ่ม	phêrm
multiplication	การคูณ	gaan khon
to multiply (vt)	คูณ	khoon

9. Numbers. Miscellaneous

digit, figure	ตัวเลข	dtua lâyk
number	เลข	lâyk
numeral	ตัวเลข	dtua lâyk
minus sign	เครื่องหมายลบ	khrêuang mǎai lóp
plus sign	เครื่องหมายบวก	khrêuang mǎai bùak
formula	สูตร	sòot
calculation	การนับ	gaan náp
to count (vi, vt)	นับ	náp
to count up	นับ	náp
to compare (vt)	เปรียบเทียบ	bprìap thîap
How much?	เท่าไหร่?	thâo rài
How many?	กี่...?	gèe...?
sum, total	ผลรวม	phǒn ruam
result	ผลลัพธ์	phǒn láp
remainder	ที่เหลือ	thêe lěua
a few (e.g., ~ years ago)	สองสาม	sǒrng sǎam
little (I had ~ time)	นิดหนอย	nít nòi
few (I have ~ friends)	นอย	nói
the rest	ที่เหลือ	thêe lěua
one and a half	หนึ่งครึ่ง	nèung khrêung
dozen	โหล	lǒh
in half (adv)	เป็นสองส่วน	bpen sǒrng sùan
equally (evenly)	เทาเทียมกัน	thâo thiam gan
half	ครึ่ง	khrêung
time (three ~s)	ครั้ง	khráng

10. The most important verbs. Part 1

to advise (vt)	แนะนำ	náe nam
to agree (say yes)	เห็นด้วย	hěn dûay
to answer (vi, vt)	ตอบ	dtòrp
to apologize (vi)	ขอโทษ	khǒr thôht
to arrive (vi)	มา	maa
to ask (~ oneself)	ถาม	thǎam
to ask (~ sb to do sth)	ขอ	khǒr
to be (vi)	เป็น	bpen
to be afraid	กลัว	glua
to be hungry	หิว	hǐw
to be interested in ...	สนใจใน	sǒn jai nai
to be needed	ต้องการ	dtôrng gaan
to be surprised	ประหลาดใจ	bprà-làat jai
to be thirsty	กระหายน้ำ	grà-hǎai náam
to begin (vt)	เริ่ม	rêrm
to belong to ...	เป็นของของ...	bpen khǒrng khǒrng...
to boast (vi)	โอ้อวด	ôh ùat
to break (split into pieces)	แตก	dtàek
to call (~ for help)	เรียก	rîak
can (v aux)	สามารถ	sǎa-mâat
to catch (vt)	จับ	jàp
to change (vt)	เปลี่ยน	bplìan
to choose (select)	เลือก	lêuak
to come down (the stairs)	ลง	long
to compare (vt)	เปรียบเทียบ	bprìap thîap
to complain (vi, vt)	บ่น	bòn
to confuse (mix up)	สับสน	sàp sǒn
to continue (vt)	ทำต่อไป	tham dtòr bpai
to control (vt)	ควบคุม	khûap khum
to cook (dinner)	ทำอาหาร	tham aa-hǎan
to cost (vt)	ราคา	raa-khaa
to count (add up)	นับ	náp
to count on ...	พึ่งพา	phêung phaa
to create (vt)	สร้าง	sâang
to cry (weep)	ร้องไห้	rórng hâi

11. The most important verbs. Part 2

to deceive (vi, vt)	หลอก	lòrk
to decorate (tree, street)	ประดับ	bprà-dàp
to defend (a country, etc.)	ปกป้อง	bpòk bpôrng

| to demand (request firmly) | เรียกร้อง | rîak rórng |
| to dig (vt) | ขุด | khùt |

to discuss (vt)	หารือ	hǎa-reu
to do (vt)	ทำ	tham
to doubt (have doubts)	สงสัย	sǒng-sǎi
to drop (let fall)	ทิ้งให้ตก	thíng hâi dtòk
to enter (room, house, etc.)	เข้า	khâo

to excuse (forgive)	ให้อภัย	hâi a-phai
to exist (vi)	มีอยู่	mee yòo
to expect (foresee)	คาดหวัง	khâat wǎng
to explain (vt)	อธิบาย	à-thí-baai
to fall (vi)	ตก	dtòk

to find (vt)	พบ	phóp
to finish (vt)	จบ	jòp
to fly (vi)	บิน	bin
to follow … (come after)	ไปตาม...	bpai dtaam...
to forget (vi, vt)	ลืม	leum

to forgive (vt)	ให้อภัย	hâi a-phai
to give (vt)	ให้	hâi
to give a hint	บอกใบ้	bòrk bâi
to go (on foot)	ไป	bpai

to go for a swim	ไปว่ายน้ำ	bpai wâai náam
to go out (for dinner, etc.)	ออกไป	òrk bpai
to guess (the answer)	คาดเดา	khâat dao

to have (vt)	มี	mee
to have breakfast	ทานอาหารเช้า	thaan aa-hǎan cháo
to have dinner	ทานอาหารเย็น	thaan aa-hǎan yen
to have lunch	ทานอาหารเที่ยง	thaan aa-hǎan thîang
to hear (vt)	ได้ยิน	dâai yin

to help (vt)	ช่วย	chûay
to hide (vt)	ซ่อน	sôrn
to hope (vi, vt)	หวัง	wǎng
to hunt (vi, vt)	ล่า	lâa
to hurry (vi)	รีบ	rêep

12. The most important verbs. Part 3

to inform (vt)	แจ้ง	jâeng
to insist (vi, vt)	ยืนยัน	yeun yan
to insult (vt)	ดูถูก	doo thòok
to invite (vt)	เชิญ	chern
to joke (vi)	ล้อเล่น	lór lên

to keep (vt)	รักษา	rák-săa
to keep silent, to hush	นิ่งเงียบ	nîng ngîap
to kill (vt)	ฆ่า	khâa
to know (sb)	รู้จัก	róo jàk
to know (sth)	รู้	róo
to laugh (vi)	หัวเราะ	hŭa rór
to liberate (city, etc.)	ปลดปล่อย	bplòt bplòi
to like (I like ...)	ชอบ	chôrp
to look for ... (search)	หา	hăa
to love (sb)	รัก	rák
to make a mistake	ทำผิด	tham phìt
to manage, to run	บริหาร	bor-rí-hăan
to mean (signify)	หมาย	măai
to mention (talk about)	กลาวถึง	glàao thĕung
to miss (school, etc.)	พลาด	phlâat
to notice (see)	สังเกต	săng-gàyt
to object (vi, vt)	ค้าน	kháan
to observe (see)	สังเกตการณ์	săng-gàyt gaan
to open (vt)	เปิด	bpèrt
to order (meal, etc.)	สั่ง	sàng
to order (mil.)	สังการ	sàng gaan
to own (possess)	เป็นเจ้าของ	bpen jâo khŏrng
to participate (vi)	มีส่วนร่วม	mee sùan rûam
to pay (vi, vt)	จาย	jàai
to permit (vt)	อนุญาต	a-nú-yâat
to plan (vt)	วางแผน	waang phăen
to play (children)	เลน	lên
to pray (vi, vt)	ภาวนา	phaa-wá-naa
to prefer (vt)	ชอบ	chôrp
to promise (vt)	สัญญา	săn-yaa
to pronounce (vt)	ออกเสียง	òrk sĭang
to propose (vt)	เสนอ	sà-nĕr
to punish (vt)	ลงโทษ	long thôht

13. The most important verbs. Part 4

to read (vi, vt)	อ่าน	àan
to recommend (vt)	แนะนำ	náe nam
to refuse (vi, vt)	ปฏิเสธ	bpà-dtì-sàyt
to regret (be sorry)	เสียใจ	sĭa jai
to rent (sth from sb)	เชา	châo
to repeat (say again)	ซ้ำ	sám
to reserve, to book	จอง	jorng
to run (vi)	วิ่ง	wîng

to save (rescue)	กู้	gôo
to say (~ thank you)	บอก	bòrk
to scold (vt)	ดุด่า	dù dàa
to see (vt)	เห็น	hěn
to sell (vt)	ขาย	khǎai
to send (vt)	ส่ง	sòng
to shoot (vi)	ยิง	ying
to shout (vi)	ตะโกน	dtà-gohn
to show (vt)	แสดง	sà-daeng
to sign (document)	ลงนาม	long naam
to sit down (vi)	นั่ง	nâng
to smile (vi)	ยิ้ม	yím
to speak (vi, vt)	พูด	phôot
to steal (money, etc.)	ขโมย	khà-moi
to stop (for pause, etc.)	หยุด	yùt
to stop (please ~ calling me)	หยุด	yùt
to study (vt)	เรียน	rian
to swim (vi)	ว่ายน้ำ	wâai náam
to take (vt)	เอา	ao
to think (vi, vt)	คิด	khít
to threaten (vt)	ขู่	khòo
to touch (with hands)	แตะต้อง	dtàe dtôrng
to translate (vt)	แปล	bplae
to trust (vt)	เชื่อ	chêua
to try (attempt)	พยายาม	phá-yaa-yaam
to turn (e.g., ~ left)	เลี้ยว	líeow
to underestimate (vt)	ดูถูก	doo thòok
to understand (vt)	เข้าใจ	khâo jai
to unite (vt)	สมาน	sà-mǎan
to wait (vt)	รอ	ror
to want (wish, desire)	ต้องการ	dtôrng gaan
to warn (vt)	เตือน	dteuan
to work (vi)	ทำงาน	tham ngaan
to write (vt)	เขียน	khǐan
to write down	จด	jòt

14. Colors

color	สี	sěe
shade (tint)	สีอ่อน	sěe òrn
hue	สีสัน	sěe sǎn
rainbow	สายรุ้ง	sǎai rúng

white (adj)	สีขาว	sěe khǎao
black (adj)	สีดำ	sěe dam
gray (adj)	สีเทา	sěe thao

green (adj)	สีเขียว	sěe khǐeow
yellow (adj)	สีเหลือง	sěe lěuang
red (adj)	สีแดง	sěe daeng

blue (adj)	สีน้ำเงิน	sěe nám ngern
light blue (adj)	สีฟ้า	sěe fáa
pink (adj)	สีชมพู	sěe chom-poo
orange (adj)	สีส้ม	sěe sôm
violet (adj)	สีม่วง	sěe mûang
brown (adj)	สีน้ำตาล	sěe nám dtaan

| golden (adj) | สีทอง | sěe thorng |
| silvery (adj) | สีเงิน | sěe ngern |

beige (adj)	สีน้ำตาลอ่อน	sěe nám dtaan òrn
cream (adj)	สีครีม	sěe khreem
turquoise (adj)	สีเขียวแกมน้ำเงิน	sěe khǐeow gaem náam ngern
cherry red (adj)	สีแดงเชอร์รี่	sěe daeng cher-rêe
lilac (adj)	สีม่วงอ่อน	sěe mûang-òrn
crimson (adj)	สีแดงเข้ม	sěe daeng khâym

light (adj)	อ่อน	òrn
dark (adj)	แก่	gàe
bright, vivid (adj)	สด	sòt

colored (pencils)	สี	sěe
color (e.g., ~ film)	สี	sěe
black-and-white (adj)	ขาวดำ	khǎao-dam
plain (one-colored)	สีเดียว	sěe dieow
multicolored (adj)	หลากสี	làak sěe

15. Questions

Who?	ใคร?	khrai
What?	อะไร?	a-rai
Where? (at, in)	ที่ไหน?	thêe nǎi
Where (to)?	ที่ไหน?	thêe nǎi
From where?	จากที่ไหน?	jàak thêe nǎi
When?	เมื่อไหร่?	mêua rài
Why? (What for?)	ทำไม?	tham-mai
Why? (~ are you crying?)	ทำไม?	tham-mai

What for?	เพื่ออะไร?	phêua a-rai
How? (in what way)	อย่างไร?	yàang rai
What? (What kind of ...?)	อะไร?	a-rai

Which?	ไหน?	nǎi
To whom?	สำหรับใคร?	sǎm-ràp khrai
About whom?	เกี่ยวกับใคร?	gìeow gàp khrai
About what?	เกี่ยวกับอะไร?	gìeow gàp a-rai
With whom?	กับใคร?	gàp khrai

How many?	กี่...?	gèe...?
How much?	เท่าไหร่?	thâo rài
Whose?	ของใคร?	khǒrng khrai

16. Prepositions

with (accompanied by)	กับ	gàp
without	ปราศจาก	bpràat-sà-jàak
to (indicating direction)	ไปที่	bpai thêe
about (talking ~ ...)	เกี่ยวกับ	gìeow gàp
before (in time)	ก่อน	gòrn
in front of ...	หน้า	nâa

under (beneath, below)	ใต้	dtâi
above (over)	เหนือ	něua
on (atop)	บน	bon
from (off, out of)	จาก	jàak
of (made from)	ทำใช้	tham chái

| in (e.g., ~ ten minutes) | ใน | nai |
| over (across the top of) | ข้าม | khâam |

17. Function words. Adverbs. Part 1

Where? (at, in)	ที่ไหน?	thêe nǎi
here (adv)	ที่นี่	thêe nêe
there (adv)	ที่นั่น	thêe nân

| somewhere (to be) | ที่ใดที่หนึ่ง | thêe dai thêe nèung |
| nowhere (not in any place) | ไม่มีที่ไหน | mâi mee thêe nǎi |

| by (near, beside) | ข้าง | khâang |
| by the window | ข้างหน้าต่าง | khâang nâa dtàang |

Where (to)?	ที่ไหน?	thêe nǎi
here (e.g., come ~!)	ที่นี่	thêe nêe
there (e.g., to go ~)	ที่นั่น	thêe nân
from here (adv)	จากที่นี่	jàak thêe nêe
from there (adv)	จากที่นั่น	jàak thêe nân

| close (adv) | ใกล้ | glâi |
| far (adv) | ไกล | glai |

near (e.g., ~ Paris)	ใกล้	glâi
nearby (adv)	ใกล้ๆ	glâi glâi
not far (adv)	ไม่ไกล	mâi glai
left (adj)	ซ้าย	sáai
on the left	ทางซ้าย	khâang sáai
to the left	ซ้าย	sáai
right (adj)	ขวา	khwǎa
on the right	ทางขวา	khâang kwǎa
to the right	ขวา	khwǎa
in front (adv)	ข้างหน้า	khâang nâa
front (as adj)	หน้า	nâa
ahead (the kids ran ~)	หน้า	nâa
behind (adv)	ข้างหลัง	khâang lǎng
from behind	จากข้างหลัง	jàak khâang lǎng
back (towards the rear)	หลัง	lǎng
middle	กลาง	glaang
in the middle	ตรงกลาง	dtrorng glaang
at the side	ข้าง	khâang
everywhere (adv)	ทุกที่	thúk thêe
around (in all directions)	รอบ	rôrp
from inside	จากข้างใน	jàak khâang nai
somewhere (to go)	ที่ไหน	thêe nǎi
straight (directly)	ตรงไป	dtrorng bpai
back (e.g., come ~)	กลับ	glàp
from anywhere	จากที่ใด	jàak thêe dai
from somewhere	จากที่ใด	jàak thêe dai
firstly (adv)	ข้อที่หนึ่ง	khôr thêe nèung
secondly (adv)	ขอที่สอง	khôr thêe sǒrng
thirdly (adv)	ขอที่สาม	khôr thêe sǎam
suddenly (adv)	ในทันที	nai than thee
at first (in the beginning)	ตอนแรก	dtorn-râek
for the first time	เป็นครั้งแรก	bpen khráng râek
long before ...	นานก่อน	naan gòrn
anew (over again)	ใหม่	mài
for good (adv)	ให้จบสิ้น	hâi jòp sîn
never (adv)	ไม่เคย	mâi khoie
again (adv)	อีกครั้งหนึ่ง	èek khráng nèung
now (at present)	ตอนนี้	dtorn-née
often (adv)	บอย	bòi
then (adv)	เวลานั้น	way-laa nán
urgently (quickly)	อย่างเรงด่วน	yàang râyng dùan

usually (adv)	มักจะ	mák jà
by the way, ...	อนึ่ง	à-nèung
possibly	เป็นไปได้	bpen bpai dâai
probably (adv)	อาจจะ	àat jà
maybe (adv)	อาจจะ	àat jà
besides ...	นอกจากนั้น...	nôrk jàak nán...
that's why ...	นั่นเป็นเหตุผลที่...	nân bpen hàyt phŏn thêe...
in spite of ...	แม้ว่า...	máe wâa...
thanks to ...	เนื่องจาก...	nêuang jàak...
what (pron.)	อะไร	a-rai
that (conj.)	ที่	thêe
something	อะไร	a-rai
anything (something)	อะไรก็ตาม	a-rai gôr dtaam
nothing	ไม่มีอะไร	mâi mee a-rai
who (pron.)	ใคร	khrai
someone	บางคน	baang khon
somebody	บางคน	baang khon
nobody	ไม่มีใคร	mâi mee khrai
nowhere (a voyage to ~)	ไม่ไปไหน	mâi bpai năi
nobody's	ไม่เป็นของของใคร	mâi bpen khŏrng khŏrng khrai
somebody's	ของคนหนึ่ง	khŏrng khon nèung
so (I'm ~ glad)	มาก	mâak
also (as well)	ด้วย	dûay
too (as well)	ด้วย	dûay

18. Function words. Adverbs. Part 2

Why?	ทำไม?	tham-mai
for some reason	เพราะเหตุผลอะไร	phrór hàyt phŏn à-rai
because ...	เพราะว่า...	phrór wâa
for some purpose	ด้วยจุดประสงค์อะไร	dûay jùt bprà-sŏng a-rai
and	และ	láe
or	หรือ	rĕu
but	แต่	dtàe
for (e.g., ~ me)	สำหรับ	săm-ràp
too (~ many people)	เกินไป	gern bpai
only (exclusively)	เท่านั้น	thâo nán
exactly (adv)	ตรง	dtrorng
about (more or less)	ประมาณ	bprà-maan
approximately (adv)	ประมาณ	bprà-maan
approximate (adj)	ประมาณ	bprà-maan
almost (adv)	เกือบ	gèuap

the rest	ที่เหลือ	thêe lĕua
the other (second)	อีก	èek
other (different)	อื่น	èun
each (adj)	ทุก	thúk
any (no matter which)	ใดๆ	dai dai
many (adj)	หลาย	lăai
much (adv)	มาก	mâak
many people	หลายคน	lăai khon
all (everyone)	ทุกๆ	thúk thúk

in return for …	ที่จะเปลี่ยนเป็น	thêe jà bplìan bpen
in exchange (adv)	แทน	thaen
by hand (made)	ใช้มือ	chái meu
hardly (negative opinion)	แทบจะไม่	thâep jà mâi

probably (adv)	อาจจะ	àat jà
on purpose (intentionally)	โดยเจตนา	doi jàyt-dtà-naa
by accident (adv)	บังเอิญ	bang-ern

very (adv)	มาก	mâak
for example (adv)	ยกตัวอย่าง	yók dtua yàang
between	ระหว่าง	rá-wàang
among	ท่ามกลาง	tâam-glaang
so much (such a lot)	มากมาย	mâak maai
especially (adv)	โดยเฉพาะ	doi chà-phór

Basic concepts. Part 2

19. Opposites

rich (adj)	รวย	ruay
poor (adj)	จน	jon
ill, sick (adj)	เจ็บป่วย	jèp bpùay
well (not sick)	สบายดี	sà-baai dee
big (adj)	ใหญ่	yài
small (adj)	เล็ก	lék
quickly (adv)	อย่างเร็ว	yàang reo
slowly (adv)	อยางชา	yàang cháa
fast (adj)	เร็ว	reo
slow (adj)	ชา	cháa
glad (adj)	ยินดี	yin dee
sad (adj)	เสียใจ	sĭa jai
together (adv)	ด้วยกัน	dûay gan
separately (adv)	ตางหาก	dtàang hàak
aloud (to read)	ออกเสียง	òrk sĭang
silently (to oneself)	อย่างเงียบๆ	yàang ngîap ngîap
tall (adj)	สูง	sŏong
low (adj)	ต่ำ	dtàm
deep (adj)	ลึก	léuk
shallow (adj)	ตื้น	dtêun
yes	ใช่	châi
no	ไม่ใช่	mâi châi
distant (in space)	ไกล	glai
nearby (adj)	ใกล	glâi
far (adv)	ไกล	glai
nearby (adv)	ใกล้ๆ	glâi glâi
long (adj)	ยาว	yaao
short (adj)	สั้น	sân
good (kindhearted)	ใจดี	jai dee
evil (adj)	เลวร้าย	leo ráai

married (adj)	แต่งงานแล้ว	dtàeng ngaan láew
single (adj)	เป็นโสด	bpen sòht
to forbid (vt)	ห้าม	hâam
to permit (vt)	อนุญาต	a-nú-yâat
end	จบ	jòp
beginning	จุดเริ่มต้น	jùt rêrm-dtôn
left (adj)	ซ้าย	sáai
right (adj)	ขวา	khwǎa
first (adj)	แรก	râek
last (adj)	สุดท้าย	sùt tháai
crime	อาชญากรรม	àat-yaa-gam
punishment	การลงโทษ	gaan long thôht
to order (vt)	สั่ง	sàng
to obey (vi, vt)	เชื่อฟัง	chêua fang
straight (adj)	ตรง	dtrorng
curved (adj)	โค้ง	khóhng
paradise	สวรรค์	sà-wǎn
hell	นรก	ná-rók
to be born	เกิด	gèrt
to die (vi)	ตาย	dtaai
strong (adj)	แข็งแรง	khǎeng raeng
weak (adj)	อ่อนแอ	òrn ae
old (adj)	แก่	gàe
young (adj)	หนุ่ม	nùm
old (adj)	เก่าแก่	gào gàe
new (adj)	ใหม่	mài
hard (adj)	แข็ง	khǎeng
soft (adj)	อ่อน	òrn
warm (tepid)	อุ่น	ùn
cold (adj)	หนาว	nǎao
fat (adj)	อ้วน	ûan
thin (adj)	ผอม	phǒrm
narrow (adj)	แคบ	khâep
wide (adj)	กว้าง	gwâang
good (adj)	ดี	dee
bad (adj)	ไม่ดี	mâi dee

| brave (adj) | กล้าหาญ | glâa hǎan |
| cowardly (adj) | ขี้ขลาด | khêe khlàat |

20. Weekdays

Monday	วันจันทร์	wan jan
Tuesday	วันอังคาร	wan ang-khaan
Wednesday	วันพุธ	wan phút
Thursday	วันพฤหัสบดี	wan phá-réu-hàt-sà-bor-dee
Friday	วันศุกร์	wan sùk
Saturday	วันเสาร์	wan sǎo
Sunday	วันอาทิตย์	wan aa-thít
today (adv)	วันนี้	wan née
tomorrow (adv)	พรุ่งนี้	phrûng-née
the day after tomorrow	วันมะรืนนี้	wan má-reun née
yesterday (adv)	เมื่อวานนี้	mêua waan née
the day before yesterday	เมื่อวานซืนนี้	mêua waan-seun née
day	วัน	wan
working day	วันทำงาน	wan tham ngaan
public holiday	วันนักขัตฤกษ์	wan nák-khàt-rêrk
day off	วันหยุด	wan yùt
weekend	วันสุดสัปดาห์	wan sùt sàp-daa
all day long	ทั้งวัน	tháng wan
the next day (adv)	วันรุ่งขึ้น	wan rûng khêun
two days ago	สองวันก่อน	sǒrng wan gòrn
the day before	วันก่อนหน้านี้	wan gòrn nâa née
daily (adj)	รายวัน	raai wan
every day (adv)	ทุกวัน	thúk wan
week	สัปดาห์	sàp-daa
last week (adv)	สัปดาห์ก่อน	sàp-daa gòrn
next week (adv)	สัปดาห์หน้า	sàp-daa nâa
weekly (adj)	รายสัปดาห์	raai sàp-daa
every week (adv)	ทุกสัปดาห์	thúk sàp-daa
twice a week	สัปดาห์ละสองครั้ง	sàp-daa lá sǒrng khráng
every Tuesday	ทุกวันอังคาร	túk wan ang-khaan

21. Hours. Day and night

morning	เช้า	cháo
in the morning	ตอนเช้า	dtorn cháo
noon, midday	เที่ยงวัน	thîang wan
in the afternoon	ตอนบ่าย	dtorn bàai
evening	เย็น	yen

in the evening	ตอนเย็น	dtorn yen
night	คืน	kheun
at night	กลางคืน	glaang kheun
midnight	เที่ยงคืน	thîang kheun
second	วินาที	wí-naa-thee
minute	นาที	naa-thee
hour	ชั่วโมง	chûa mohng
half an hour	ครึ่งชั่วโมง	khrêung chûa mohng
a quarter-hour	สิบห้านาที	sìp hâa naa-thee
fifteen minutes	สิบห้านาที	sìp hâa naa-thee
24 hours	24 ชั่วโมง	yêe sìp sèe · chûa mohng
sunrise	พระอาทิตย์ขึ้น	phrá aa-thít khêun
dawn	ใกล้รุ่ง	glâi rûng
early morning	เช้า	cháo
sunset	พระอาทิตย์ตก	phrá aa-thít dtòk
early in the morning	ตอนเช้า	dtorn cháo
this morning	เช้านี้	cháo née
tomorrow morning	พรุ่งนี้เช้า	phrûng-née cháo
this afternoon	บ่ายนี้	bàai née
in the afternoon	ตอนบ่าย	dtorn bàai
tomorrow afternoon	พรุ่งนี้บ่าย	phrûng-née bàai
tonight (this evening)	คืนนี้	kheun née
tomorrow night	คืนพรุ่งนี้	kheun phrûng-née
at 3 o'clock sharp	3 โมงตรง	săam mohng dtrorng
about 4 o'clock	ประมาณ 4 โมง	bprà-maan sèe mohng
by 12 o'clock	ภายใน 12 โมง	phaai nai sìp sŏng mohng
in 20 minutes	อีก 20 นาที	èek yêe sìp naa-thee
in an hour	อีกหนึ่งชั่วโมง	èek nèung chûa mohng
on time (adv)	ทันเวลา	than way-laa
a quarter to …	อีกสิบห้านาที	èek sìp hâa naa-thee
within an hour	ภายในหนึ่ง	phaai nai nèung
	ชั่วโมง	chûa mohng
every 15 minutes	ทุก 15 นาที	thúk sìp hâa naa-thee
round the clock	ทั้งวัน	tháng wan

22. Months. Seasons

January	มกราคม	mók-gà-raa khom
February	กุมภาพันธ์	gum-phaa phan
March	มีนาคม	mee-naa khom
April	เมษายน	may-săa-yon
May	พฤษภาคม	phréut-sà-phaa khom
June	มิถุนายน	mí-thù-naa-yon

July	กรกฎาคม	gà-rá-gà-daa-khom
August	สิงหาคม	sǐng hǎa khom
September	กันยายน	gan-yaa-yon
October	ตุลาคม	dtù-laa khom
November	พฤศจิกายน	phréut-sà-jì-gaa-yon
December	ธันวาคม	than-waa khom

spring	ฤดูใบไม้ผลิ	réu-doo bai máai phlì
in spring	ฤดูใบไม้ผลิ	réu-doo bai máai phlì
spring (as adj)	ฤดูใบไม้ผลิ	réu-doo bai máai phlì

summer	ฤดูร้อน	réu-doo rórn
in summer	ฤดูร้อน	réu-doo rórn
summer (as adj)	ฤดูร้อน	réu-doo rórn

fall	ฤดูใบไม้ร่วง	réu-doo bai máai rûang
in fall	ฤดูใบไม้ร่วง	réu-doo bai máai rûang
fall (as adj)	ฤดูใบไม้ร่วง	réu-doo bai máai rûang

winter	ฤดูหนาว	réu-doo nǎao
in winter	ฤดูหนาว	réu-doo nǎao
winter (as adj)	ฤดูหนาว	réu-doo nǎao

month	เดือน	deuan
this month	เดือนนี้	deuan née
next month	เดือนหน้า	deuan nâa
last month	เดือนที่แล้ว	deuan thêe láew

a month ago	หนึ่งเดือน ก่อนหน้านี้	nèung deuan gòrn nâa née
in a month (a month later)	อีกหนึ่งเดือน	èek nèung deuan
in 2 months (2 months later)	อีกสองเดือน	èek sǒrng deuan
the whole month	ทั้งเดือน	tháng deuan
all month long	ตลอดทั้งเดือน	dtà-lòrt tháng deuan

monthly (~ magazine)	รายเดือน	raai deuan
monthly (adv)	ทุกเดือน	thúk deuan
every month	ทุกเดือน	thúk deuan
twice a month	เดือนละสองครั้ง	deuan lá sǒrng kráng

year	ปี	bpee
this year	ปีนี้	bpee née
next year	ปีหน้า	bpee nâa
last year	ปีที่แล้ว	bpee thêe láew

a year ago	หนึ่งปีก่อน	nèung bpee gòrn
in a year	อีกหนึ่งปี	èek nèung bpee
in two years	อีกสองปี	èek sǒng bpee
the whole year	ทั้งปี	tháng bpee
all year long	ตลอดทั้งปี	dtà-lòrt tháng bpee

every year	ทุกปี	thúk bpee
annual (adj)	รายปี	raai bpee
annually (adv)	ทุกปี	thúk bpee
4 times a year	ปีละสี่ครั้ง	bpee lá sèe kráng

date (e.g., today's ~)	วันที่	wan thêe
date (e.g., ~ of birth)	วันเดือนปี	wan deuan bpee
calendar	ปฏิทิน	bpà-dtì-thin

half a year	ครึ่งปี	khrêung bpee
six months	หกเดือน	hòk deuan
season (summer, etc.)	ฤดูกาล	réu-doo gaan
century	ศตวรรษ	sà-dtà-wát

23. Time. Miscellaneous

time	เวลา	way-laa
moment	ครูหนึ่ง	khrôo nèung
instant (n)	ครูเดียว	khrôo dieow
instant (adj)	เพียงครูเดียว	phiang khrôo dieow
lapse (of time)	ช่วงเวลา	chûang way-laa
life	ชีวิต	chee-wít
eternity	ตลอดกาล	dtà-lòrt gaan

epoch	สมัย	sà-mǎi
era	ยุค	yúk
cycle	วัฏจักร	wát-dtà-jàk
period	ช่วง	chûang
term (short-~)	ระยะเวลา	rá-yá way-laa

the future	อนาคต	a-naa-khót
future (as adj)	อนาคตุ	a-naa-khót
next time	ครั้งหน้า	khráng nâa
the past	อดีต	a-dèet
past (recent)	ที่ผ่านมา	thêe phàan maa
last time	ครั้งที่แล้ว	khráng thêe láew

later (adv)	ภายหลัง	phaai lǎng
after (prep.)	หลังจาก	lǎng jàak
nowadays (adv)	เวลานี้	way-laa née
now (at this moment)	ตอนนี้	dtorn-née
immediately (adv)	ทันที	than thee
soon (adv)	อีกไม่นาน	èek mâi naan
in advance (beforehand)	ล่วงหน้า	lûang nâa

a long time ago	นานมาแล้ว	naan maa láew
recently (adv)	เมื่อเร็ว ๆ นี้	mêua reo reo née
destiny	ชะตากรรม	chá-dtaa gam
memories (childhood ~)	ความทรงจำ	khwaam song jam
archives	จดหมายเหตุ	jòt mǎai hàyt

during ...	ระหว่าง...	rá-wàang...
long, a long time (adv)	นาน	naan
not long (adv)	ไม่นาน	mâi naan
early (in the morning)	ล่วงหน้า	lûang nâa
late (not early)	ช้า	cháa

forever (for good)	ตลอดกาล	dtà-lòrt gaan
to start (begin)	เริ่ม	rêrm
to postpone (vt)	เลื่อน	lêuan

at the same time	ในเวลาเดียวกัน	nai way-laa dieow gan
permanently (adv)	อย่างถาวร	yàang thǎa-won
constant (noise, pain)	ต่อเนื่อง	dtòr nêuang
temporary (adj)	ชั่วคราว	chûa khraao

sometimes (adv)	บางครั้ง	baang khráng
rarely (adv)	ไม่บ่อย	mâi bòi
often (adv)	บ่อย	bòi

24. Lines and shapes

square	สี่เหลี่ยมจัตุรัส	sèe lìam jàt-dtù-ràt
square (as adj)	สี่เหลี่ยมจัตุรัส	sèe lìam jàt-dtù-ràt
circle	วงกลม	wong glom
round (adj)	กลม	glom
triangle	รูปสามเหลี่ยม	rôop sǎam lìam
triangular (adj)	สามเหลี่ยม	sǎam lìam

oval	รูปกลมรี	rôop glom ree
oval (as adj)	กลมรี	glom ree
rectangle	สี่เหลี่ยมมุมฉาก	sèe lìam mum chàak
rectangular (adj)	สี่เหลี่ยมมุมฉาก	sèe lìam mum chàak

pyramid	พีระมิด	phee-rá-mít
rhombus	รูปสี่เหลี่ยม ขนมเปียกปูน	rôop sèe lìam khà-nǒm bpìak bpoon
trapezoid	รูปสี่เหลี่ยมคางหมู	rôop sèe lìam khaang mǒo
cube	ลูกบาศก์	lôok bàat
prism	ปริซึม	bprì seum

circumference	เส้นรอบวง	sên rôrp wong
sphere	ทรงกลม	song glom
ball (solid sphere)	ลูกกลม	lôok glom
diameter	เส้นผ่านศูนย์กลาง	sên phàan sǒon-glaang
radius	เส้นรัศมี	sên rát-sà-mǐe

perimeter (circle's ~)	เส้นรอบวง	sên rôrp wong
center	กลาง	glaang
horizontal (adj)	แนวนอน	naew norn
vertical (adj)	แนวตั้ง	naew dtâng

| parallel (n) | เส้นขนาน | sên khà-nǎan |
| parallel (as adj) | ขนาน | khà-nǎan |

line	เส้น	sên
stroke	เส้น	sên
straight line	เส้นตรง	sên dtrorng
curve (curved line)	เส้นโค้ง	sên khóhng
thin (line, etc.)	บาง	baang
contour (outline)	เส้นขอบ	sâyn khòrp

intersection	เส้นตัด	sên dtàt
right angle	มุมฉาก	mum chàak
segment	เซกเมนต์	sâyk-mayn
sector (circular ~)	เซกเตอร์	sâyk-dtêr
side (of triangle)	ข้าง	khâang
angle	มุม	mum

25. Units of measurement

weight	น้ำหนัก	nám nàk
length	ความยาว	khwaam yaao
width	ความกว้าง	khwaam gwâang
height	ความสูง	khwaam sǒong
depth	ความลึก	khwaam léuk
volume	ปริมาณ	bpà-rí-maan
area	บริเวณ	bor-rí-wayn

gram	กรัม	gram
milligram	มิลลิกรัม	min-lí gram
kilogram	กิโลกรัม	gì-loh gram
ton	ตัน	dtan
pound	ปอนด์	bporn
ounce	ออนซ์	orn

meter	เมตร	máyt
millimeter	มิลลิเมตร	min-lí mâyt
centimeter	เซ็นติเมตร	sen dtì mâyt
kilometer	กิโลเมตร	gì-loh máyt
mile	ไมล์	mai

inch	นิ้ว	níw
foot	ฟุต	fút
yard	หลา	lǎa

square meter	ตารางเมตร	dtaa-raang máyt
hectare	เฮกตาร์	hêek dtaa
liter	ลิตร	lít
degree	องศา	ong-sǎa
volt	โวลต์	wohn
ampere	แอมแปร์	aem-bpae

horsepower	แรงม้า	raeng máa

quantity	จำนวน	jam-nuan
a little bit of ...	นิดนอย	nít nói
half	ครึ่ง	khrêung
dozen	โหล	lŏh
piece (item)	สวน	sùan

| size | ขนาด | khà-nàat |
| scale (map ~) | มาตราสวน | mâat-dtraa sùan |

minimal (adj)	นอยที่สุด	nói thêe sùt
the smallest (adj)	เล็กที่สุด	lék thêe sùt
medium (adj)	กลาง	glaang
maximal (adj)	สูงสุด	sŏong sùt
the largest (adj)	ใหญ่ที่สุด	yài têe sùt

26. Containers

canning jar (glass ~)	ขวดโหล	khùat lŏh
can	กระป๋อง	grà-bpŏrng
bucket	ถัง	thăng
barrel	ถัง	thăng

wash basin (e.g., plastic ~)	กะทะ	gà-thá
tank (100L water ~)	ถังเก็บน้ำ	thăng gèp nám
hip flask	กระติกน้ำ	grà-dtìk nám
jerrycan	ภาชนะ	phaa-chá-ná
tank (e.g., tank car)	ถังบรรจุ	thăng ban-jù

mug	แก้ว	gâew
cup (of coffee, etc.)	ถวย	thûay
saucer	จานรอง	jaan rorng
glass (tumbler)	แก้ว	gâew
wine glass	แก้วไวน์	gâew wai
stock pot (soup pot)	หมอ	môr

| bottle (~ of wine) | ขวด | khùat |
| neck (of the bottle, etc.) | ปาก | bpàak |

carafe (decanter)	คนโท	khon-thoh
pitcher	เหยือก	yèuak
vessel (container)	ภาชนะ	phaa-chá-ná
pot (crock, stoneware ~)	หมอ	môr
vase	แจกัน	jae-gan
flacon, bottle (perfume ~)	กระติก	grà-dtìk
vial, small bottle	ขวดเล็ก	khùat lék
tube (of toothpaste)	หลอด	lòrt
sack (bag)	ถุง	thŭng
bag (paper ~, plastic ~)	ถุง	thŭng

pack (of cigarettes, etc.)	ซอง	sorng
box (e.g., shoebox)	กล่อง	glòrng
crate	ลัง	lang
basket	ตะกร้า	dtà-grâa

27. Materials

material	วัสดุ	wát-sà-dù
wood (n)	ไม้	máai
wood-, wooden (adj)	ไม้	máai
glass (n)	แก้ว	gâew
glass (as adj)	แก้ว	gâew
stone (n)	หิน	hǐn
stone (as adj)	หิน	hǐn
plastic (n)	พลาสติก	pláat-dtìk
plastic (as adj)	พลาสติก	pláat-dtìk
rubber (n)	ยาง	yaang
rubber (as adj)	ยาง	yaang
cloth, fabric (n)	ผ้า	phâa
fabric (as adj)	ผ้า	phâa
paper (n)	กระดาษ	grà-dàat
paper (as adj)	กระดาษ	grà-dàat
cardboard (n)	กระดาษแข็ง	grà-dàat khǎeng
cardboard (as adj)	กระดาษแข็ง	grà-dàat khǎeng
polyethylene	โพลีเอทิลีน	phoh-lee-ay-thí-leen
cellophane	เซลโลเฟน	sayn loh-fayn
linoleum	เสื่อน้ำมัน	sèua náam man
plywood	ไม้อัด	máai àt
porcelain (n)	เครื่องเคลือบดินเผา	khrêuang khlêuap din phǎo
porcelain (as adj)	เครื่องเคลือบดินเผา	khrêuang khlêuap din phǎo
clay (n)	ดินเหนียว	din nǐeow
clay (as adj)	ดินเหนียว	din nǐeow
ceramic (n)	เซรามิก	say-raa mík
ceramic (as adj)	เซรามิก	say-raa mík

28. Metals

metal (n)	โลหะ	loh-hà
metal (as adj)	โลหะ	loh-hà
alloy (n)	โลหะสัมฤทธิ์	loh-hà sǎm-rít
gold (n)	ทอง	thorng
gold, golden (adj)	ทอง	thorng
silver (n)	เงิน	ngern
silver (as adj)	เงิน	ngern
iron (n)	เหล็ก	lèk
iron-, made of iron (adj)	เหล็ก	lèk
steel (n)	เหล็กกล้า	lèk glâa
steel (as adj)	เหล็กกลา	lèk glâa
copper (n)	ทองแดง	thorng daeng
copper (as adj)	ทองแดง	thorng daeng
aluminum (n)	อะลูมิเนียม	a-loo-mí-niam
aluminum (as adj)	อะลูมิเนียม	a-loo-mí-niam
bronze (n)	ทองบรอนซ์	thorng-bron
bronze (as adj)	ทองบรอนซ์	thorng-bron
brass	ทองเหลือง	thorng lěuang
nickel	นิกเกิล	ník-gêrn
platinum	ทองคำขาว	thorng kham khǎao
mercury	ปรอท	bpa -ròrt
tin	ดีบุก	dee-bùk
lead	ตะกั่ว	dtà-gùa
zinc	สังกะสี	sǎng-gà-sěe

HUMAN BEING

Human being. The body

29. Humans. Basic concepts

human being	มนุษย์	má-nút
man (adult male)	ผู้ชาย	phôo chaai
woman	ผู้หญิง	phôo yǐng
child	เด็ก, ลูก	dèk, lôok
girl	เด็กผู้หญิง	dèk phôo yǐng
boy	เด็กผู้ชาย	dèk phôo chaai
teenager	วัยรุ่น	wai rûn
old man	ชายชรา	chaai chá-raa
old woman	หญิงชรา	yǐng chá-raa

30. Human anatomy

organism (body)	ร่างกาย	râang gaai
heart	หัวใจ	hǔa jai
blood	เลือด	lêuat
artery	เส้นเลือดแดง	sâyn lêuat daeng
vein	เส้นเลือดดำ	sâyn lêuat dam
brain	สมอง	sà-mǒrng
nerve	เส้นประสาท	sên bprà-sàat
nerves	เส้นประสาท	sên bprà-sàat
vertebra	กระดูกสันหลัง	grà-dòok sǎn-lǎng
spine (backbone)	สันหลัง	sǎn lǎng
stomach (organ)	กระเพาะอาหาร	grà phór aa-hǎan
intestines, bowels	ลำไส้	lam sâi
intestine (e.g., large ~)	ลำไส้	lam sâi
liver	ตับ	dtàp
kidney	ไต	dtai
bone	กระดูก	grà-dòok
skeleton	โครงกระดูก	khrohng grà-dòok
rib	ซี่โครง	sêe khrohng
skull	กะโหลก	gà-lòhk
muscle	กล้ามเนื้อ	glâam néua
biceps	กล้ามเนื้อไบเซ็ปส์	glâam néua bai-sép

triceps	กล้ามเนื้อไทรเซปส์	gglâam néua thrai-sâyp
tendon	เส้นเอ็น	sâyn en
joint	ข้อต่อ	khôr dtòr
lungs	ปอด	bpòrt
genitals	อวัยวะเพศ	a-wai-wá phâyt
skin	ผิวหนัง	phǐw nǎng

31. Head

head	หัว	hǔa
face	หน้า	nâa
nose	จมูก	jà-mòok
mouth	ปาก	bpàak

eye	ตา	dtaa
eyes	ตา	dtaa
pupil	รูม่านตา	roo mâan dtaa
eyebrow	คิ้ว	khíw
eyelash	ขนตา	khǒn dtaa
eyelid	เปลือกตา	bplèuak dtaa

tongue	ลิ้น	lín
tooth	ฟัน	fan
lips	ริมฝีปาก	rim fǐe bpàak
cheekbones	โหนกแก้ม	nòhk gâem
gum	เหงือก	ngèuak
palate	เพดานปาก	phay-daan bpàak

nostrils	รูจมูก	roo jà-mòok
chin	คาง	khaang
jaw	ขากรรไกร	khǎa gan-grai
cheek	แก้ม	gâem

forehead	หน้าผาก	nâa phàak
temple	ขมับ	khà-màp
ear	หู	hǒo
back of the head	หลังศีรษะ	lǎng sěe-sà
neck	คอ	khor
throat	ลำคอ	lam khor

hair	ผม	phǒm
hairstyle	ทรงผม	song phǒm
haircut	ทรงผม	song phǒm
wig	ผมปลอม	phǒm bplorm

mustache	หนวด	nùat
beard	เครา	krao
to have (a beard, etc.)	ลองไว้	lorng wái
braid	ผมเปีย	phǒm bpia
sideburns	จอน	jorn

red-haired (adj)	ผมแดง	phŏm daeng
gray (hair)	ผมหงอก	phŏm ngòrk
bald (adj)	หัวล้าน	hŭa láan
bald patch	หัวล้าน	hŭa láan
ponytail	ผมทรงหางม้า	phŏm song hăang máa
bangs	ผมม้า	phŏm máa

32. Human body

hand	มือ	meu
arm	แขน	khăen
finger	นิ้ว	níw
toe	นิ้วเท้า	níw tháo
thumb	นิ้วโป้ง	níw bpôhng
little finger	นิ้วก้อย	níw gôi
nail	เล็บ	lép
fist	กำปั้น	gam bpân
palm	ฝ่ามือ	fàa meu
wrist	ข้อมือ	khôr meu
forearm	แขนช่วงล่าง	khăen chûang lâang
elbow	ข้อศอก	khôr sòrk
shoulder	ไหล่	lài
leg	ขา	khăa
foot	เท้า	tháo
knee	หัวเข่า	hŭa khào
calf (part of leg)	น่อง	nôrng
hip	สะโพก	sà-phôhk
heel	ส้นเท้า	sôn tháo
body	ร่างกาย	râang gaai
stomach	ท้อง	thórng
chest	อก	òk
breast	หน้าอก	nâa òk
flank	ข้าง	khâang
back	หลัง	lăng
lower back	หลังส่วนล่าง	lăng sùan lâang
waist	เอว	eo
navel (belly button)	สะดือ	sà-deu
buttocks	ก้น	gôn
bottom	ก้น	gôn
beauty mark	ไฝเสน่ห์	făi sà-này
birthmark (café au lait spot)	ปาน	bpaan
tattoo	รอยสัก	roi sàk
scar	แผลเป็น	phlăe bpen

Clothing & Accessories

33. Outerwear. Coats

clothes	เสื้อผ้า	sêua phâa
outerwear	เสื้อนอก	sêua nôk
winter clothing	เสื้อกันหนาว	sêua gan nǎao
coat (overcoat)	เสื้อโค้ท	sêua khóht
fur coat	เสื้อโค้ทขนสัตว์	sêua khóht khǒn sàt
fur jacket	แจคเก็ตขนสัตว์	jáek-gèt khǒn sàt
down coat	แจ็คเก็ตกันหนาว	jàek-gèt gan nǎao
jacket (e.g., leather ~)	แจ็คเก็ต	jáek-gèt
raincoat (trenchcoat, etc.)	เสื้อกันฝน	sêua gan fǒn
waterproof (adj)	ซึ่งกันน้ำได้	sêung gan náam dâai

34. Men's & women's clothing

shirt (button shirt)	เสื้อ	sêua
pants	กางเกง	gaang-gayng
jeans	กางเกงยีนส์	gaang-gayng yeen
suit jacket	แจ็คเก็ตสูท	jàek-gèt sòot
suit	ชุดสูท	chút sòot
dress (frock)	ชุดเดรส	chút draet
skirt	กระโปรง	grà bprohng
blouse	เสื้อ	sêua
knitted jacket (cardigan, etc.)	แจคเก็ตถัก	jáek-gèt thàk
jacket (of woman's suit)	แจ็คเก็ต	jáek-gèt
T-shirt	เสื้อยืด	sêua yêut
shorts (short trousers)	กางเกงขาสั้น	gaang-gayng khǎa sân
tracksuit	ชุดวอร์ม	chút wom
bathrobe	เสื้อคลุมอาบน้ำ	sêua khlum àap náam
pajamas	ชุดนอน	chút norn
sweater	เสื้อไหมพรม	sêua mǎi phrom
pullover	เสื้อกันหนาวแบบสวม	sêua gan nǎao bàep sǔam
vest	เสื้อกั๊ก	sêua gák
tailcoat	เสื้อเทลโค้ต	sêua thayn-khóht
tuxedo	ชุดทักซิโด	chút thák sí dôh

uniform	เครื่องแบบ	khrêuang bàep
workwear	ชุดทำงาน	chút tam ngaan
overalls	ชุดเอี๊ยม	chút íam
coat (e.g., doctor's smock)	เสื้อคลุม	sêua khlum

35. Clothing. Underwear

underwear	ชุดชั้นใน	chút chán nai
boxers, briefs	กางเกงในชาย	gaang-gayng nai chaai
panties	กางเกงในสตรี	gaang-gayng nai sàt-dtree
undershirt (A-shirt)	เสื้อชั้นใน	sêua chán nai
socks	ถุงเท้า	thǔng tháo

nightdress	ชุดนอนสตรี	chút norn sàt-dtree
bra	ยกทรง	yók song
knee highs (knee-high socks)	ถุงเท้ายาว	thǔng tháo yaao
pantyhose	ถุงน่องเต็มตัว	thǔng nôrng dtem dtua
stockings (thigh highs)	ถุงน่อง	thǔng nôrng
bathing suit	ชุดว่ายน้ำ	chút wâai náam

36. Headwear

hat	หมวก	mùak
fedora	หมวก	mùak
baseball cap	หมวกเบสบอล	mùak bàyt-bon
flatcap	หมวกติงลี่	mùak dting lêe

beret	หูมวกเบเร่ต์	mùak bay-rây
hood	ฮูด	hóot
panama hat	หมวกปานามา	mùak bpaa-naa-maa
knit cap (knitted hat)	หมวกไหมพรม	mùak mǎi phrom

headscarf	ผ้าโพกศีรษะ	phâa phôhk sěe-sà
women's hat	หมวกสตรี	mùak sàt-dtree
hard hat	หมวกนิรภัย	mùak ní-rá-phai
garrison cap	หมวกหนีบ	mùak nèep
helmet	หมวกกันน็อค	mùak ní-rá-phai

| derby | หมวกกลมทรงสูง | mùak glom song sǒong |
| top hat | หมวกทรงสูง | mùak song sǒong |

37. Footwear

| footwear | รองเท้า | rorng tháo |
| shoes (men's shoes) | รองเท้า | rorng tháo |

shoes (women's shoes)	รองเท้า	rorng tháo
boots (e.g., cowboy ~)	รองเท้าบูท	rorng tháo bòot
slippers	รองเทาแตะในบ้าน	rorng tháo dtàe nai bâan
tennis shoes (e.g., Nike ~)	รองเท้ากีฬา	rorng tháo gee-laa
sneakers (e.g., Converse ~)	รองเทาผาใบ	rorng tháo phâa bai
sandals	รองเท้าแตะ	rorng tháo dtàe
cobbler (shoe repairer)	คนซ่อมรองเท้า	khon sôrm rorng tháo
heel	สนรองเทา	sôn rorng tháo
pair (of shoes)	คู่	khôo
shoestring	เชือกรองเท้า	chêuak rorng tháo
to lace (vt)	ผูกเชือกรองเท้า	phòok chêuak rorng tháo
shoehorn	ที่ชอนรองเทา	thêe chón rorng tháo
shoe polish	ยาขัดรองเทา	yaa khàt rorng tháo

38. Textile. Fabrics

cotton (n)	ฝ้าย	fâai
cotton (as adj)	ฝาย	fâai
flax (n)	แฟลกซ์	fláek
flax (as adj)	แฟลกซ์	fláek
silk (n)	ไหม	măi
silk (as adj)	ไหม	măi
wool (n)	ขนสัตว์	khŏn sàt
wool (as adj)	ขนสัตว	khŏn sàt
velvet	กำมะหยี่	gam-má-yèe
suede	หนังกลับ	năng glàp
corduroy	ผาลูกฟูก	phâa lôok fôok
nylon (n)	ไนลอน	nai-lorn
nylon (as adj)	ไนลอน	nai-lorn
polyester (n)	โพลีเอสเตอร์	poh-lee-àyt-dtêr
polyester (as adj)	โพลีเอสเตอร	poh-lee-àyt-dtêr
leather (n)	หนัง	năng
leather (as adj)	หนัง	năng
fur (n)	ขนสัตว์	khŏn sàt
fur (e.g., ~ coat)	ขนสัตว	khŏn sàt

39. Personal accessories

gloves	ถุงมือ	thŭng meu
mittens	ถุงมือ	thŭng meu

scarf (muffler)	ผ้าพันคอ	phâa phan khor
glasses (eyeglasses)	แว่นตา	wâen dtaa
frame (eyeglass ~)	กรอบแว่น	gròrp wâen
umbrella	ร่ม	rôm
walking stick	ไม้เท้า	máai tháo
hairbrush	แปรงหวีผม	bpraeng wĕe phŏm
fan	พัด	phát

tie (necktie)	เนคไท	nâyk-thai
bow tie	โบว์หูกระต่าย	boh hŏo grà-dtàai
suspenders	สายเอี๊ยม	săai íam
handkerchief	ผ้าเช็ดหน้า	phâa chét-nâa

comb	หวี	wĕe
barrette	ที่หนีบผม	têe nèep phŏm
hairpin	กิ๊บ	gíp
buckle	หัวเข็มขัด	hŭa khĕm khàt

| belt | เข็มขัด | khĕm khàt |
| shoulder strap | สายกระเป๋า | săai grà-bpăo |

bag (handbag)	กระเป๋า	grà-bpăo
purse	กระเป๋าถือ	grà-bpăo thĕu
backpack	กระเป๋าสะพายหลัง	grà-bpăo sà-phaai lăng

40. Clothing. Miscellaneous

fashion	แฟชั่น	fae-chân
in vogue (adj)	ดานิยม	khâa ní-yom
fashion designer	นักออกแบบแฟชั่น	nák òrk bàep fae-chân

collar	คอปกเสื้อ	khor bpòk sêua
pocket	กระเป๋า	grà-bpăo
pocket (as adj)	กระเป๋า	grà-bpăo
sleeve	แขนเสื้อ	khăen sêua
hanging loop	ที่แขวนเสื้อ	têe khwăen sêua
fly (on trousers)	ซิปกางเกง	síp gaang-gayng

zipper (fastener)	ซิป	síp
fastener	ซิป	síp
button	กระดุม	grà dum
buttonhole	รูกระดุม	roo grà dum
to come off (ab. button)	หลุดออก	lùt òrk

to sew (vi, vt)	เย็บ	yép
to embroider (vi, vt)	ปัก	bpàk
embroidery	ลายปัก	laai bpàk
sewing needle	เข็มเย็บผ้า	khĕm yép phâa
thread	เส้นด้าย	sêy-dâai
seam	รอยเย็บ	roi yép

to get dirty (vi)	สกปรก	sòk-gà-bpròk
stain (mark, spot)	รอยเปื้อน	roi bpêuan
to crease, crumple (vt)	พับเป็นรอยยน	pháp bpen roi yôn
to tear, to rip (vt)	ฉีก	chèek
clothes moth	แมลงกินผ้า	má-laeng gin phâa

41. Personal care. Cosmetics

toothpaste	ยาสีฟัน	yaa sěe fan
toothbrush	แปรงสีฟัน	bpraeng sěe fan
to brush one's teeth	แปรงฟัน	bpraeng fan
razor	มีดโกน	mêet gohn
shaving cream	ครีมโกนหนวด	khreem gohn nùat
to shave (vi)	โกน	gohn
soap	สบู่	sà-bòo
shampoo	แชมพู	chaem-phoo
scissors	กรรไกร	gan-grai
nail file	ตะไบเล็บ	dtà-bai lép
nail clippers	กรรไกรตัดเล็บ	gan-grai dtàt lép
tweezers	แหนบ	nàep
cosmetics	เครื่องสำอาง	khrêuang sǎm-aang
face mask	มาสก์หน้า	mâak nâa
manicure	การแตงเล็บ	gaan dtàeng lép
to have a manicure	แตงเล็บ	dtàeng lép
pedicure	การแตงเล็บเท้า	gaan dtàeng lép táo
make-up bag	กระเป๋าเครื่องสำอาง	grà-bpǎo khrêuang sǎm-aang
face powder	แป้งฝุ่น	bpâeng-fùn
powder compact	ตลับแป้ง	dtà-làp bpâeng
blusher	แป้งทาแก้ม	bpâeng thaa gâem
perfume (bottled)	น้ำหอม	nám hǒrm
toilet water (lotion)	น้ำหอมออนๆ	náam hǒrm òn òn
lotion	โลชั่น	loh-chân
cologne	โคโลญจ์	khoh-lohn
eyeshadow	อายแชโดว์	aai-chae-doh
eyeliner	อายไลเนอร์	aai lai-ner
mascara	มาสคารา	mâat-khaa-râa
lipstick	ลิปสติก	líp-sà-dtìk
nail polish, enamel	น้ำยาทาเล็บ	nám yaa-thaa lép
hair spray	สเปรย์ฉีดผม	sà-bpray chèet phǒm
deodorant	ยาดับกลิ่น	yaa dàp glìn
cream	ครีม	khreem

face cream	ครีมทาหน้า	khreem thaa nâa
hand cream	ครีมทามือ	khreem thaa meu
anti-wrinkle cream	ครีมลดริ้วรอย	khreem lót ríw roi
day cream	ครีมกลางวัน	khreem klaang wan
night cream	ครีมกลางคืน	khreem klaang kheun
day (as adj)	กลางวัน	glaang wan
night (as adj)	กลางคืน	glaang kheun
tampon	ผ้าอนามัยแบบสอด	phâa a-naa-mai bàep sòrt
toilet paper (toilet roll)	กระดาษชำระ	grà-dàat cham-rá
hair dryer	เครื่องเป่าผม	khrêuang bpào phŏm

42. Jewelry

jewelry, jewels	เครื่องเพชรพลอย	khrêuang phét phloi
precious (e.g., ~ stone)	เพชรพลอย	phét phloi
hallmark stamp	ตราฮอลมาร์ค	dtraa hon-mâak
ring	แหวน	wăen
wedding ring	แหวนแต่งงาน	wăen dtàeng ngaan
bracelet	กำไลขอมือ	gam-lai khôr meu
earrings	ตุ้มหู	dtûm hŏo
necklace (~ of pearls)	สร้อยคอ	sôi khor
crown	มงกุฎ	mong-gùt
bead necklace	สร้อยคอลูกปัด	sôi khor lôok bpàt
diamond	เพชร	phét
emerald	มรกต	mor-rá-gòt
ruby	พลอยสีทับทิม	phloi sĕe tháp-thim
sapphire	ไพลิน	phai-lin
pearl	ไข่มุก	khài múk
amber	อำพัน	am phan

43. Watches. Clocks

watch (wristwatch)	นาฬิกา	naa-lí-gaa
dial	หน้าปัด	nâa bpàt
hand (of clock, watch)	เข็ม	khĕm
metal watch band	สายนาฬิกาข้อมือ	săi naa-lí-gaa khôr meu
watch strap	สายรัดข้อมือ	săi rát khôr meu
battery	แบตเตอรี่	bàet-dter-rêe
to be dead (battery)	หมด	mòt
to change a battery	เปลี่ยนแบตเตอรี่	bplìan bàet-dter-rêe
to run fast	เดินเร็วเกินไป	dern reo gern bpai
to run slow	เดินช้า	dern cháa
wall clock	นาฬิกา แขวนผนัง	naa-lí-gaa khwăen phà-năng

hourglass	นาฬิกาทราย	naa-lí-gaa saai
sundial	นาฬิกาแดด	naa-lí-gaa dàet
alarm clock	นาฬิกาปลุก	naa-lí-gaa bplùk
watchmaker	ช่างซ่อมนาฬิกา	châang sôrm naa-lí-gaa
to repair (vt)	ซ่อม	sôrm

Food. Nutricion

44. Food

meat	เนื้อ	néua
chicken	ไก่	gài
Rock Cornish hen (poussin)	เนื้อลูกไก่	néua lôok gài
duck	เป็ด	bpèt
goose	หาน	hàan
game	สัตว์ที่ล่า	sàt thêe lâa
turkey	ไก่งวง	gài nguang
pork	เนื้อหมู	néua mŏo
veal	เนื้อลูกวัว	néua lôok wua
lamb	เนื้อแกะ	néua gàe
beef	เนื้อวัว	néua wua
rabbit	เนื้อกระต่าย	néua grà-dtàai
sausage (bologna, etc.)	ไส้กรอก	sâi gròrk
vienna sausage (frankfurter)	ไสกรอกเวียนนา	sâi gròrk wian-naa
bacon	หมูเบคอน	mŏo bay-khorn
ham	แฮม	haem
gammon	แฮมแกมมอน	haem gaem-morn
pâté	ปาเต	bpaa dtay
liver	ตับ	dtàp
hamburger (ground beef)	เนื้อสับ	néua sàp
tongue	ลิ้น	lín
egg	ไข่	khài
eggs	ไข	khài
egg white	ไข่ขาว	khài khăao
egg yolk	ไขแดง	khài daeng
fish	ปลา	bplaa
seafood	อาหารทะเล	aa hăan thá-lay
crustaceans	สัตว์พวกกุ้งกั้งปู	sàt phûak gûng gâng bpoo
caviar	ไขปลา	khài-bplaa
crab	ปู	bpoo
shrimp	กุ้ง	gûng
oyster	หอยนางรม	hŏi naang rom
spiny lobster	กุ้งมังกร	gûng mang-gon
octopus	ปลาหมึก	bplaa mèuk

squid	ปลาหมึกกล้วย	bplaa mèuk-glûay
sturgeon	ปลาสเตอรเจียน	bpláa sà-dtêr jian
salmon	ปลาแซลมอน	bplaa saen-morn
halibut	ปลาตาเดียว	bplaa dtaa-dieow
cod	ปลาค็อด	bplaa khót
mackerel	ปลาแม็คเคอเร็ล	bplaa máek-kay-a-rěn
tuna	ปลาทูนา	bplaa thoo-nâa
eel	ปลาไหล	bplaa lǎi
trout	ปลาเทราท์	bplaa thrau
sardine	ปลาซาร์ดีน	bplaa saa-deen
pike	ปลาไพค์	bplaa phai
herring	ปลาเฮอร์ริ่ง	bplaa her-ring
bread	ขนมปัง	khà-nǒm bpang
cheese	เนยแข็ง	noie khǎeng
sugar	น้ำตาล	nám dtaan
salt	เกลือ	gleua
rice	ข้าว	khâao
pasta (macaroni)	พาสต้า	phâat-dtâa
noodles	ก๋วยเตี๋ยว	gǔay-dtǐeow
butter	เนย	noie
vegetable oil	น้ำมันพืช	nám man phêut
sunflower oil	น้ำมันดอก ทานตะวัน	nám man dòrk thaan dtà-wan
margarine	เนยเทียม	noie thiam
olives	มะกอก	má-gòrk
olive oil	น้ำมันมะกอก	nám man má-gòrk
milk	นม	nom
condensed milk	นมข้น	nom khôn
yogurt	โยเกิร์ต	yoh-gèrt
sour cream	ซาวร์ครีม	saao khreem
cream (of milk)	ครีม	khreem
mayonnaise	มายองเนส	maa-yorng-nâyt
buttercream	สวนผสมของเนย และน้ำตาล	sùan phà-sǒm khǒrng noie láe nám dtaan
groats (barley ~, etc.)	เมล็ดธัญพืช	má-lét than-yá-phêut
flour	แป้ง	bpâeng
canned food	อาหารกระป๋อง	aa-hǎan grà-bpǒrng
cornflakes	คอร์นเฟลค	khorn-flâyk
honey	น้ำผึ้ง	nám phêung
jam	แยม	yaem
chewing gum	หมากฝรั่ง	màak fà-ràng

45. Drinks

water	น้ำ	nám
drinking water	น้ำดื่ม	nám dèum
mineral water	น้ำแร่	nám râe

still (adj)	ไม่มีฟอง	mâi mee forng
carbonated (adj)	น้ำอัดลม	nám àt lom
sparkling (adj)	มีฟอง	mee forng
ice	น้ำแข็ง	nám khǎeng
with ice	ใส่น้ำแข็ง	sài nám khǎeng

non-alcoholic (adj)	ไม่มีแอลกอฮอล์	mâi mee aen-gor-hor
soft drink	เครื่องดื่มที่ไม่มีแอลกอฮอล์	krêuang dèum têe mâi mee aen-gor-hor
refreshing drink	เครื่องดื่มให้ความสดชื่น	khrêuang dèum hâi khwaam sòt chêun
lemonade	น้ำเลมอนเนด	nám lay-morn-nâyt

liquors	เหล้า	lǎu
wine	ไวน์	wai
white wine	ไวน์ขาว	wai khǎao
red wine	ไวน์แดง	wai daeng

liqueur	สุรา	sù-raa
champagne	แชมเปญ	chaem-bpayn
vermouth	เหล้าองุ่นขาวซึ่งมีกลิ่นหอม	lâo a-ngùn khǎao sêung mee glìn hǒrm

whiskey	เหล้าวิสกี้	lǎu wít-sa -gêe
vodka	เหล้าวอดกา	lǎu wórt-gâa
gin	เหล้ายิน	lǎu yin
cognac	เหล้าคอนยัก	lǎu khorn yák
rum	เหลารัม	lǎu ram

coffee	กาแฟ	gaa-fae
black coffee	กาแฟดำ	gaa-fae dam
coffee with milk	กาแฟใส่นม	gaa-fae sài nom
cappuccino	กาแฟคาปูชิโน	gaa-fae khaa bpoo chí noh
instant coffee	กาแฟสำเร็จรูป	gaa-fae sǎm-rèt rôop

milk	นม	nom
cocktail	ค็อกเทล	khók-tayn
milkshake	มิลค์เชค	min-châyk

juice	น้ำผลไม้	nám phǒn-lá-máai
tomato juice	น้ำมะเขือเทศ	nám má-khěua thâyt
orange juice	น้ำส้ม	nám sôm
freshly squeezed juice	น้ำผลไม้คั้นสด	nám phǒn-lá-máai khán sòt

| beer | เบียร์ | bia |

| light beer | เบียร์ไลท์ | bia lai |
| dark beer | เบียร์ดารัค | bia dàak |

tea	ชา	chaa
black tea	ชาดำ	chaa dam
green tea	ชาเขียว	chaa khĭeow

46. Vegetables

| vegetables | ผัก | phàk |
| greens | ผักใบเขียว | phàk bai khĭeow |

tomato	มะเขือเทศ	má-khĕua thâyt
cucumber	แตงกวา	dtaeng-gwaa
carrot	แครอท	khae-rót
potato	มันฝรั่ง	man fà-ràng
onion	หัวหอม	hŭa hŏrm
garlic	กระเทียม	grà-thiam

cabbage	กะหล่ำปลี	gà-làm bplee
cauliflower	ดอกกะหล่ำ	dòrk gà-làm
Brussels sprouts	กะหล่ำดาว	gà-làm-daao
broccoli	บร็อคโคลี่	bròrk-khoh-lêe
beet	บีทรูท	bee-trôot
eggplant	มะเขือยาว	má-khĕua-yaao
zucchini	แตงซูคินี	dtaeng soo-khí-nee
pumpkin	ฟักทอง	fák-thorng
turnip	หัวผักกาด	hŭa-phàk-gàat

parsley	ผักชีฝรั่ง	phàk chee fà-ràng
dill	ผักชีลาว	phàk-chee-laao
lettuce	ผักกาดหอม	phàk gàat hŏrm
celery	คื่นช่าย	khêun-châai
asparagus	หน่อไม้ฝรั่ง	nòr máai fà-ràng
spinach	ผักขม	phàk khŏm
pea	ถั่วลันเตา	thùa-lan-dtao
beans	ถั่ว	thùa
corn (maize)	ข้าวโพด	khâao-phôht
kidney bean	ถั่วรูปไต	thùa rôop dtai

bell pepper	พริกหยวก	phrík-yùak
radish	หัวไชเทา	hŭa chai tháo
artichoke	อาร์ติโชค	aa dtì chôhk

47. Fruits. Nuts

| fruit | ผลไม้ | phŏn-lá-máai |
| apple | แอปเปิ้ล | àep-bpêrn |

pear	แพร์	phae
lemon	มะนาว	má-naao
orange	ส้ม	sôm
strawberry (garden ~)	สตรอว์เบอร์รี่	sà-dtror-ber-rêe

mandarin	ส้มแมนดาริน	sôm maen daa rin
plum	พลัม	phlam
peach	ลูกทอ	lôok thór
apricot	แอปริคอท	ae-bprì-khôrt
raspberry	ราสเบอร์รี่	râat-ber-rêe
pineapple	สับปะรด	sàp-bpà-rót

banana	กล้วย	glûay
watermelon	แตงโม	dtaeng moh
grape	องุ่น	a-ngùn
sour cherry	เชอร์รี่	cher-rêe
sweet cherry	เชอร์รี่ป่า	cher-rêe bpàa
melon	เมลอน	may-lorn

grapefruit	ส้มโอ	sôm oh
avocado	อะโวคาโด	a-who-khaa-doh
papaya	มะละกอ	má-lá-gor
mango	มะม่วง	má-mûang
pomegranate	ทับทิม	tháp-thim

redcurrant	เรดเคอร์แรนท์	râyt-khêr-raen
blackcurrant	แบล็คเคอูรแรนท์	blàek khêr-raen
gooseberry	กูสเบอร์รี่	gòot-ber-rêe
bilberry	บิลเบอร์รี่	bil-ber-rêe
blackberry	แบล็คเบอร์รี่	blàek ber-rêe

raisin	ลูกเกด	lôok gàyt
fig	มะเดื่อฝรั่ง	má dèua fà-ràng
date	ลูกอินทผลัม	lôok in-thá-plăm

peanut	ถั่วลิสง	thùa-lí-sŏng
almond	อัลมอนด์	an-morn
walnut	วอลนัต	wor-lá-nát
hazelnut	เฮเซลนัท	hay sayn nát
coconut	มะพร้าว	má-phráao
pistachios	ถั่วพิสตาชิโอ	thùa phít dtaa chí oh

48. Bread. Candy

bakers' confectionery (pastry)	ขนม	khà-nŏm
bread	ขนมปัง	khà-nŏm bpang
cookies	คุกกี้	khúk-gêe
chocolate (n)	ช็อกโกแลต	chók-goh-láet
chocolate (as adj)	ช็อกโกแลต	chók-goh-láet

candy (wrapped)	ลูกกวาด	lôok gwàat
cake (e.g., cupcake)	ขนมคัก	khà-nŏm kháyk
cake (e.g., birthday ~)	ขนมเค้ก	khà-nŏm kháyk

| pie (e.g., apple ~) | ขนมพาย | khà-nŏm phaai |
| filling (for cake, pie) | ไส้ในขนม | sâi nai khà-nŏm |

jam (whole fruit jam)	แยม	yaem
marmalade	แยมผิวส้ม	yaem phĭw sôm
wafers	วาฟเฟิล	waaf-fern
ice-cream	ไอศกรีม	ai-sà-greem
pudding	พุดดิ้ง	phút-dîng

49. Cooked dishes

course, dish	มื้ออาหาร	méu aa-hăan
cuisine	อาหาร	aa-hăan
recipe	ตำราอาหาร	dtam-raa aa-hăan
portion	ส่วน	sùan

| salad | สลัด | sà-làt |
| soup | ซุป | súp |

clear soup (broth)	ซุปน้ำใส	súp nám-săi
sandwich (bread)	แซนด์วิช	saen-wít
fried eggs	ไข่ทอด	khài thôrt

| hamburger (beefburger) | แฮมเบอร์เกอร์ | haem-ber-gêr |
| beefsteak | สเต็กเนื้อ | sà-dtèk néua |

side dish	เครื่องเคียง	khrêuang khiang
spaghetti	สปาเก็ตตี้	sà-bpaa-gèt-dtêe
mashed potatoes	มันฝรั่งบด	man fà-ràng bòt
pizza	พิซซา	phít-sâa
porridge (oatmeal, etc.)	ข้าวต้ม	khâao-dtôm
omelet	ไข่เจียว	khài jieow

boiled (e.g., ~ beef)	ต้ม	dtôm
smoked (adj)	รมควัน	rom khwan
fried (adj)	ทอด	thôrt
dried (adj)	ตากแห้ง	dtàak hâeng
frozen (adj)	แช่แข็ง	châe khăeng
pickled (adj)	ดอง	dorng

sweet (sugary)	หวาน	wăan
salty (adj)	เค็ม	khem
cold (adj)	เย็น	yen
hot (adj)	ร้อน	rórn
bitter (adj)	ขม	khŏm
tasty (adj)	อร่อย	à-ròi

to cook in boiling water	ต้ม	dtôm
to cook (dinner)	ทำอาหาร	tham aa-hǎan
to fry (vt)	ทอด	thôrt
to heat up (food)	อุ่น	ùn
to salt (vt)	ใส่เกลือ	sài gleua
to pepper (vt)	ใส่พริกไทย	sài phrík thai
to grate (vt)	ขูด	khòot
peel (n)	เปลือก	bplèuak
to peel (vt)	ปอกเปลือก	bpòrk bplêuak

50. Spices

salt	เกลือ	gleua
salty (adj)	เค็ม	khem
to salt (vt)	ใส่เกลือ	sài gleua
black pepper	พริกไทย	phrík thai
red pepper (milled ~)	พริกแดง	phrík daeng
mustard	มัสตาร์ด	mát-dtàat
horseradish	ฮอสแรดิช	hórt rae dìt
condiment	เครื่องปรุงรส	khrêuang bprung rót
spice	เครื่องเทศ	khrêuang thâyt
sauce	ซอส	sós
vinegar	น้ำส้มสายชู	nám sôm sǎai choo
anise	เทียนสัตตบุษย์	thian-sàt-dtà-bùt
basil	ใบโหระพา	bai hǒh rá phaa
cloves	กานพลู	gaan-phloo
ginger	ขิง	khǐng
coriander	ผักชีลา	pàk-chee-laa
cinnamon	อบเชย	òp-choie
sesame	งา	ngaa
bay leaf	ใบกระวาน	bai grà-waan
paprika	พริกป่น	phrík bpòn
caraway	เทียนตากบ	thian dtaa gòp
saffron	หญ้าฝรั่น	yâa fà-ràn

51. Meals

food	อาหาร	aa-hǎan
to eat (vi, vt)	กิน	gin
breakfast	อาหารเช้า	aa-hǎan cháo
to have breakfast	ทานอาหารเช้า	thaan aa-hǎan cháo

lunch	ข้าวเที่ยง	khâao thîang
to have lunch	ทานอาหารเที่ยง	thaan aa-hǎan thîang
dinner	อาหารเย็น	aa-hǎan yen
to have dinner	ทานอาหารเย็น	thaan aa-hǎan yen
appetite	ความอยากอาหาร	kwaam yàak aa hǎan
Enjoy your meal!	กินให้อร่อย!	gin hâi a-ròi
to open (~ a bottle)	เปิด	bpèrt
to spill (liquid)	ทำหก	tham hòk
to spill out (vi)	ทำหกออกมา	tham hòk òrk maa
to boil (vi)	ต้ม	dtôm
to boil (vt)	ต้ม	dtôm
boiled (~ water)	ต้ม	dtôm
to chill, cool down (vt)	แช่เย็น	châe yen
to chill (vi)	แช่เย็น	châe yen
taste, flavor	รสชาติ	rót châat
aftertaste	รส	rót
to slim down (lose weight)	ลดน้ำหนัก	lót nám nàk
diet	อาหารพิเศษ	aa-hǎan phí-sàyt
vitamin	วิตามิน	wí-dtaa-min
calorie	แคลอรี่	khae-lor-rêe
vegetarian (n)	คนกินเจ	khon gin jay
vegetarian (adj)	มังสวิรัติ	mang-sà-wí-rát
fats (nutrient)	ไขมัน	khǎi man
proteins	โปรตีน	bproh-dteen
carbohydrates	คาร์โบไฮเดรต	kaa-boh-hai-dràyt
slice (of lemon, ham)	แผ่น	phàen
piece (of cake, pie)	ชิ้น	chín
crumb	เศษ	sàyt
(of bread, cake, etc.)		

52. Table setting

spoon	ช้อน	chórn
knife	มีด	mêet
fork	ส้อม	sôrm
cup (e.g., coffee ~)	แก้ว	gâew
plate (dinner ~)	จาน	jaan
saucer	จานรอง	jaan rorng
napkin (on table)	ผ้าเช็ดปาก	phâa chét bpàak
toothpick	ไม้จิ้มฟัน	máai jîm fan

53. Restaurant

restaurant	ร้านอาหาร	ráan aa-hăan
coffee house	ร้านกาแฟ	ráan gaa-fae
pub, bar	ร้านเหล้า	ráan lâo
tearoom	ร้านน้ำชา	ráan nám chaa
waiter	คนเสิร์ฟชาย	khon sèrf chaai
waitress	คนเสิร์ฟหญิง	khon sèrf yĭng
bartender	บาร์เทนเดอร์	baa-thayn-dêr
menu	เมนู	may-noo
wine list	รายการไวน์	raai gaan wai
to book a table	จองโต๊ะ	jorng dtó
course, dish	มื้ออาหาร	méu aa-hăan
to order (meal)	สั่ง	sàng
to make an order	สั่งอาหาร	sàng aa-hăan
aperitif	เครื่องดื่มเหล้า กอนอาหาร	khrêuang dèum lâo gòrn aa-hăan
appetizer	ของกินเล่น	khŏrng gin lâyn
dessert	ของหวาน	khŏrng wăan
check	คิดเงิน	khít ngern
to pay the check	จวยคาอาหาร	jàai khâa aa hăan
to give change	ให้เงินทอน	hâi ngern thorn
tip	เงินทิป	ngern thíp

Family, relatives and friends

54. Personal information. Forms

name (first name)	ชื่อ	chêu
surname (last name)	นามสกุล	naam sà-gun
date of birth	วันเกิด	wan gèrt
place of birth	สถานที่เกิด	sà-thăan thêe gèrt
nationality	สัญชาติ	săn-châat
place of residence	ที่อยู่อาศัย	thêe yòo aa-săi
country	ประเทศ	bprà-thâyt
profession (occupation)	อาชีพ	aa-chêep
gender, sex	เพศ	phâyt
height	ความสูง	khwaam sŏong
weight	น้ำหนัก	nám nàk

55. Family members. Relatives

mother	มารดา	maan-daa
father	บิดา	bì-daa
son	ลูกชาย	lôok chaai
daughter	ลูกสาว	lôok săao
younger daughter	ลูกสาวคนเล็ก	lôok săao khon lék
younger son	ลูกชายคนเล็ก	lôok chaai khon lék
eldest daughter	ลูกสาวคนโต	lôok săao khon dtoh
eldest son	ลูกชายคนโต	lôok chaai khon dtoh
elder brother	พี่ชาย	phêe chaai
younger brother	น้องชาย	nórng chaai
elder sister	พี่สาว	phêe săao
younger sister	น้องสาว	nórng săao
cousin (masc.)	ลูกพี่ลูกน้อง	lôok phêe lôok nórng
cousin (fem.)	ลูกพี่ลูกน้อง	lôok phêe lôok nórng
mom, mommy	แม่	mâe
dad, daddy	พ่อ	phôr
parents	พ่อแม่	phôr mâe
child	เด็ก, ลูก	dèk, lôok
children	เด็กๆ	dèk dèk
grandmother	ยา, ยาย	yâa, yaai

grandfather	ปู่, ตา	bpòo, dtaa
grandson	หลานชาย	lǎan chaai
granddaughter	หลานสาว	lǎan sǎao
grandchildren	หลานๆ	lǎan

uncle	ลุง	lung
aunt	ป้า	bpâa
nephew	หลานชาย	lǎan chaai
niece	หลานสาว	lǎan sǎao
mother-in-law (wife's mother)	แม่ยาย	mâe yaai
father-in-law (husband's father)	พ่อสามี	phôr sǎa-mee
son-in-law (daughter's husband)	ลูกเขย	lôok khǒie
stepmother	แม่เลี้ยง	mâe líang
stepfather	พอเลี้ยง	phôr líang

infant	ทารก	thaa-rók
baby (infant)	เด็กเล็ก	dèk lék
little boy, kid	เด็ก	dèk

wife	ภรรยา	phan-rá-yaa
husband	สามี	sǎa-mee
spouse (husband)	สามี	sǎa-mee
spouse (wife)	ภรรยา	phan-rá-yaa

married (masc.)	แต่งงานแล้ว	dtàeng ngaan láew
married (fem.)	แตงงานแลว	dtàeng ngaan láew
single (unmarried)	เป็นโสด	bpen sòht
bachelor	ชายโสด	chaai sòht
divorced (masc.)	หย่าแล้ว	yàa láew
widow	แม่หม้าย	mâe mâai
widower	พอหม้าย	phôr mâai

relative	ญาติ	yâat
close relative	ญาติใกล้ชิด	yâat glâi chít
distant relative	ญาติหางๆ	yâat hàang hàang
relatives	ญาติๆ	yâat

orphan (boy)	เด็กชายกำพร้า	dèk chaai gam phráa
orphan (girl)	เด็กหญิงกำพรา	dèk yǐng gam phráa
guardian (of a minor)	ผูปกครอง	phôo bpòk khrorng
to adopt (a boy)	บุญธรรม	bun tham
to adopt (a girl)	บุญธรรม	bun tham

56. Friends. Coworkers

| friend (masc.) | เพื่อน | phêuan |
| friend (fem.) | เพื่อน | phêuan |

friendship	มิตรภาพ	mít-dtrà-phâap
to be friends	เป็นเพื่อน	bpen phêuan
buddy (masc.)	เพื่อนสนิท	phêuan sà-nìt
buddy (fem.)	เพื่อนสนิท	phêuan sà-nìt
partner	หุ้นส่วน	hûn sùan
chief (boss)	หัวหน้า	hǔa-nâa
superior (n)	ผู้บังคับบัญชา	phôo bang-kháp ban-chaa
owner, proprietor	เจ้าของ	jâo khǒrng
subordinate (n)	ลูกน้อง	lôok nórng
colleague	เพื่อนร่วมงาน	phêuan rûam ngaan
acquaintance (person)	ผู้คุ้นเคย	phôo khún khoie
fellow traveler	เพื่อนร่วมทาง	pêuan rûam thaang
classmate	เพื่อนรุ่น	phêuan rûn
neighbor (masc.)	เพื่อนบ้านผู้ชาย	phêuan bâan pôo chaai
neighbor (fem.)	เพื่อนบ้านผู้หญิง	phêuan bâan phôo yǐng
neighbors	เพื่อนบ้าน	phêuan bâan

57. Man. Woman

woman	ผู้หญิง	phôo yǐng
girl (young woman)	หญิงสาว	yǐng sǎao
bride	เจ้าสาว	jâo sǎao
beautiful (adj)	สวย	sǔay
tall (adj)	สูง	sǒong
slender (adj)	ผอม	phǒrm
short (adj)	เตี้ย	dtîa
blonde (n)	ผมสีทอง	phǒm sěe thorng
brunette (n)	ผมสีคล้ำ	phǒm sěe khlám
ladies' (adj)	สตรี	sàt-dtree
virgin (girl)	บริสุทธิ์	bor-rí-sùt
pregnant (adj)	ตั้งครรภ์	dtâng khan
man (adult male)	ผู้ชาย	phôo chaai
blond (n)	ผมสีทอง	phǒm sěe thorng
brunet (n)	ผมสีคล้ำ	phǒm sěe khlám
tall (adj)	สูง	sǒong
short (adj)	เตี้ย	dtîa
rude (rough)	หยาบคาย	yàap kaai
stocky (adj)	แข็งแรง	khǎeng raeng
robust (adj)	กำยำ	gam-yam
strong (adj)	แข็งแรง	khǎeng raeng
strength	ความแข็งแรง	khwaam khǎeng raeng

stout, fat (adj)	ท้วม	thúam
swarthy (adj)	ผิวดำ	phǐw dam
slender (well-built)	ผอม	phǒrm
elegant (adj)	สง่า	sà-ngàa

58. Age

age	อายุ	aa-yú
youth (young age)	วัยเยาว์	wai yao
young (adj)	หนุ่ม	nùm
younger (adj)	อายุน้อยกว่า	aa-yú nói gwàa
older (adj)	อายุสูงกว่า	aa-yú sǒong gwàa
young man	ชายหนุ่ม	chaai nùm
teenager	วัยรุ่น	wai rûn
guy, fellow	คนหนุ่ม	khon nùm
old man	ชายชรา	chaai chá-raa
old woman	หญิงชรา	yǐng chá-raa
adult (adj)	ผู้ใหญ่	phôo yài
middle-aged (adj)	วัยกลาง	wai glaang
elderly (adj)	วัยชรา	wai chá-raa
old (adj)	แก่	gàe
retirement	การเกษียณอายุ	gaan gà-sǐan aa-yú
to retire (from job)	เกษียณ	gà-sǐan
retiree	ผู้เกษียณอายุ	phôo gà-sǐan aa-yú

59. Children

child	เด็ก, ลูก	dèk, lôok
children	เด็กๆ	dèk dèk
twins	แฝด	fàet
cradle	เปล	bplay
rattle	ของเล่นกุ๊งกิ๊ง	khǒrng lên gúng-gîng
diaper	ผ้าอ้อม	phâa ôrm
pacifier	จุกนม	jùk-nom
baby carriage	รถเข็นเด็ก	rót khěn dèk
kindergarten	โรงเรียนอนุบาล	rohng rian a-nú-baan
babysitter	คนเฝ้าเด็ก	khon fâo dèk
childhood	วัยเด็ก	wai dèk
doll	ตุ๊กตา	dtúk-dtaa
toy	ของเล่น	khǒrng lên

construction set (toy)	ชุดของเล่นก่อสร้าง	chút khǒrng lên gòr sâang
well-bred (adj)	มีกิริยา	mee gì-rí-yaa
	มารยาทดี	maa-rá-yâat dee
ill-bred (adj)	ไม่มีมารยาท	mâi mee maa-rá-yâat
spoiled (adj)	เสียคน	sǐa khon
to be naughty	ซน	son
mischievous (adj)	ซน	son
mischievousness	ความเกเร	kwaam gay-ray
mischievous child	เด็กเกเร	dèk gay-ray
obedient (adj)	ที่เชื่อฟัง	thêe chêua fang
disobedient (adj)	ที่ไม่เชื่อฟัง	thêe mâi chêua fang
docile (adj)	ที่เชื่อฟังผู้ใหญ่	thée chêua fang phôo yài
clever (smart)	ฉลาด	chà-làat
child prodigy	เด็กมีพรสวรรค์	dèk mee phon sà-wǎn

60. Married couples. Family life

to kiss (vt)	จูบ	jòop
to kiss (vi)	จูบ	jòop
family (n)	ครอบครัว	khrôrp khrua
family (as adj)	ครอบครัว	khrôrp khrua
couple	ผัวเมีย	phǔa mia
marriage (state)	การแต่งงาน	gaan dtàeng ngaan
hearth (home)	บ้าน	bâan
dynasty	วงศตระกูล	wong dtrà-goon
date	การออกเดท	gaan òrk dàyt
kiss	การจูบ	gaan jòop
love (for sb)	ความรัก	khwaam rák
to love (sb)	รัก	rák
beloved	ที่รัก	thêe rák
tenderness	ความละเมียดละไม	khwaam lá-mîat lá-mai
tender (affectionate)	ละเมียดละไม	lá-mîat lá-mai
faithfulness	ความซื่อ	khwaam sêu
faithful (adj)	ซื่อ	sêu
care (attention)	การดูแล	gaan doo lae
caring (~ father)	ชอบดูแล	chôrp doo lae
newlyweds	ดูแต่งงานใหม่	khôo dtàeng ngaan mài
honeymoon	ฮันนีมูน	han-nee-moon
to get married (ab. woman)	แต่งงาน	dtàeng ngaan
to get married (ab. man)	แต่งงาน	dtàeng ngaan
wedding	การสมรส	gaan sǒm rót
golden wedding	การสมรสครบรอบ50ปี	gaan sǒm rót khróp rôrp hâa-sìp bpee

anniversary	วันครบรอบ	wan khróp rôrp
lover (masc.)	ชู้รัก	khôo rák
mistress (lover)	เมียน้อย	mia nói

adultery	การคบชู้	gaan khóp chóo
to cheat on ... (commit adultery)	คบชู้	khóp chóo
jealous (adj)	หึงหวง	hĕung hŭang
to be jealous	หึง	hĕung
divorce	การหย่าร้าง	gaan yàa ráang
to divorce (vi)	หย่า	yàa

to quarrel (vi)	ทะเลาะ	thá-lór
to be reconciled (after an argument)	ประนีประนอม	bprà-nee-bprà-nom
together (adv)	ด้วยกัน	dûay gan
sex	เพศสัมพันธ์	phâyt sǎm-phan

happiness	ความสุข	khwaam sùk
happy (adj)	มีความสุข	mee khwaam sùk
misfortune (accident)	เหตุร้าย	hàyt ráai
unhappy (adj)	ไม่มีความสุข	mâi mee khwaam sùk

Character. Feelings. Emotions

61. Feelings. Emotions

feeling (emotion)	ความรู้สึก	khwaam róo sèuk
feelings	ความรู้สึก	khwaam róo sèuk
to feel (vt)	รู้สึก	róo sèuk
hunger	ความหิว	khwaam hǐw
to be hungry	หิว	hǐw
thirst	ความกระหาย	khwaam grà-hǎai
to be thirsty	กระหาย	grà-hǎai
sleepiness	ความง่วง	khwaam ngûang
to feel sleepy	ง่วง	ngûang
tiredness	ความเหนื่อย	khwaam nèuay
tired (adj)	เหนื่อย	nèuay
to get tired	เหนื่อย	nèuay
mood (humor)	อารมณ์	aa-rom
boredom	ความเบื่อ	khwaam bèua
to be bored	เบื่อ	bèua
seclusion	ความเหงา	khwaam ngǎo
to seclude oneself	ปลีกวิเวก	bplèek wí-wâyk
to worry (make anxious)	ทำให้...เป็นห่วง	tham hâi...bpen hùang
to be worried	กังวล	gang-won
worrying (n)	ความเป็นห่วง	khwaam bpen hùang
anxiety	ความวิตกกังวล	khwaam wí-dtòk gang-won
preoccupied (adj)	เป็นห่วงใหญ่	bpen hùang yài
to be nervous	กระวนกระวาย	grà won grà waai
to panic (vi)	ตื่นตระหนก	dtèun dtrà-nòk
hope	ความหวัง	khwaam wǎng
to hope (vi, vt)	หวัง	wǎng
certainty	ความแน่ใจ	khwaam nâe jai
certain, sure (adj)	แน่ใจ	nâe jai
uncertainty	ความไม่มั่นใจ	khwaam mâi mân jai
uncertain (adj)	ไม่มั่นใจ	mâi mân jai
drunk (adj)	เมา	mao
sober (adj)	ไม่เมา	mâi mao
weak (adj)	อ่อนแอ	òrn ae
happy (adj)	มีความสุข	mee khwaam sùk
to scare (vt)	ทำให้...กลัว	tham hâi...glua

fury (madness)	ความโกรธเคือง	khwaam gròht kheuang
rage (fury)	ความเดือดดาล	khwaam dèuat daan
depression	ความหดหู่	khwaam hòt-hòo
discomfort (unease)	อึดอัด	èut àt
comfort	สบาย	sà-baai
to regret (be sorry)	เสียดาย	sĭa daai
regret	ความเสียดาย	khwaam sĭa daai
bad luck	โชคราย	chôhk ráai
sadness	ความเศรา	khwaam sâo
shame (remorse)	ความละอายใจ	khwaam lá-aai jai
gladness	ความปีติ	khwaam bpì-dtì
enthusiasm, zeal	ความกระตือรือร้น	khwaam grà-dteu-reu-rón
enthusiast	คนที่กระตือรือรน	khon thêe grà-dteu-reu-rón
to show enthusiasm	แสดงความ	sà-daeng khwaam
	กระตือรือรน	grà-dteu-reu-rón

62. Character. Personality

character	นิสัย	ní-sǎi
character flaw	ขอเสีย	khôr sĭa
mind	สติ	sà-dtì
reason	สติ	sà-dtì
conscience	มโนธรรม	má-noh tham
habit (custom)	นิสัย	ní-sǎi
ability (talent)	ความสามารถ	khwaam sǎa-mâat
can (e.g., ~ swim)	สามารถ	sǎa-mâat
patient (adj)	อดทน	òt thon
impatient (adj)	ใจรอนใจเร็ว	jai rórn jai reo
curious (inquisitive)	อยากรู้อยากเห็น	yàak róo yàak hěn
curiosity	ความอยาก	khwaam yàak
	รู้อยากเห็น	róo yàak hěn
modesty	ความถอมตน	khwaam thòrm dton
modest (adj)	ถอมตน	thòrm dton
immodest (adj)	หยาบโลน	yàap lohn
laziness	ความขี้เกียจ	khwaam khêe gìat
lazy (adj)	ขี้เกียจ	khêe gìat
lazy person (masc.)	คนขี้เกียจ	khon khêe gìat
cunning (n)	ความเจ้าเล่ห์	khwaam jâo lây
cunning (as adj)	เจาเลห	jâo lây
distrust	ความหวาดระแวง	khwaam wàat rá-waeng
distrustful (adj)	เคลือบแคลงลง	khlêuap-khlaeng
generosity	ความเอื้อเฟื้อ	khwaam êua féua
generous (adj)	มีน้ำใจ	mee nám jai

talented (adj)	มีพรสวรรค์	mee phon sà-wăn
talent	พรสวรรค	phon sà-wăn
courageous (adj)	กล้าหาญ	glâa hăan
courage	ความกล้าหาญ	khwaam glâa hăan
honest (adj)	ซื่อสัตย์	sêu sàt
honesty	ความซื่อสัตย์	khwaam sêu sàt
careful (cautious)	ระมัดระวัง	rá mát rá-wang
brave (courageous)	กล้า	glâa
serious (adj)	เอาจริงเอาจัง	ao jing ao jang
strict (severe, stern)	เขมงวด	khêm ngûat
decisive (adj)	เด็ดเดี่ยว	dèt dìeow
indecisive (adj)	ไม่เด็ดขาด	mâi dèt khàat
shy, timid (adj)	อาย	aai
shyness, timidity	ความขวยอาย	khwaam khŭay aai
confidence (trust)	ความไว้ใจ	khwaam wái jai
to believe (trust)	ไว้เนื้อเชื่อใจ	wái néua chêua jai
trusting (credulous)	เชื่อใจ	chêua jai
sincerely (adv)	อย่างจริงใจ	yàang jing jai
sincere (adj)	จริงใจ	jing jai
sincerity	ความจริงใจ	khwaam jing jai
open (person)	เปิดเผย	bpèrt phŏie
calm (adj)	ใจเย็น	jai yen
frank (sincere)	จริงใจ	jing jai
naïve (adj)	หลงเชื่อ	lŏng chêua
absent-minded (adj)	ใจลอย	jai loi
funny (odd)	ตลก	dtà-lòk
greed, stinginess	ความโลภ	khwaam lôhp
greedy, stingy (adj)	โลภ	lôhp
stingy (adj)	ขี้เหนียว	khêe nĭeow
evil (adj)	เลว	leo
stubborn (adj)	ดื้อ	dêu
unpleasant (adj)	ไม่น่าพึงพอใจ	mâi nâa pheung phor jai
selfish person (masc.)	คนที่เห็นแก่ตัว	khon thêe hĕn gàe dtua
selfish (adj)	เห็นแก่ตัว	hĕn gàe dtua
coward	คนขี้ขลาด	khon khêe khlàat
cowardly (adj)	ขี้ขลาด	khêe khlàat

63. Sleep. Dreams

to sleep (vi)	นอน	norn
sleep, sleeping	ความนอน	khwaam norn
dream	ความฝัน	khwaam făn

| to dream (in sleep) | ฝัน | făn |
| sleepy (adj) | ง่วง | ngûang |

bed	เตียง	dtiang
mattress	ฟูกนอน	fôok norn
blanket (comforter)	ผ้าห่ม	phâa hòm
pillow	หมอน	mŏrn
sheet	ผ้าปูที่นอน	phâa bpoo thêe norn

insomnia	อาการนอนไม่หลับ	aa-gaan norn mâi làp
sleepless (adj)	นอนไม่หลับ	norn mâi làp
sleeping pill	ยานอนหลับ	yaa-norn-làp
to take a sleeping pill	กินยานอนหลับ	gin yaa-norn-làp

to feel sleepy	ง่วง	ngûang
to yawn (vi)	หาว	hăao
to go to bed	ไปนอน	bpai norn
to make up the bed	ปูที่นอน	bpoo thêe norn
to fall asleep	หลับ	làp

nightmare	ฝันร้าย	făn ráai
snore, snoring	การกรน	gaan-kron
to snore (vi)	กรน	gron

alarm clock	นาฬิกาปลุก	naa-lí-gaa bplùk
to wake (vt)	ปลุก	bplùk
to wake up	ตื่น	dtèun
to get up (vi)	ลุกขึ้น	lúk khêun
to wash up (wash face)	ล้างหน้าล้างตา	láang nâa láang dtaa

64. Humour. Laughter. Gladness

humor (wit, fun)	อารมณ์ขัน	aa-rom khăn
sense of humor	อารมณ์	aa-rom
to enjoy oneself	เริงรื่น	rerng rêun
cheerful (merry)	เริงรื่น	rerng rêun
merriment (gaiety)	ความรื่นเริง	khwaam rêun-rerng

smile	รอยยิ้ม	roi yím
to smile (vi)	ยิ้ม	yím
to start laughing	เริ่มหัวเราะ	rêrm hŭa rór
to laugh (vi)	หัวเราะ	hŭa rór
laugh, laughter	การหัวเราะ	gaan hŭa rór

anecdote	เรื่องขำขัน	rêuang khăm khăn
funny (anecdote, etc.)	ตลก	dtà-lòk
funny (odd)	ขบขัน	khòp khăn

| to joke (vi) | ล้อเล่น | lór lên |
| joke (verbal) | ตลก | dtà-lòk |

joy (emotion)	ความสุขสันต์	khwaam sùk-săn
to rejoice (vi)	โมทนา	moh-thá-naa
joyful (adj)	ยินดี	yin dee

65. Discussion, conversation. Part 1

| communication | การสื่อสาร | gaan sèu săan |
| to communicate | สื่อสาร | sèu săan |

conversation	การสนทนา	gaan sŏn-thá-naa
dialog	บทสนทนา	bòt sŏn-thá-naa
discussion (discourse)	การหารือ	gaan hăa-reu
dispute (debate)	การโต้แย้ง	gaan dtôh yáeng
to dispute	โต้แย้ง	dtôh yáeng

interlocutor	คู่สนทนา	khôo sŏn-tá-naa
topic (theme)	หัวข้อ	hŭa khôr
point of view	แง่คิด	ngâe khít
opinion (point of view)	ความคิดเห็น	khwaam khít hěn
speech (talk)	สุนทรพจน์	sŭn tha ra phót

discussion (of report, etc.)	การหารือ	gaan hăa-reu
to discuss (vt)	หารือ	hăa-reu
talk (conversation)	การสนทนา	gaan sŏn-thá-naa
to talk (to chat)	คุยกัน	khui gan
meeting (encounter)	การพบกัน	gaan phóp gan
to meet (vi, vt)	พบ	phóp

proverb	สุภาษิต	sù-phaa-sìt
saying	คำกล่าว	kham glàao
riddle (poser)	ปริศนา	bprìt-sà-năa
to pose a riddle	ถามปริศนา	thăam bprìt-sà-năa
password	รหัสผ่าน	rá-hàt phàan
secret	ความลับ	khwaam láp

oath (vow)	คำสาบาน	kham săa-baan
to swear (an oath)	สาบาน	săa baan
promise	คำสัญญา	kham săn-yaa
to promise (vt)	สัญญา	săn-yaa

advice (counsel)	คำแนะนำ	kham náe nam
to advise (vt)	แนะนำ	náe nam
to follow one's advice	ทำตาม คำแนะนำ	tham dtaam kham náe nam
to listen to ... (obey)	เชื่อฟัง	chêua fang

news	ข่าว	khàao
sensation (news)	ข่าวดัง	khàao dang
information (report)	ข้อมูล	khôr moon
conclusion (decision)	ข้อสรุป	khôr sà-rùp

voice	เสียง	sĭang
compliment	คำชมเชย	kham chom choie
kind (nice)	ใจดี	jai dee

word	คำ	kham
phrase	วลี	wá-lee
answer	คำตอบ	kham dtòrp

truth	ความจริง	khwaam jing
lie	การโกหก	gaan goh-hòk

thought	ความคิด	khwaam khít
idea (inspiration)	ความคิด	khwaam khít
fantasy	จินตนาการ	jin-dtà-naa gaan

66. Discussion, conversation. Part 2

respected (adj)	ที่นับถือ	thêe náp thĕu
to respect (vt)	นับถือ	náp thĕu
respect	ความนับถือ	khwaam náp thĕu
Dear ... (letter)	ทาน	thâan

to introduce (sb to sb)	แนะนำ	náe nam
to make acquaintance	รู้จัก	róo jàk

intention	ความตั้งใจ	khwaam dtâng jai
to intend (have in mind)	ตั้งใจ	dtâng jai
wish	การขอพร	gaan khŏr phon
to wish (~ good luck)	ขอ	khŏr

surprise (astonishment)	ความประหลาดใจ	khwaam bprà-làat jai
to surprise (amaze)	ทำให้...ประหลาดใจ	tham hâi...bprà-làat jai
to be surprised	ประหลาดใจ	bprà-làat jai

to give (vt)	ให้	hâi
to take (get hold of)	รับ	ráp
to give back	ให้คืน	hâi kheun
to return (give back)	เอาคืน	ao kheun

to apologize (vi)	ขอโทษ	khŏr thôht
apology	คำขอโทษ	kham khŏr thôht
to forgive (vt)	ให้อภัย	hâi a-phai

to talk (speak)	คุยกัน	khui gan
to listen (vi)	ฟัง	fang
to hear out	ฟังจนจบ	fang jon jòp
to understand (vt)	เขาใจ	khâo jai

to show (to display)	แสดง	sà-daeng
to look at ...	ดู	doo

to call (yell for sb)	เรียก	rîak
to distract (disturb)	รบกวน	róp guan
to disturb (vt)	รุบกวน	róp guan
to pass (to hand sth)	ส่ง	sòng

demand (request)	ข้อร้องขอ	khôr rórng khŏr
to request (ask)	ร้องขอ	rórng khŏr
demand (firm request)	ขอเรียกร้อง	khôr rîak rórng
to demand (request firmly)	เรียกร้อง	rîak rórng

to tease (call names)	แซว	saew
to mock (make fun of)	ล้อเลียน	lór lian
mockery, derision	ข้อล้อเลียน	khôr lór lian
nickname	ชื่อเล่น	chêu lên

insinuation	การพูดเป็นนัย	gaan phôot bpen nai
to insinuate (imply)	พูดเป็นนัย	phôot bpen nai
to mean (vt)	หมายความว่า	măai khwaam wâa

description	คำพรรณนา	kham phan-ná-naa
to describe (vt)	พรรณนา	phan-ná-naa
praise (compliments)	คำชม	kham chom
to praise (vt)	ชม	chom

disappointment	ความผิดหวัง	khwaam phìt wăng
to disappoint (vt)	ทำให้...ผิดหวัง	tham hâi...phìt wăng
to be disappointed	ผิดหวัง	phìt wăng

supposition	ข้อสมมุติ	khôr sŏm mút
to suppose (assume)	สมมุติ	sŏm mút
warning (caution)	คำเตือน	kham dteuan
to warn (vt)	เตือน	dteuan

67. Discussion, conversation. Part 3

| to talk into (convince) | เกลี้ยกล่อม | glîak-glôrm |
| to calm down (vt) | ทำให้...สงบ | tham hâi...sà-ngòp |

silence (~ is golden)	ความเงียบ	khwaam ngîap
to be silent (not speaking)	เงียบ	ngîap
to whisper (vi, vt)	กระซิบ	grà síp
whisper	เสียงกระซิบ	sĭang grà síp

frankly, sincerely (adv)	พูดตรงๆ	phôot dtrorng dtrorng
in my opinion ...	ในสายตาของ	nai săai dtaa-kŏrng
	ผม/ฉัน...	phŏm/chăn...

detail (of the story)	รายละเอียด	raai lá-ìat
detailed (adj)	โดยละเอียด	doi lá-ìat
in detail (adv)	อย่างละเอียด	yàang lá-ìat

hint, clue	คำบอกใบ้	kham bòrk bâi
to give a hint	บอกใบ้	bòrk bâi
look (glance)	การมอง	gaan morng
to have a look	มอง	morng
fixed (look)	จอง	jôrng
to blink (vi)	กระพริบตา	grà phríp dtaa
to wink (vi)	ขยิบตา	khà-yìp dtaa
to nod (in assent)	พยักหน้า	phá-yák nâa
sigh	การถอนหายใจ	gaan thŏrn hăai jai
to sigh (vi)	ถอนหายใจ	thŏrn hăai-jai
to shudder (vi)	สั่น	sàn
gesture	อิริยาบถ	i-rí-yaa-bòt
to touch (one's arm, etc.)	สัมผัส	săm-phàt
to seize	จับ	jàp
(e.g., ~ by the arm)		
to tap (on the shoulder)	แตะ	dtàe
Look out!	ระวัง!	rá-wang
Really?	จริงหรือ?	jing rĕu
Are you sure?	คุณแน่ใจหรือ?	khun nâe jai rĕu
Good luck!	ขอให้โชคดี!	khŏr hâi chôhk dee
I see!	ฉันเขาใจ!	chăn khâo jai
What a pity!	น่าเสียดาย!	nâa sĭa-daai

68. Agreement. Refusal

consent	การยินยอม	gaan yin yorm
to consent (vi)	ยินยอม	yin yorm
approval	คำอนุมัติ	kham a-nú-mát
to approve (vt)	อนุมัติ	a-nú-mát
refusal	คำปฏิเสธ	kham bpà-dtì-sàyt
to refuse (vi, vt)	ปฏิเสธ	bpà-dtì-sàyt
Great!	เยี่ยม!	yîam
All right!	ดีเลย!	dee loie
Okay! (I agree)	โอเค!	oh-khay
forbidden (adj)	ไม่ได้รับอนุญาต	mâi dâai ráp a-nú-yâat
it's forbidden	หาม	hâam
it's impossible	มันเป็นไปไม่ได้	man bpen bpai mâi dâai
incorrect (adj)	ไมถูกต้อง	mâi thòok dtôrng
to reject (~ a demand)	ปฏิเสธ	bpà-dtì-sàyt
to support (cause, idea)	สนับสนุน	sà-nàp-sà-nŭn
to accept (~ an apology)	ยอมรับ	yorm ráp
to confirm (vt)	ยืนยัน	yeun yan
confirmation	คำยืนยัน	kham yeun yan

permission	คำอนุญาต	kham a-nú-yâat
to permit (vt)	อนุญาต	a-nú-yâat
decision	การตัดสินใจ	gaan dtàt sĭn jai
to say nothing (hold one's tongue)	ไม่พูดอะไร	mâi phôot a-rai
condition (term)	เงื่อนไข	ngêuan khăi
excuse (pretext)	ขออ้าง	khŏr âang
praise (compliments)	คำชม	kham chom
to praise (vt)	ชม	chom

69. Success. Good luck. Failure

success	ความสำเร็จ	khwaam săm-rèt
successfully (adv)	ให้เป็นผลสำเร็จ	hâi bpen phŏn săm-rèt
successful (adj)	ที่สำเร็จ	thêe săm-rèt
luck (good luck)	โชค	chôhk
Good luck!	ขอให้โชคดี!	khŏr hâi chôhk dee
lucky (e.g., ~ day)	มีโชค	mee chôhk
lucky (fortunate)	มีโชคดี	mee chôhk dee
failure	ความล้มเหลว	khwaam lóm lĕo
misfortune	โชคร้าย	chôhk ráai
bad luck	โชคร้าย	chôhk ráai
unsuccessful (adj)	ไม่ประสบ ความสำเร็จ	mâi bprà-sòp khwaam săm-rèt
catastrophe	ความล้มเหลว	khwaam lóm lĕo
pride	ความภาคภูมิใจ	khwaam phâak phoom jai
proud (adj)	ภูมิใจ	phoom jai
to be proud	ภูมิใจ	phoom jai
winner	ผู้ชนะ	phôo chá-ná
to win (vi)	ชนะ	chá-ná
to lose (not win)	แพ้	pháe
try	ความพยายาม	khwaam phá-yaa-yaam
to try (vi)	พยายาม	phá-yaa-yaam
chance (opportunity)	โอกาส	oh-gàat

70. Quarrels. Negative emotions

shout (scream)	เสียงตะโกน	sĭang dtà-gohn
to shout (vi)	ตะโกน	dtà-gohn
to start to cry out	เริ่มตะโกน	rêrm dtà-gohn
quarrel	การทะเลาะ	gaan thá-lór
to quarrel (vi)	ทะเลาะ	thá-lór

fight (squabble)	ความทะเลาะ	khwaam thá-lór
to make a scene	ตีโพยตีพาย	dtee phoi dtee phaai
conflict	ความขัดแย้ง	khwaam khàt yáeng
misunderstanding	การเขาใจผิด	gaan khâo jai phìt
insult	คำดูถูก	kham doo thòok
to insult (vt)	ดูถูก	doo thòok
insulted (adj)	โดนดูถูก	dohn doo thòok
resentment	ความเคียดแค้น	khwaam khîat-kháen
to offend (vt)	ลวงเกิน	lûang gern
to take offense	ถือสา	thěu sǎa
indignation	ความโกรธแค้น	khwaam gròht kháen
to be indignant	ขุนเคือง	khùn kheuang
complaint	คำร้อง	kham rórng
to complain (vi, vt)	บ่น	bòn
apology	คำขอโทษ	kham khǒr thôht
to apologize (vi)	ขอโทษ	khǒr thôht
to beg pardon	ขออภัย	khǒr a-phai
criticism	คำวิจารณ์	kham wí-jaan
to criticize (vt)	วิจารณ์	wí-jaan
accusation (charge)	การกลาวหา	gaan glàao hǎa
to accuse (vt)	กลาวหา	glàao hǎa
revenge	การแก้แค้น	gaan gâe kháen
to avenge (get revenge)	แก้แค้น	gâe kháen
to pay back	แก้แค้น	gâe kháen
disdain	ความดูหมิ่น	khwaam doo mìn
to despise (vt)	ดูหมิ่น	doo mìn
hatred, hate	ความเกลียดชัง	khwaam glìat chang
to hate (vt)	เกลียด	glìat
nervous (adj)	กระวนกระวาย	grà won grà waai
to be nervous	กระวนกระวาย	grà won grà waai
angry (mad)	โกรธ	gròht
to make angry	ทำให้...โกรธ	tham hâi...gròht
humiliation	ความเสียดเย้ย	khwaam sìat yóie
to humiliate (vt)	ฉีกหน้า	chèek nâa
to humiliate oneself	ฉีกหน้าตนเอง	chèek nâa dton ayng
shock	ความตกตะลึง	khwaam dtòk dtà-leung
to shock (vt)	ทำให้...ตกตะลึง	tham hâi...dtòk dtà-leung
trouble (e.g., serious ~)	ปัญหา	bpan-hǎa
unpleasant (adj)	ไม่นาพึงพอใจ	mâi nâa pheung phor jai
fear (dread)	ความกลัว	khwaam glua
terrible (storm, heat)	แย่	yâe

scary (e.g., ~ story)	น่ากลัว	nâa glua
horror	ความกลัว	khwaam glua
awful (crime, news)	แย่มาก	yâe mâak
to begin to tremble	เริ่มตัวสั่น	rêrm dtua sàn
to cry (weep)	ร้องไห้	rórng hâi
to start crying	เริ่มร้องไห้	rêrm rórng hâi
tear	น้ำตา	nám dtaa
fault	ความผิด	khwaam phìt
guilt (feeling)	ผิด	phìt
dishonor (disgrace)	เสียเกียรติ	sĭa gìat
protest	การประท้วง	gaan bprà-thúang
stress	ความว้าวุ่นใจ	khwaam wáa-wûn-jai
to disturb (vt)	รบกวน	róp guan
to be furious	โกรธจัด	gròht jàt
mad, angry (adj)	โกรธ	gròht
to end (~ a relationship)	ยุติ	yút-dtì
to swear (at sb)	ดุด่า	dù dàa
to scare (become afraid)	ตกใจ	dtòk jai
to hit (strike with hand)	ตี	dtee
to fight (street fight, etc.)	สู้	sôo
to settle (a conflict)	ยุติ	yút-dtì
discontented (adj)	ไม่พอใจ	mâi phor jai
furious (adj)	โกรธจัด	gròht jàt
It's not good!	มันไม่ค่อยดี	man mâi khôi dee
It's bad!	มันไม่ดีเลย	man mâi dee loie

Medicine

71. Diseases

sickness	โรค	rôhk
to be sick	ป่วย	bpùay
health	สุขภาพ	sùk-khà-phâap
runny nose (coryza)	น้ำมูกไหล	nám môok lǎi
tonsillitis	ตอมทอนซิลอักเสบ	dtòm thorn-sin àk-sàyp
cold (illness)	หวัด	wàt
to catch a cold	เป็นหวัด	bpen wàt
bronchitis	โรคหลอดลมอักเสบ	rôhk lòrt lom àk-sàyp
pneumonia	โรคปอดบวม	rôhk bpòrt-buam
flu, influenza	ไขหวัดใหญ	khâi wàt yài
nearsighted (adj)	สายตาสั้น	sǎai dtaa sân
farsighted (adj)	สายตายาว	sǎai dtaa yaao
strabismus (crossed eyes)	ตาเหล	dtaa lày
cross-eyed (adj)	เป็นตาเหล	bpen dtaa kǎy rĕu lày
cataract	ตูอกระจก	dtôr grà-jòk
glaucoma	ตอหิน	dtôr hĭn
stroke	โรคหลอดเลือดสมอง	rôhk lòrt lêuat sà-mŏrng
heart attack	อาุการหัวใจวาย	aa-gaan hǔa jai waai
myocardial infarction	กลามเนื้อหัวใจตาย เหตุขาดเลือด	glâam néua hǔa jai dtaai hàyt khàat lêuat
paralysis	อัมพูาต	am-má-phâat
to paralyze (vt)	ทำใหเป็น อัมพาต	tham hâi bpen am-má-phâat
allergy	ภูมิแพ้	phoom pháe
asthma	โรคหืด	rôhk hèut
diabetes	โรคเบาหวาน	rôhk bao wǎan
toothache	อาการปวดฟัน	aa-gaan bpùat fan
caries	ฟันผุ	fan phù
diarrhea	อาการทูองเสีย	aa-gaan thórng sĭa
constipation	อาการทองผูก	aa-gaan thórng phòok
stomach upset	อาการปวดทอง	aa-gaan bpùat thórng
food poisoning	ภาวะอาหารเป็นพิษ	phaa-wá aa hǎan bpen pít
to get food poisoning	กินอาหารเป็นพิษ	gin aa hǎan bpen phít
arthritis	โรคขออักเสบ	rôhk khôr àk-sàyp
rickets	โรคกระดูกออน	rôhk grà-dòok òrn

rheumatism	โรครูมาติก	rôhk roo-maa-dtìk
atherosclerosis	ภาวะหลอดเลือดแข็ง	phaa-wá lòrt lêuat khǎeng
gastritis	โรคกระเพาะอาหาร	rôhk grà-phór aa-hǎan
appendicitis	ไส้ติ่งอักุเสบ	sâi dtìng àk-sàyp
cholecystitis	โรคถุงน้ำดี อักเสบ	rôhk thǔng nám dee àk-sàyp
ulcer	แผลเปื่อย	phlǎe bpèuay
measles	โรคหัด	rôhk hàt
rubella (German measles)	โรคหัดเยอรมัน	rôhk hàt yer-rá-man
jaundice	โรคดีซ่าน	rôhk dee sâan
hepatitis	โรคตับอักเสบ	rôhk dtàp àk-sàyp
schizophrenia	โรคจิตเภท	rôhk jìt-dtà-phâyt
rabies (hydrophobia)	โรคพิษสุนัขบ้า	rôhk phít sù-nák bâa
neurosis	โรคประสาท	rôhk bprà-sàat
concussion	สมองกระทบ กระเทือน	sà-mǒrng grà-thóp grà-theuan
cancer	มะเร็ง	má-reng
sclerosis	กูวรแข็งตัวของ เนื้อเยื่อรางกาย	gaan kǎeng dtua kǒng néua yêua râang gaai
multiple sclerosis	โรคปลอกประสาท เสื่อมแข็ง	rôhk bplòk bprà-sàat sèuam kǎeng
alcoholism	โรคพิษสุราเรื้อรัง	rôhk phít sù-raa réua rang
alcoholic (n)	คนขี้เหล้า	khon khêe lâo
syphilis	โรคซิฟิลิส	rôhk sí-fí-lít
AIDS	โรคเอดส	rôhk àyt
tumor	เนื้องอก	néua ngôk
malignant (adj)	ร้าย	ráai
benign (adj)	ไม่ร้าย	mâi ráai
fever	ไข้	khâi
malaria	ไข้มาลาเรีย	kâi maa-laa-ria
gangrene	เนื้อตายเน่า	néua dtaai nâo
seasickness	ภาวะเมาคลื่น	phaa-wá mao khlêun
epilepsy	โรคลมบ้าหมู	rôhk lom bâa-mǒo
epidemic	โรคระบาด	rôhk rá-bàat
typhus	โรครากสาดใหญ่	rôhk râak-sàat yài
tuberculosis	วัณโรค	wan-ná-rôhk
cholera	อหิวาตกโรค	a-hì-wâat-gà-rôhk
plague (bubonic ~)	กาฬโรค	gaan-lá-rôhk

72. Symptoms. Treatments. Part 1

symptom	อาการ	aa-gaan
temperature	อุณหภูมิ	un-hà-phoom

high temperature (fever)	อุณหภูมิสูง	un-hà-phoom sŏong
pulse (heartbeat)	ชีพจร	chêep-phá-jon
dizziness (vertigo)	อาการเวียนหัว	aa-gaan wian hŭa
hot (adj)	รอน	rórn
shivering	หนาวสั่น	năao sàn
pale (e.g., ~ face)	หนาเซียว	nâa sieow
cough	การไอ	gaan ai
to cough (vi)	ไอ	ai
to sneeze (vi)	จาม	jaam
faint	การเป็นลม	gaan bpen lom
to faint (vi)	เป็นลม	bpen lom
bruise (hématome)	ฟกช้ำ	fók chám
bump (lump)	บวม	buam
to bang (bump)	ชน	chon
contusion (bruise)	รอยฟกช้ำ	roi fók chám
to get a bruise	ได้รอยช้ำ	dâai roi chám
to limp (vi)	กะโผลกกะเผลก	gà-phlòhk-gà-phlàyk
dislocation	ขอหลุด	khôr lùt
to dislocate (vt)	ทำขอหลุด	tham khôr lùt
fracture	กระดูกหัก	grà-dòok hàk
to have a fracture	หักกระดูก	hàk grà-dòok
cut (e.g., paper ~)	รอยบาด	roi bàat
to cut oneself	ทำบาด	tham bàat
bleeding	การเลือดไหล	gaan lêuat lăi
burn (injury)	แผลไฟไหม้	phlăe fai mâi
to get burned	ได้รับแผลไฟไหม้	dâai ráp phlăe fai mâi
to prick (vt)	ตำ	dtam
to prick oneself	ตำตัวเอง	dtam dtua ayng
to injure (vt)	ทำให้บาดเจ็บ	tham hâi bàat jèp
injury	การบาดเจ็บ	gaan bàat jèp
wound	แผล	phlăe
trauma	แผลบาดเจ็บ	phlăe bàat jèp
to be delirious	คลุ้มคลั่ง	khlúm khlâng
to stutter (vi)	พูดตะกุกตะกัก	phôot dtà-gùk-dtà-gàk
sunstroke	โรคลมแดด	rôhk lom dàet

73. Symptoms. Treatments. Part 2

pain, ache	ความเจ็บปวด	khwaam jèp bpùat
splinter (in foot, etc.)	เสี้ยน	sîan
sweat (perspiration)	เหงื่อ	ngèua
to sweat (perspire)	เหงื่อออก	ngèua òrk

vomiting	การอาเจียน	gaan aa-jian
convulsions	การชัก	gaan chák
pregnant (adj)	ตั้งครรภ์	dtâng khan
to be born	เกิด	gèrt
delivery, labor	การคลอด	gaan khlôrt
to deliver (~ a baby)	คลอดบุตร	khlôrt bùt
abortion	การแทงบุตร	gaan tháeng bùt
breathing, respiration	การหายใจ	gaan hăai-jai
in-breath (inhalation)	การหายใจเข้า	gaan hăai-jai khâo
out-breath (exhalation)	การหายใจออก	gaan hăai-jai òrk
to exhale (breathe out)	หายใจออก	hăai-jai òrk
to inhale (vi)	หายใจเข้า	hăai-jai khâo
disabled person	คนพิการ	khon phí-gaan
cripple	พิการ	phí-gaan
drug addict	ผู้ติดยาเสพติด	phôo dtìt yaa-sàyp-dtìt
deaf (adj)	หูหนวก	hŏo nùak
mute (adj)	เป็นใบ้	bpen bâi
deaf mute (adj)	หูหนวกเป็นใบ้	hŏo nùak bpen bâi
mad, insane (adj)	บ้า	bâa
madman (demented person)	คนบ้า	khon bâa
madwoman	คนบ้า	khon bâa
to go insane	เสียสติ	sĭa sà-dtì
gene	ยีน	yeun
immunity	ภูมิคุ้มกัน	phoom khúm gan
hereditary (adj)	เป็นกรรมพันธุ์	bpen gam-má-phan
congenital (adj)	แต่กำเนิด	dtàe gam-nèrt
virus	เชื้อไวรัส	chéua wai-rát
microbe	จุลินทรีย์	jù-lin-see
bacterium	แบคทีเรีย	bàek-tee-ria
infection	การติดเชื้อ	gaan dtìt chéua

74. Symptoms. Treatments. Part 3

hospital	โรงพยาบาล	rohng phá-yaa-baan
patient	ผู้ป่วย	phôo bpùay
diagnosis	การวินิจฉัยโรค	gaan wí-nít-chăi rôhk
cure	การรักษา	gaan rák-săa
medical treatment	การรักษาทางการแพทย์	gaan rák-săa thaang gaan phâet
to get treatment	รับการรักษา	ráp gaan rák-săa
to treat (~ a patient)	รักษา	rák-săa

to nurse (look after)	รักษา	rák-săa
care (nursing ~)	การดูแลรักษา	gaan doo lae rák-săa
operation, surgery	การผ่าตัด	gaan phàa dtàt
to bandage (head, limb)	พันแผล	phan phlăe
bandaging	การพันแผล	gaan phan phlăe
vaccination	การฉีดวัคซีน	gaan chèet wák-seen
to vaccinate (vt)	ฉีดวัคซีน	chèet wák-seen
injection, shot	การฉีดยา	gaan chèet yaa
to give an injection	ฉีดยา	chèet yaa
attack	มีอาการเฉียบพลัน	mee aa-gaan chìap phlan
amputation	การตัดอวัยวะออก	gaan dtàt a-wai-wá òrk
to amputate (vt)	ตัด	dtàt
coma	อาการโคม่า	aa-gaan khoh-mâa
to be in a coma	อยู่ในอาการโคม่า	yòo nai aa-gaan khoh-mâa
intensive care	หนวยอภิบาล	nùay à-phí-baan
to recover (~ from flu)	ฟื้นตัว	féun dtua
condition (patient's ~)	อาการ	aa-gaan
consciousness	สติสัมปชัญญะ	sà-dtì săm-bpà-chan-yá
memory (faculty)	ความทรงจำ	khwaam song jam
to pull out (tooth)	ถอน	thŏrn
filling	การอุด	gaan ùt
to fill (a tooth)	อุด	ùt
hypnosis	การสะกดจิต	gaan sà-gòt jìt
to hypnotize (vt)	สะกดจิต	sà-gòt jìt

75. Doctors

doctor	แพทย์	phâet
nurse	พยาบาล	phá-yaa-baan
personal doctor	แพทย์สวนตัว	phâet sùan dtua
dentist	ทันตแพทย์	than-dtà phâet
eye doctor	จักษุแพทย์	jàk-sù phâet
internist	อายุรแพทย์	aa-yú-rá-phâet
surgeon	ศัลยแพทย์	săn-yá-phâet
psychiatrist	จิตแพทย์	jìt-dtà-phâet
pediatrician	กุมารแพทย์	gù-maan phâet
psychologist	นักจิตวิทยา	nák jìt wít-thá-yaa
gynecologist	นรีแพทย์	ná-ree phâet
cardiologist	หทัยแพทย์	hà-thai phâet

76. Medicine. Drugs. Accessories

medicine, drug	ยา	yaa
remedy	ยา	yaa
to prescribe (vt)	จ่ายยา	jàai yaa
prescription	ใบสั่งยา	bai sàng yaa
tablet, pill	ยาเม็ด	yaa mét
ointment	ยาทา	yaa thaa
ampule	หลอดยา	lòrt yaa
mixture, solution	ยาส่วนผสม	yaa sùan phà-sŏm
syrup	น้ำเชื่อม	nám chêuam
capsule	ยาเม็ด	yaa mét
powder	ยาผง	yaa phŏng
gauze bandage	ผ้าพันแผล	phâa phan phlăe
cotton wool	สำลี	săm-lee
iodine	ไอโอดีน	ai oh-deen
Band-Aid	พลาสเตอร์	phláat-dtêr
eyedropper	ที่หยอดตา	thêe yòrt dtaa
thermometer	ปรอท	bpa -ròrt
syringe	เข็มฉีดยา	khĕm chèet-yaa
wheelchair	รถเข็นคนพิการ	rót khĕn khon phí-gaan
crutches	ไม้ค้ำยัน	máai khám yan
painkiller	ยาแก้ปวด	yaa gâe bpùat
laxative	ยาระบาย	yaa rá-baai
spirits (ethanol)	เอธานอล	ay-thaa-norn
medicinal herbs	สมุนไพรทางการแพทย์	sà-mŭn phrai thaang gaan phâet
herbal (~ tea)	สมุนไพร	sà-mŭn phrai

77. Smoking. Tobacco products

tobacco	ยาสูบ	yaa sòop
cigarette	บุหรี่	bù rèe
cigar	ซิการ์	sí-gâa
pipe	ไปป์	bpai
pack (of cigarettes)	ซอง	sorng
matches	ไม้ขีด	máai khèet
matchbox	กล่องไม้ขีด	glòrng máai khèet
lighter	ไฟแช็ก	fai cháek
ashtray	ที่เขี่ยบุหรี่	thêe khìa bù rèe
cigarette case	กล่องใส่บุหรี่	glòrng sài bù rèe
cigarette holder	ที่ตอบุหรี่	thêe dtòr bù rèe
filter (cigarette tip)	ตัวกรองบุหรี่	dtua grorng bù rèe

to smoke (vi, vt)	สูบ	sòop
to light a cigarette	จุดบุหรี่	jùt bù rèe
smoking	การสูบบุหรี่	gaan sòop bù rèe
smoker	ผู้สูบบุหรี่	pôo sòop bù rèe
stub, butt (of cigarette)	ก้นบุหรี่	gôn bù rèe
smoke, fumes	ควันบุหรี่	khwan bù rèe
ash	ขี้บุหรี่	khêe bù rèe

HUMAN HABITAT

City

city, town	เมือง	meuang
capital city	เมืองหลวง	meuang lŭang
village	หมู่บ้าน	mòo bâan

city map	แผนที่เมือง	phăen thêe meuang
downtown	ใจกลางเมือง	jai glaang-meuang
suburb	ชานเมือง	chaan meuang
suburban (adj)	ชานเมือง	chaan meuang

outskirts	รอบนอกเมือง	rôrp nôrk meuang
environs (suburbs)	เขตรอบเมือง	khàyt rôrp-meuang
city block	บล็อกผังเมือง	blòrk phăng meuang
residential block (area)	บล็อกที่อยู่อาศัย	blòrk thêe yòo aa-săi

traffic	การจราจร	gaan jà-raa-jon
traffic lights	ไฟจราจร	fai jà-raa-jon
public transportation	ขนส่งมวลชน	khŏn sòng muan chon
intersection	สี่แยก	sèe yâek

crosswalk	ทางม้าลาย	thaang máa laai
pedestrian underpass	อุโมงค์คนเดิน	u-mohng kon dern
to cross (~ the street)	ข้าม	khâam
pedestrian	คนเดินเท้า	khon dern tháo
sidewalk	ทางเท้า	thaang tháo

bridge	สะพาน	sà-phaan
embankment (river walk)	ทางเลียบแม่น้ำ	thaang lîap mâe náam
fountain	น้ำพุ	nám phú

allée (garden walkway)	ทางเลียบสวน	thaang lîap sŭan
park	สวน	sŭan
boulevard	ถนนกว้าง	thà-nŏn gwâang
square	จัตุรัส	jàt-dtù-ràt
avenue (wide street)	ถนนใหญ่	thà-nŏn yài
street	ถนน	thà-nŏn
side street	ซอย	soi
dead end	ทางตัน	thaang dtan
house	บ้าน	bâan
building	อาคาร	aa-khaan

skyscraper	ตึกระฟ้า	dtèuk rá-fáa
facade	ดานหนาอาคาร	dâan-nâa aa-khaan
roof	หลังคา	lăng khaa
window	หูนาตาง	nâa dtàang
arch	ชุมประตู	súm bprà-dtoo
column	เสา	săo
corner	มุม	mum

store window	หน้าต่างร้านค้า	nâa dtàang ráan kháa
signboard (store sign, etc.)	ป้ายราน	bpâai ráan
poster (e.g., playbill)	โปสเตอร	bpòht-dtêr
advertising poster	ป้ายโฆษณา	bpâai khôht-sà-naa
billboard	กระดานปิดประกาศโฆษณา	grà-daan bpìt bprà-gàat khôht-sà-naa

garbage, trash	ขยะ	khà-yà
trash can (public ~)	ถังขยะ	thăng khà-yà
to litter (vi)	ทิ้งขยะ	thíng khà-yà
garbage dump	ที่ทิ้งขยะ	thêe thíng khà-yà

phone booth	ตู้โทรศัพท์	dtôo thoh-rá-sàp
lamppost	เสาโคม	săo khohm
bench (park ~)	มานั่ง	máa nâng

police officer	เจ้าหน้าที่ตำรวจ	jâo nâa-thêe dtam-rùat
police	ตำรวจ	dtam-rùat
beggar	ขอทาน	khŏr thaan
homeless (n)	คนไรบาน	khon rái bâan

79. Urban institutions

store	ร้านค้า	ráan kháa
drugstore, pharmacy	ร้านขายยา	ráan khăai yaa
eyeglass store	รานตัดแวน	ráan dtàt wâen
shopping mall	ศูนยการคา	sŏon gaan kháa
supermarket	ซูเปอรมารเก็ต	soo-bper-maa-gèt

bakery	ร้านขนมปัง	ráan khà-nŏm bpang
baker	คนอบขนมปัง	khon òp khà-nŏm bpang
pastry shop	รานขนม	ráan khà-nŏm
grocery store	รานขายของชำ	ráan khăai khŏrng oham
butcher shop	รานขายเนื้อ	ráan khăai néua

| produce store | ร้านขายผัก | ráan khăai phàk |
| market | ตลาด | dtà-làat |

coffee house	ร้านกาแฟ	ráan gaa-fae
restaurant	รานอาหาร	ráan aa-hăan
pub, bar	บาร	baa
pizzeria	รานพิชซา	ráan phís-sâa

hair salon	ร้านทำผม	ráan tham phŏm
post office	โรงไปรษณีย์	rohng bprai-sà-nee
dry cleaners	ร้านซักแหง	ráan sák hâeng
photo studio	หองถายภาพ	hôrng thàai phâap
shoe store	ร้านขายรองเท้า	ráan khăai rorng táo
bookstore	ร้านขายหนังสือ	ráan khăai năng-sĕu
sporting goods store	ร้านขาย อุปกรณ์กีฬา	ráan khăai u-bpà-gon gee-laa
clothes repair shop	ร้านซ่อมเสื้อผ้า	ráan sôrm sêua phâa
formal wear rental	ร้านเชาเสื้อออกงาน	ráan châo sêua òrk ngaan
video rental store	รานเชาวิดีโอ	ráan châo wí-dee-oh
circus	โรงละครสัตว์	rohng lá-khon sàt
zoo	สวนสัตว์	sŭan sàt
movie theater	โรงภาพยนุตร์	rohng phâap-phá-yon
museum	พิพิธภัณฑ	phí-phítha phan
library	หองสมุด	hôrng sà-mùt
theater	โรงละคร	rohng lá-khon
opera (opera house)	โรงอุปรากร	rohng ù-bpà-raa-gon
nightclub	ไนทคลับ	nai-khláp
casino	คาสิโน	khaa-sì-noh
mosque	สุเหร่า	sù-rào
synagogue	โบสถยิว	bòht yiw
cathedral	อาสนวิหาร	aa sŏn wí-hăan
temple	วิหาร	wí-hăan
church	โบสถ	bòht
college	วิทยาลัย	wít-thá-yaa-lai
university	มหาวิทยาลัย	má-hăa wít-thá-yaa-lai
school	โรงเรียน	rohng rian
prefecture	ศาลากลางจังหวัด	săa-laa glaang jang-wàt
city hall	ศาลาเทศบาล	săa-laa thâyt-sà-baan
hotel	โรงแรม	rohng raem
bank	ธนาคาร	thá-naa-khaan
embassy	สถานทูต	sà-thăan thôot
travel agency	บริษัททัวร์	bor-rí-sàt thua
information office	สำนักงาน ศูนยขอมูล	săm-nák ngaan sŏon khôr moon
currency exchange	รานแลกเงิน	ráan lâek ngern
subway	รถไฟใต้ดิน	rót fai dtâi din
hospital	โรงพยาบาล	rohng phá-yaa-baan
gas station	ปั้มน้ำมัน	bpám náam man
parking lot	ลานจอดรถ	laan jòrt rót

80. Signs

signboard (store sign, etc.)	ป้ายร้าน	bpâai ráan
notice (door sign, etc.)	ป้ายเตือน	bpâai dteuan
poster	โปสเตอร์	bpòht-dtêr
direction sign	ป้ายบอกทาง	bpâai bòrk thaang
arrow (sign)	ลูกศร	lôok sŏn
caution	คำเตือน	kham dteuan
warning sign	ป้ายเตือน	bpâai dteuan
to warn (vt)	เตือน	dteuan
rest day (weekly ~)	วันหยุด	wan yùt
timetable (schedule)	ตารางเวลา	dtaa-raang way-laa
opening hours	เวลาทำการ	way-laa tham gaan
WELCOME!	ยินดีต้อนรับ!	yin dee dtôrn ráp
ENTRANCE	ทางเขา	thaang khâo
EXIT	ทางออก	thaang òrk
PUSH	ผลัก	phlàk
PULL	ดึง	deung
OPEN	เปิด	bpèrt
CLOSED	ปิด	bpìt
WOMEN	หญิง	yĭng
MEN	ชาย	chaai
DISCOUNTS	ลดราคา	lót raa-khaa
SALE	ขายของลดราคา	khăai khŏrng lót raa-khaa
NEW!	ใหม่!	mài
FREE	ฟรี	free
ATTENTION!	โปรดทราบ!	bpròht sâap
NO VACANCIES	ไม่มีห้องว่าง	mâi mee hôrng wâang
RESERVED	จองแล้ว	jorng láew
ADMINISTRATION	สำนักงาน	săm-nák ngaan
STAFF ONLY	เฉพาะพนักงาน	chà-phór phá-nák ngaan
BEWARE OF THE DOG!	ระวังสุนัข!	rá-wang sù-nák
NO SMOKING	ห้ามสูบบุหรี่	hâam sòop bù rèe
DO NOT TOUCH!	ห้ามแตะ!	hâam dtàe
DANGEROUS	อันตราย	an-dtà-raai
DANGER	อันตราย	an-dtà-raai
HIGH VOLTAGE	ไฟฟ้าแรงสูง	fai fáa raeng sŏong
NO SWIMMING!	ห้ามวายน้ำ!	hâam wâai náam
OUT OF ORDER	เสีย	sĭa
FLAMMABLE	อันตรายติดไฟ	an-dtà-raai dtìt fai
FORBIDDEN	ห้าม	hâam

| NO TRESPASSING! | ห้ามผ่าน! | hâam phàan |
| WET PAINT | สีพื้นเปียก | sĕe phéun bpìak |

81. Urban transportation

bus	รถเมล์	rót may
streetcar	รถราง	rót raang
trolley bus	รถโดยสารประจำ ทางไฟฟ้า	rót doi săan bprà-jam thaang fai fáa
route (of bus, etc.)	เส้นทาง	sên thaang
number (e.g., bus ~)	หมายเลข	măai lâyk
to go by ...	ไปด้วย	bpai dûay
to get on (~ the bus)	ขึ้น	khêun
to get off ...	ลง	long
stop (e.g., bus ~)	ป้าย	bpâai
next stop	ป้ายถัดไป	bpâai thàt bpai
terminus	ป้ายสุดท้าย	bpâai sùt tháai
schedule	ตารางเวลา	dtaa-raang way-laa
to wait (vt)	รอ	ror
ticket	ตั๋ว	dtŭa
fare	ค่าตั๋ว	khâa dtŭa
cashier (ticket seller)	คนขายตั๋ว	khon khăai dtŭa
ticket inspection	การตรวจตั๋ว	gaan dtrùat dtŭa
ticket inspector	พนักงานตรวจตั๋ว	phá-nák ngaan dtrùat dtŭa
to be late (for ...)	ไปสาย	bpai săai
to miss (~ the train, etc.)	พลาด	phlâat
to be in a hurry	รีบเร่ง	rêep râyng
taxi, cab	แท็กซี่	tháek-sêe
taxi driver	คนขับแท็กซี่	khon khàp tháek-sêe
by taxi	โดยแท็กซี่	doi tháek-sêe
taxi stand	ป้ายจอดแท็กซี่	bpâai jòrt tháek sêe
to call a taxi	เรียกแท็กซี่	rîak tháek sêe
to take a taxi	ขึ้นรถแท็กซี่	khêun rót tháek-sêe
traffic	การจราจร	gaan jà-raa-jon
traffic jam	การจราจรติดขัด	gaan jà-raa-jon dtìt khàt
rush hour	ชั่วโมงเร่งด่วน	chûa mohng râyng dùan
to park (vi)	จอด	jòrt
to park (vt)	จอด	jòrt
parking lot	ลานจอดรถ	laan jòrt rót
subway	รถไฟใต้ดิน	rót fai dtâi din
station	สถานี	sà-thăa-nee
to take the subway	ขึ้นรถไฟใต้ดิน	khêun rót fai dtâi din

train	รถไฟ	rót fai
train station	สถานีรถไฟ	sà-thǎa-nee rót fai

82. Sightseeing

monument	อนุสาวรีย์	a-nú-sǎa-wá-ree
fortress	ป้อม	bpôrm
palace	วัง	wang
castle	ปราสาท	bpraa-sàat
tower	หอ	hǒr
mausoleum	สุสาน	sù-sǎan
architecture	สถาปัตยกรรม	sà-thǎa-bpàt-dtà-yá-gam
medieval (adj)	ยุคกลาง	yúk glaang
ancient (adj)	โบราณ	boh-raan
national (adj)	แห่งชาติ	hàeng châat
famous (monument, etc.)	ที่มีชื่อเสียง	thêe mee chêu-sǐang
tourist	นักท่องเที่ยว	nák thôrng thîeow
guide (person)	มัคคุเทศก์	mák-khú-thâyt
excursion, sightseeing tour	ทัศนศึกษา	thát-sà-ná-sèuk-sǎa
to show (vt)	แสดง	sà-daeng
to tell (vt)	เล่า	lâo
to find (vt)	หาพบ	hǎa phóp
to get lost (lose one's way)	หลงทาง	lǒng thaang
map (e.g., subway ~)	แผนที่	phǎen thêe
map (e.g., city ~)	แผนที่	phǎen thêe
souvenir, gift	ของที่ระลึก	khǒrng thêe rá-léuk
gift shop	ร้านขาย ของที่ระลึก	ráan khǎai khǒrng thêe rá-léuk
to take pictures	ถ่ายภาพ	thàai phâap
to have one's picture taken	ได้รับการ ถ่ายภาพให้	dâai ráp gaan thàai phâap hâi

83. Shopping

to buy (purchase)	ซื้อ	séu
purchase	ของซื้อ	khǒrng séu
to go shopping	ไปซื้อของ	bpai séu khǒrng
shopping	การชอปปิง	gaan chóp bping
to be open (ab. store)	เปิด	bpèrt
to be closed	ปิด	bpìt
footwear, shoes	รองเท้า	rorng tháo
clothes, clothing	เสื้อผ้า	sêua phâa

cosmetics	เครื่องสำอาง	khrêuang sǎm-aang
food products	อาหาร	aa-hǎan
gift, present	ของขวัญ	khǒng khwǎn
salesman	พนักงานขาย	phá-nák ngaan khǎai
saleswoman	พนักงานขาย	phá-nák ngaan khǎai
check out, cash desk	ที่จ่ายเงิน	thêe jàai ngern
mirror	กระจก	grà-jòk
counter (store ~)	เคาน์เตอร์	khao-dtêr
fitting room	หองลองเสื้อผ้า	hôrng lorng sêua phâa
to try on	ลอง	lorng
to fit (ab. dress, etc.)	เหมาะ	mò
to like (I like ...)	ชอบ	chôrp
price	ราคา	raa-khaa
price tag	ป้ายราคา	bpâai raa-khaa
to cost (vt)	ราคา	raa-khaa
How much?	ราคาเท่าไหร่?	raa-khaa thâo rài
discount	ลดราคา	lót raa-khaa
inexpensive (adj)	ไม่แพง	mâi phaeng
cheap (adj)	ถูก	thòok
expensive (adj)	แพง	phaeng
It's expensive	มันราคาแพง	man raa-khaa phaeng
rental (n)	การเช่า	gaan châo
to rent (~ a tuxedo)	เช่า	châo
credit (trade credit)	สินเชื่อ	sǐn chêua
on credit (adv)	ซื้อเงินเชื่อ	séu ngern chêua

84. Money

money	เงิน	ngern
currency exchange	การแลกเปลี่ยนสกุลเงิน	gaan lâek bplìan sà-gun ngern
exchange rate	อัตราแลกเปลี่ยนสกุลเงิน	àt-dtraa lâek bplìan sà-gun ngern
ATM	เอทีเอ็ม	ay-thee-em
coin	เหรียญ	rǐan
dollar	ดอลลาร์	dorn-lâa
euro	ยูโร	yoo-roh
lira	ลีราอิตาลี	lee-raa ì-dtaa-lee
Deutschmark	มาร์ค	mâak
franc	ฟรังค์	frang
pound sterling	ปอนด์สเตอร์ลิง	bporn sà-dtêr-ling
yen	เยน	yayn

debt	หนี้	nêe
debtor	ลูกหนี้	lôok nêe
to lend (money)	ให้ยืม	hâi yeum
to borrow (vi, vt)	ขอยืม	khǒr yeum

bank	ธนาคาร	thá-naa-khaan
account	บัญชี	ban-chee
to deposit (vt)	ฝาก	fàak
to deposit into the account	ฝากเงินเข้าบัญชี	fàak ngern khâo ban-chee
to withdraw (vt)	ถอน	thǒrn

credit card	บัตรเครดิต	bàt khray-dìt
cash	เงินสด	ngern sòt
check	เช็ค	chék
to write a check	เขียนเช็ค	khǐan chék
checkbook	สมุดเช็ค	sà-mùt chék

wallet	กระเป๋าเงิน	grà-bpǎo ngern
change purse	กระเป๋าสตางค์	grà-bpǎo sà-dtaang
safe	ตู้เซฟ	dtôo sâyf

heir	ทายาท	thaa-yâat
inheritance	มรดก	mor-rá-dòrk
fortune (wealth)	เงินจำนวนมาก	ngern jam-nuan mâak

lease	สัญญาเช่า	sǎn-yaa châo
rent (money)	ค่าเช่า	kâa châo
to rent (sth from sb)	เช่า	châo

price	ราคา	raa-khaa
cost	ราคา	raa-khaa
sum	จำนวนเงินรวม	jam-nuan ngern ruam

to spend (vt)	จ่าย	jàai
expenses	ค่าจ่าย	khâa jàai
to economize (vi, vt)	ประหยัด	bprà-yàt
economical	ประหยัด	bprà-yàt

to pay (vi, vt)	จ่าย	jàai
payment	การจ่ายเงิน	gaan jàai ngern
change (give the ~)	เงินทอน	ngern thorn

tax	ภาษี	phaa-sěe
fine	ค่าปรับ	khâa bpràp
to fine (vt)	ปรับ	bpràp

85. Post. Postal service

| post office | โรงไปรษณีย์ | rohng bprai-sà-nee |
| mail (letters, etc.) | จดหมาย | jòt mǎai |

mailman	บุรุษไปรษณีย์	bù-rùt bprai-sà-nee
opening hours	เวลาทำการ	way-laa tham gaan
letter	จดหมาย	jòt măai
registered letter	จดหมายลงทะเบียน	jòt măai long thá-bian
postcard	ไปรษณียบัตร	bprai-sà-nee-yá-bàt
telegram	โทรเลข	thoh-rá-lâyk
package (parcel)	พัสดุ	phát-sà-dù
money transfer	การโอนเงิน	gaan ohn ngern
to receive (vt)	รับ	ráp
to send (vt)	ฝาก	fàak
sending	การฝาก	gaan fàak
address	ที่อยู่	thêe yòo
ZIP code	รหัสไปรษณีย์	rá-hàt bprai-sà-nee
sender	ผู้ฝาก	phôo fàak
receiver	ผู้รับ	phôo ráp
name (first name)	ชื่อ	chêu
surname (last name)	นามสกุล	naam sà-gun
postage rate	อัตราค่าส่งไปรษณีย์	àt-dtraa khâa sòng bprai-sà-nee
standard (adj)	มาตรฐาน	mâat-dtrà-thăan
economical (adj)	ประหยัด	bprà-yàt
weight	น้ำหนัก	nám nàk
to weigh (~ letters)	มีน้ำหนัก	mee nám nàk
envelope	ซอง	sorng
postage stamp	แสตมป์ไปรษณีย์	sà-dtaem bprai-sà-nee
to stamp an envelope	แสตมป์ตราประทับบนซอง	sà-dtaem dtraa bprà-tháp bon song

Dwelling. House. Home

86. House. Dwelling

house	บ้าน	bâan
at home (adv)	ที่บ้าน	thêe bâan
yard	สนาม	sà-nǎam
fence (iron ~)	รั้ว	rúa
brick (n)	อิฐ	ìt
brick (as adj)	อิฐ	ìt
stone (n)	หิน	hǐn
stone (as adj)	หิน	hǐn
concrete (n)	คอนกรีต	khorn-grèet
concrete (as adj)	คอนกรีต	khorn-grèet
new (new-built)	ใหม่	mài
old (adj)	เก่า	gào
decrepit (house)	เสื่อมสภาพ	sèuam sà-phâap
modern (adj)	ทันสมัย	than sà-mǎi
multistory (adj)	ที่มีหลายชั้น	thêe mee lǎai chán
tall (~ building)	สูง	sǒong
floor, story	ชั้น	chán
single-story (adj)	ชั้นเดียว	chán dieow
1st floor	ชั้นล่าง	chán lâang
top floor	ชั้นบนสุด	chán bon sùt
roof	หลังคา	lǎng khaa
chimney	ปล่องควัน	bplòrng khwan
roof tiles	กระเบื้องหลังคา	grà-bêuang lǎng khaa
tiled (adj)	กระเบื้อง	grà-bêuang
attic (storage place)	ห้องใต้หลังคา	hôrng dtâi lǎng-khaa
window	หน้าต่าง	nâa dtàang
glass	แก้ว	gâew
window ledge	ชั้นติดผนัง	chán dtìt phà-nǎng
	ใต้หน้าต่าง	dtâi nâa dtàang
shutters	ชัตเตอร์	chát-dtêr
wall	ฝาผนัง	fǎa phà-nǎng
balcony	ระเบียง	rá-biang
downspout	รางน้ำ	raang náam
upstairs (to be ~)	ชั้นบน	chán bon
to go upstairs	ขึ้นไปข้างบน	khêun bpai khâang bon

to come down (the stairs)	ลง	long
to move (to new premises)	ย้ายไป	yáai bpai

87. House. Entrance. Lift

entrance	ทางเข้า	thaang khâo
stairs (stairway)	บันได	ban-dai
steps	ขั้นบันได	khân ban-dai
banister	ราวบันได	raao ban-dai
lobby (hotel ~)	ห้องโถง	hôrng thŏhng
mailbox	ตู้จดหมาย	dtôo jòt măai
garbage can	ถังขยะ	thăng khà-yà
trash chute	ช่องทิ้งขยะ	chôrng thíng khà-yà
elevator	ลิฟต์	líf
freight elevator	ลิฟต์ขนของ	líf khŏn khŏrng
elevator cage	กรงลิฟต์	grorng líf
to take the elevator	ขึ้นลิฟต์	khêun líf
apartment	อพาร์ตเมนต์	a-phâat-mayn
residents (~ of a building)	ผู้อาศัย	phôo aa-săi
neighbor (masc.)	เพื่อนบ้าน	phêuan bâan
neighbor (fem.)	เพื่อนบ้าน	phêuan bâan
neighbors	เพื่อนบ้าน	phêuan bâan

88. House. Electricity

electricity	ไฟฟ้า	fai fáa
light bulb	หลอดไฟฟ้า	lòrt fai fáa
switch	ปุ่มปิดเปิดไฟ	bpùm bpìt bpèrt fai
fuse (plug fuse)	ฟิวส์	fiw
cable, wire (electric ~)	สายไฟฟ้า	săai fai fáa
wiring	การเดินสายไฟ	gaan dern săai fai
electricity meter	มิเตอร์วัดไฟฟ้า	mí-dtêr wát fai fáa
readings	ค่ามิเตอร์	khâa mí-dtêr

89. House. Doors. Locks

door	ประตู	bprà-dtoo
gate (vehicle ~)	ประตูรั้ว	bprà-dtoo rúa
handle, doorknob	ลูกบิดประตู	lôok bìt bprà-dtoo
to unlock (unbolt)	ไข	khăi
to open (vt)	เปิด	bpèrt
to close (vt)	ปิด	bpìt

key	ลูกกุญแจ	lôok gun-jae
bunch (of keys)	พวง	phuang
to creak (door, etc.)	ออดแอด	órt-áet
creak	เสียงออดแอด	sĭang órt-áet
hinge (door ~)	บานพับ	baan pháp
doormat	ที่เช็ดเท้า	thêe chét tháo

door lock	แม่กุญแจ	mâe gun-jae
keyhole	รูกุญแจ	roo gun-jae
crossbar (sliding bar)	ไม้ที่วางขวาง	máai thêe waang khwăng
door latch	กลอนประตู	glorn bprà-dtoo
padlock	ดอกกุญแจ	dòrk gun-jae

to ring (~ the door bell)	กดออด	gòt òrt
ringing (sound)	เสียงดัง	sĭang dang
doorbell	กระดิ่งประตู	grà-dìng bprà-dtoo
doorbell button	ปุ่มออดหน้าประตู	bpùm òrt nâa bprà-dtoo
knock (at the door)	เสียงเคาะ	sĭang khór
to knock (vi)	เคาะ	khór

code	รหัส	rá-hàt
combination lock	กุญแจรหัส	gun-jae rá-hàt
intercom	อินเตอร์คอม	in-dtêr-khom
number (on the door)	เลข	lâyk
doorplate	ป้ายหน้าประตู	bpâai nâa bprà-dtoo
peephole	ช่องตาแมว	chôrng dtaa maew

90. Country house

village	หมู่บ้าน	mòo bâan
vegetable garden	สวนผัก	sŭan phàk
fence	รั้ว	rúa
picket fence	รั้วปักดิน	rúa bpàk din
wicket gate	ประตูรั้วเล็กๆ	bprà-dtoo rúa lék lék

granary	ยุ้งฉาง	yúng chăang
root cellar	ห้องใต้ดิน	hôrng dtâi din
shed (garden ~)	โรงนา	rohng naa
water well	บ่อน้ำ	bòr náam

| stove (wood-fired ~) | เตา | dtao |
| to stoke the stove | จุดไฟ | jùt fai |

| firewood | ฟืน | feun |
| log (firewood) | ท่อน | thôrn |

veranda	เฉลียงหน้าบ้าน	chà-lĭang nâa bâan
deck (terrace)	ระเบียง	rá-biang
stoop (front steps)	บันไดทางเข้าบ้าน	ban-dai thaang khâo bâan
swing (hanging seat)	ชิงช้า	ching cháa

91. Villa. Mansion

country house	บ้านสไตล์คันทรี่	bâan sà-dtai khan trêe
villa (seaside ~)	คฤหาสน์	khá-réu-hàat
wing (~ of a building)	สวน	sùan
garden	สวน	sŭan
park	สวน	sŭan
conservatory (greenhouse)	เรือนกระจกเขตร้อน	reuan grà-jòk khàyt rórn
to look after (garden, etc.)	ดูแล	doo lae
swimming pool	สระว่ายน้ำ	sà wâai náam
gym (home gym)	โรงยิม	rohng-yim
tennis court	สนามเทนนิส	sà-năam then-nít
home theater (room)	ห้องฉายหนัง	hôrng chăai năng
garage	โรงรถ	rohng rót
private property	ทรัพย์สินส่วนบุคคล	sáp sĭn sùan bùk-khon
private land	ที่ดินส่วนบุคคล	thêe din sùan bùk-khon
warning (caution)	คำเตือน	kham dteuan
warning sign	ป้ายเตือน	bpâai dteuan
security	ผู้รักษา ความปลอดภัย	phôo rák-săa khwaam bplòrt phai
security guard	ยาม	yaam
burglar alarm	สัญญาณกันขโมย	săn-yaan gan khà-moi

92. Castle. Palace

castle	ปราสาท	bpraa-sàat
palace	วัง	wang
fortress	ป้อม	bpôrm
wall (round castle)	กำแพง	gam-phaeng
tower	หอ	hŏr
keep, donjon	หอกลาง	hŏr klaang
portcullis	ประตูชักรอก	bprà-dtoo chák rôrk
underground passage	ทางใต้ดิน	taang dtâi din
moat	ดูเมือง	khoo meuang
chain	โซ่	sôh
arrow loop	ช่องยิงธนู	chôrng ying thá-noo
magnificent (adj)	ภัทร	phát
majestic (adj)	โอโถง	òh thŏhng
impregnable (adj)	ที่ไม่สวมารถ เจาะเขาไปถึง	thêe mâi săa-mâat jòr khăo bpai thĕung
medieval (adj)	ยุคกลาง	yúk glaang

93. Apartment

apartment	อพาร์ตเมนต์	a-phâat-mayn
room	ห้อง	hôrng
bedroom	ห้องนอน	hôrng norn
dining room	ห้องรับประทาน อาหาร	hôrng ráp bprà-thaan aa-hǎan
living room	ห้องนั่งเล่น	hôrng nâng lên
study (home office)	ห้องทำงาน	hôrng tham ngaan
entry room	ห้องเข้า	hôrng khâo
bathroom (room with a bath or shower)	ห้องน้ำ	hôrng náam
half bath	ห้องส้วม	hôrng sûam
ceiling	เพดาน	phay-daan
floor	พื้น	phéun
corner	มุม	mum

94. Apartment. Cleaning

to clean (vi, vt)	ทำความสะอาด	tham khwaam sà-àat
to put away (to stow)	เก็บ	gèp
dust	ฝุ่น	fùn
dusty (adj)	มีฝุ่นเยอะ	mee fùn yúh
to dust (vt)	ปัดกวาด	bpàt gwàat
vacuum cleaner	เครื่องดูดฝุ่น	khrêuang dòot fùn
to vacuum (vt)	ดูดฝุ่น	dòot fùn
to sweep (vi, vt)	กวาด	gwàat
sweepings	ฝุ่นกวาด	fùn gwàat
order	ความสะอาด	khwaam sà-àat
disorder, mess	ความไม่เป็นระเบียบ	khwaam mâi bpen rá-bìap
mop	ไม้ถูพื้น	mái thǒo phéun
dust cloth	ผ้าเช็ดพื้น	phâa chét phéun
short broom	ไม้กวาดสั้น	máai gwàat sân
dustpan	ที่ตักผง	têe dtàk phǒng

95. Furniture. Interior

furniture	เครื่องเรือน	khrêuang reuan
table	โต๊ะ	dtó
chair	เก้าอี้	gâo-êe
bed	เตียง	dtiang
couch, sofa	โซฟา	soh-faa

armchair	เก้าอี้เท้าแขน	gâo-êe tháo khǎen
bookcase	ตู้หนังสือ	dtôo nǎng-sěu
shelf	ชั้นวาง	chán waang

wardrobe	ตู้เสื้อผ้า	dtôo sêua phâa
coat rack (wall-mounted ~)	ที่แขวนเสื้อ	thêe khwǎen sêua
coat stand	ไม้แขวนเสื้อ	mái khwǎen sêua

| bureau, dresser | ตู้ลิ้นชัก | dtôo lín chák |
| coffee table | โต๊ะกาแฟ | dtó gaa-fae |

mirror	กระจก	grà-jòk
carpet	พรม	phrom
rug, small carpet	พรมเช็ดเท้า	phrom chét tháo

fireplace	เตาผิง	dtao phǐng
candle	เทียน	thian
candlestick	เชิงเทียน	cherng thian

drapes	ผ้าแขวน	phâa khwǎen
wallpaper	วอลเปเปอร์	worn-bpay-bper
blinds (jalousie)	บานเกล็ดหน้าต่าง	baan glèt nâa dtàang

table lamp	โคมไฟตั้งโต๊ะ	khohm fai dtâng dtó
wall lamp (sconce)	ไฟติดผนัง	fai dtìt phà-nǎng
floor lamp	โคมไฟตั้งพื้น	khohm fai dtâng phéun
chandelier	โคมระย้า	khohm rá-yáa

leg (of chair, table)	ขา	khǎa
armrest	ที่พักแขน	thêe phák khǎen
back (backrest)	พนักพิง	phá-nák phing
drawer	ลิ้นชัก	lín chák

96. Bedding

bedclothes	ชุดผ้าปูที่นอน	chút phâa bpoo thêe norn
pillow	หมอน	mǒrn
pillowcase	ปลอกหมอน	bplòk mǒrn
duvet, comforter	ผ้าผวย	phâa phǔay
sheet	ผ้าปู	phâa bpoo
bedspread	ผ้าคลุมเตียง	phâa khlum dtiang

97. Kitchen

kitchen	ห้องครัว	hôrng khrua
gas	แก๊ส	gáet
gas stove (range)	เตาแก๊ส	dtao gàet
electric stove	เตาไฟฟ้า	dtao fai-fáa

oven	เตาอบ	dtao òp
microwave oven	เตาอบไมโครเวฟ	dtao òp mai-khroh-we p

refrigerator	ตู้เย็น	dtôo yen
freezer	ตู้แช่แข็ง	dtôo châe khǎeng
dishwasher	เครื่องล้างจาน	khrêuang láang jaan

meat grinder	เครื่องบดเนื้อ	khrêuang bòt néua
juicer	เครื่องคั้น	khrêuang khán
	น้ำผลไม้	náam phǒn-lá-mái
toaster	เครื่องปิ้ง	khrêuang bpîng
	ขนมปัง	khà-nǒm bpang
mixer	เครื่องปั่น	khrêuang bpàn

coffee machine	เครื่องชงกาแฟ	khrêuang chong gaa-fae
coffee pot	หม้อกาแฟ	môr gaa-fae
coffee grinder	เครื่องบดกาแฟ	khrêuang bòt gaa-fae

kettle	กาน้ำ	gaa náam
teapot	กาน้ำชา	gaa náam chaa
lid	ฝา	fǎa
tea strainer	ที่กรองชา	thêe grorng chaa

spoon	ช้อน	chórn
teaspoon	ช้อนชา	chórn chaa
soup spoon	ช้อนซุป	chórn súp
fork	ส้อม	sôrm
knife	มีด	mêet

tableware (dishes)	ถ้วยชาม	thûay chaam
plate (dinner ~)	จาน	jaan
saucer	จานรอง	jaan rorng

shot glass	แก้วช็อต	gâew chórt
glass (tumbler)	แก้ว	gâew
cup	ถ้วย	thûay

sugar bowl	โถน้ำตาล	thǒh náam dtaan
salt shaker	กระปุกเกลือ	grà-bpùk gleua
pepper shaker	กระปุกพริกไทย	grà-bpùk phrík thai
butter dish	ที่ใส่เนย	thêe sài noie

stock pot (soup pot)	หม้อต้ม	môr dtôm
frying pan (skillet)	กระทะ	grà-thá
ladle	กระบวย	grà-buay
colander	กระชอน	grà chorn
tray (serving ~)	ถาด	thàat

bottle	ขวด	khùat
jar (glass)	ขวดโหล	khùat lǒh
can	กระป๋อง	grà-bpǒrng
bottle opener	ที่เปิดขวด	thêe bpèrt khùat

can opener	ที่เปิดกระป๋อง	thêe bpèrt grà-bpŏrng
corkscrew	ที่เปิดจุก	thêe bpèrt jùk
filter	ที่กรอง	thêe grorng
to filter (vt)	กรอง	grorng
trash, garbage (food waste, etc.)	ขยะ	khà-yà
trash can (kitchen ~)	ถังขยะ	thăng khà-yà

98. Bathroom

bathroom	ห้องน้ำ	hôrng náam
water	น้ำ	nám
faucet	ก็อกน้ำ	gòk náam
hot water	น้ำร้อน	nám rórn
cold water	น้ำเย็น	nám yen
toothpaste	ยาสีฟัน	yaa sĕe fan
to brush one's teeth	แปรงฟัน	bpraeng fan
toothbrush	แปรงสีฟัน	bpraeng sĕe fan
to shave (vi)	โกน	gohn
shaving foam	โฟมโกนหนวด	fohm gohn nùat
razor	มีดโกน	mêet gohn
to wash (one's hands, etc.)	ล้าง	láang
to take a bath	อาบ	àap
shower	ฝักบัว	fàk bua
to take a shower	อาบน้ำฝักบัว	àap náam fàk bua
bathtub	อ่างอาบน้ำ	àang àap náam
toilet (toilet bowl)	โถชักโครก	thŏh chák khrôhk
sink (washbasin)	อ่างล้างหน้า	àang láang-nâa
soap	สบู่	sà-bòo
soap dish	ที่ใส่สบู่	thêe sài sà-bòo
sponge	ฟองน้ำ	forng náam
shampoo	แชมพู	chaem-phoo
towel	ผ้าเช็ดตัว	phâa chét dtua
bathrobe	เสื้อคลุมอาบน้ำ	sêua khlum àap náam
laundry (laundering)	การซักผ้า	gaan sák phâa
washing machine	เครื่องซักผ้า	khrêuang sák phâa
to do the laundry	ซักผ้า	sák phâa
laundry detergent	ผงซักฟอก	phŏng sák-fôrk

99. Household appliances

TV set	ทีวี	thee-wee
tape recorder	เครื่องบันทึกเทป	khrêuang ban-théuk thâyp
VCR (video recorder)	เครื่องบันทึก วิดีโอ	khrêuang ban-théuk wí-dee-oh
radio	วิทยุ	wít-thá-yú
player (CD, MP3, etc.)	เครื่องเล่น	khrêuang lên
video projector	โปรเจ็คเตอร์	bproh-jèk-dtêr
home movie theater	เครื่องฉาย ภาพยนตร์ที่บ้าน	khhrêuang chǎai phâap-phá yon thêe bâan
DVD player	เครื่องเล่น DVD	khrêuang lên dee-wee-dee
amplifier	เครื่องขยายเสียง	khrêuang khà-yǎi sǐang
video game console	เครื่องเกม คอนโซล	khrêuang gaym khorn sohn
video camera	กล้องถ่ายวิดีโอ	glôrng thàai wí-dee-oh
camera (photo)	กล้องถ่ายรูป	glôrng thàai rôop
digital camera	กล้องดิจิตอล	glôrng dì-jì-dton
vacuum cleaner	เครื่องดูดฝุ่น	khrêuang dòot fùn
iron (e.g., steam ~)	เตารีด	dtao rêet
ironing board	กระดานรองรีด	grà-daan rorng rêet
telephone	โทรศัพท์	thoh-rá-sàp
cell phone	มือถือ	meu thěu
typewriter	เครื่องพิมพ์ดีด	khrêuang phim dèet
sewing machine	จักรเย็บผ้า	jàk yép phâa
microphone	ไมโครโฟน	mai-khroh-fohn
headphones	หูฟัง	hǒo fang
remote control (TV)	รีโมตทีวี	ree môht thee wee
CD, compact disc	CD	see-dee
cassette, tape	เทป	thâyp
vinyl record	จานเสียง	jaan sǐang

100. Repairs. Renovation

renovations	การซ่อมแซม	gaan sôrm saem
to renovate (vt)	ซ่อมแซม	sôrm saem
to repair, to fix (vt)	ซ่อมแซม	sôrm saem
to put in order	สะสาง	sà-sǎang
to redo (do again)	ทำใหม่	tham mài
paint	สี	sěe
to paint (~ a wall)	ทาสี	thaa sěe
house painter	ช่างทาสีบ้าน	châang thaa sěe bâan

paintbrush	แปรงทาสี	bpraeng thaa sěe
whitewash	สารฟอกขาว	sǎan fôrk khǎao
to whitewash (vt)	ฟอกขาว	fôrk khǎao

wallpaper	วอลเปเปอร์	worn-bpay-bper
to wallpaper (vt)	ติดวอลเปเปอร์	dtìt wor lá-bpay-bper
varnish	น้ำมันชักเงา	náam man chák ngao
to varnish (vt)	เคลือบ	khlêuap

101. Plumbing

water	น้ำ	nám
hot water	น้ำร้อน	nám rórn
cold water	น้ำเย็น	nám yen
faucet	ก็อกน้ำ	gòk náam

drop (of water)	หยด	yòt
to drip (vi)	ตก	dtòk
to leak (ab. pipe)	รั่ว	rûa
leak (pipe ~)	การรั่ว	gaan rûa
puddle	หลมน้ำ	lòm nám

pipe	ท่อ	thôr
valve (e.g., ball ~)	วาล์ว	waao
to be clogged up	อุดตัน	ùt dtan

tools	เครื่องมือ	khrêuang meu
adjustable wrench	ประแจคอม้า	bprà-jae kor máa
to unscrew (lid, filter, etc.)	คลายเกลียวออก	khlaai glieow òrk
to screw (tighten)	ขันให้แน่น	khǎn hâi nâen

to unclog (vt)	แก้การอุดตัน	gâe gaan ùt dtan
plumber	ช่างประปา	châang bprà-bpaa
basement	ชั้นใต้ดิน	chán dtâi din
sewerage (system)	ระบบท่อน้ำทิ้ง	rá-bòp thôr náam thíng

102. Fire. Conflagration

fire (accident)	ไฟไหม้	fai mâi
flame	เปลวไฟ	bpleo fai
spark	ประกายไฟ	bprà-gaai fai
smoke (from fire)	ควัน	khwan
torch (flaming stick)	คบเพลิง	khóp phlerng
campfire	กองไฟ	gorng fai

gas, gasoline	น้ำมันเชื้อเพลิง	nám man chéua phlerng
kerosene (type of fuel)	น้ำมันก๊าด	nám man gáat
flammable (adj)	ติดไฟได้	dtìt fai dâai

explosive (adj)	ที่ระเบิดได้	thêe rá-bèrt dâai
NO SMOKING	ห้ามสูบบุหรี่	hâam sòop bù rèe
safety	ความปลอดภัย	khwaam bplòrt phai
danger	อันตราย	an-dtà-raai
dangerous (adj)	อันตราย	an-dtà-raai
to catch fire	ติดไฟ	dtìt fai
explosion	การระเบิด	gaan rá-bèrt
to set fire	เผา	phǎo
arsonist	ผู้ลอบวางเพลิง	phôo lôp waang phlerng
arson	การลอบวางเพลิง	gaan lôp waang phlerng
to blaze (vi)	ไฟลุกโชน	fai lúk-chohn
to burn (be on fire)	ไหม้	mâi
to burn down	เผาให้ราบ	phǎo hâi râap
to call the fire department	เรียกนักดับเพลิง	rîak nák dàp phlerng
firefighter, fireman	นักดับเพลิง	nák dàp phlerng
fire truck	รถดับเพลิง	rót dàp phlerng
fire department	สถานีดับเพลิง	sà-thǎa-nee dàp phlerng
fire truck ladder	บันไดรถดับเพลิง	ban-dai rót dàp phlerng
fire hose	ท่อดับเพลิง	thôr dàp phlerng
fire extinguisher	ที่ดับเพลิง	thêe dàp phlerng
helmet	หมวกนิรภัย	mùak ní-rá-phai
siren	สัญญาณเตือนภัย	sǎn-yaan dteuan phai
to cry (for help)	ร้อง	rórng
to call for help	ขอช่วย	khǒr chûay
rescuer	นักกู้ภัย	nák gôo phai
to rescue (vt)	ช่วยชีวิต	chûay chee-wít
to arrive (vi)	มา	maa
to extinguish (vt)	ดับเพลิง	dàp phlerng
water	น้ำ	nám
sand	ทราย	saai
ruins (destruction)	ซาก	sâak
to collapse (building, etc.)	ถล่ม	thà-lòm
to fall down (vi)	ถล่มทลาย	thà-lòm thá-laai
to cave in (ceiling, floor)	ถล่ม	thà-lòm
piece of debris	ส่วนสะเก็ด	sùan sà-gèt
ash	ขี้เถ้า	khêe thâo
to suffocate (die)	ขาดอากาศตาย	khàat aa-gàat dtaai
to be killed (perish)	เสียชีวิต	sǐa chee-wít

HUMAN ACTIVITIES

Job. Business. Part 1

103. Office. Working in the office

office (company ~)	สำนักงาน	sǎm-nák ngaan
office (of director, etc.)	ห้องทำงาน	hôrng tham ngaan
reception desk	แผนกต้อนรับ	phà-nàek dtôrn ráp
secretary	เลขา	lay-khǎa
secretary (fem.)	เลขา	lay-khǎa
director	ผู้อำนวยการ	phôo am-nuay gaan
manager	ผู้จัดการ	phôo jàt gaan
accountant	คนทำบัญชี	khon tham ban-chee
employee	พนักงาน	phá-nák ngaan
furniture	เครื่องเรือน	khrêuang reuan
desk	โต๊ะ	dtó
desk chair	เก้าอี้สำนักงาน	gâo-êe sǎm-nák ngaan
drawer unit	ตู้มีลิ้นชัก	dtôo mee lín chák
coat stand	ไม้แขวนเสื้อ	mái khwǎen sêua
computer	คอมพิวเตอร์	khorm-phiw-dtêr
printer	เครื่องพิมพ์	khrêuang phim
fax machine	เครื่องโทรสาร	khrêuang thoh-rá-sǎan
photocopier	เครื่องอัดสำเนา	khrêuang àt sǎm-nao
paper	กระดาษ	grà-dàat
office supplies	เครื่องใช้สำนักงาน	khrêuang chái sǎm-nák ngaan
mouse pad	แผ่นรองเมาส์	phàen rorng mao
sheet (of paper)	ใบ	bai
binder	แฟ้ม	fáem
catalog	บัญชีรายชื่อ	ban-chee raai chêu
phone directory	สมุดโทรศัพท์	sà-mùt thoh-rá-sàp
documentation	เอกสาร	àyk sǎan
brochure (e.g., 12 pages ~)	โบรชัวร์	broh-chua
leaflet (promotional ~)	ใบปลิว	bai bpliw
sample	ตัวอย่าง	dtua yàang
training meeting	การประชุมฝึกอบรม	gaan bprà-chum fèuk òp-rom

meeting (of managers)	การประชุม	gaan bprà-chum
lunch time	การพักเที่ยง	gaan phák thîang
to make a copy	ทำสำเนา	tham săm-nao
to make multiple copies	ทำสำเนา หลายฉบับ	tham săm-nao lăai chà-bàp
to receive a fax	รับโทรสาร	ráp thoh-rá-săan
to send a fax	ส่งโทรสาร	sòng thoh-rá-săan
to call (by phone)	โทรศัพท์	thoh-rá-sàp
to answer (vt)	รับสาย	ráp săai
to put through	โอนสาย	ohn săai
to arrange, to set up	นัด	nát
to demonstrate (vt)	สาธิต	săa-thít
to be absent	ขาด	khàat
absence	การขาด	gaan khàat

104. Business processes. Part 1

business	ธุรกิจ	thú-rá gìt
occupation	อาชีพ	aa-chêep
firm	บริษัท	bor-rí-sàt
company	บริษัท	bor-rí-sàt
corporation	บริษัท	bor-rí-sàt
enterprise	บริษัท	bor-rí-sàt
agency	สำนักงาน	săm-nák ngaan
agreement (contract)	ข้อตกลง	khôr dtòk long
contract	สัญญา	săn-yaa
deal	ข้อตกลง	khôr dtòk long
order (to place an ~)	การสั่ง	gaan sàng
terms (of the contract)	เงื่อนไข	ngêuan khăi
wholesale (adv)	ขายส่ง	khăai sòng
wholesale (adj)	ขายส่ง	khăai sòng
wholesale (n)	การขายส่ง	gaan khăai sòng
retail (adj)	ขายปลีก	khăai bplèek
retail (n)	การขายปลีก	gaan khăai bplèek
competitor	คู่แข่ง	khôo khàong
competition	การแข่งขัน	gaan khàeng khăn
to compete (vi)	แข่งขัน	khàeng khăn
partner (associate)	พันธมิตร	phan-thá-mít
partnership	ห้างหุ้นส่วน	hâang hûn sùan
crisis	วิกฤติ	wí-grìt
bankruptcy	การล้มละลาย	gaan lóm lá-laai

to go bankrupt	ล้มละลาย	lóm lá-laai
difficulty	ความยากลำบาก	khwaam yâak lam-bàak
problem	ปัญหา	bpan-hǎa
catastrophe	ความหายนะ	khwaam hǎa-yá-ná

economy	เศรษฐกิจ	sàyt-thà-gìt
economic (~ growth)	ทางเศรษฐกิจ	thaang sàyt-thà-gìt
economic recession	เศรษฐกิจถดถอย	sàyt-thà-gìt thòt thǒi

| goal (aim) | เป้าหมาย | bpâo mǎai |
| task | งาน | ngaan |

to trade (vi)	แลกเปลี่ยน	lâek bplìan
network (distribution ~)	เครือขาย	khreua khàai
inventory (stock)	คลังสินค้า	khlang sǐn kháa
range (assortment)	ประเภทสินค้าตางๆ	bprà-phàyt sǐn kháa dtàang dtàang

leader (leading company)	ผู้นำ	phôo nam
large (~ company)	ขนาดใหญ่	khà-nàat yài
monopoly	การผูกขาด	gaan phòok khàat

theory	ทฤษฎี	thrít-sà-dee
practice	การดำเนินการ	gaan dam-nern gaan
experience (in my ~)	ประสบการณ์	bprà-sòp gaan
trend (tendency)	แนวโน้ม	naew nóhm
development	การพัฒนา	gaan phát-thá-naa

105. Business processes. Part 2

| profit (foregone ~) | กำไร | gam-rai |
| profitable (~ deal) | กำไร | gam-rai |

delegation (group)	คณะผู้แทน	khá-ná phôo thaen
salary	เงินเดือน	ngern deuan
to correct (an error)	แก้ไข	gâe khǎi
business trip	การเดินทางไปทำธุรกิจ	gaan dern taang bpai tham thú-rá gìt
commission	คณะ	khá-ná

to control (vt)	ควบคุม	khûap khum
conference	งานประชุม	ngaan bprà-chum
license	ใบอนุญาต	bai a-nú-yâat
reliable (~ partner)	พึ่งพาได้	phêung phaa dâai

initiative (undertaking)	การริเริ่ม	gaan rí-rêrm
norm (standard)	มาตรฐาน	mâat-dtrà-thǎan
circumstance	ภาวะ	phaa-wá
duty (of employee)	หน้าที่	nâa thêe
organization (company)	องค์การ	ong gaan

organization (process)	การจัด	gaan jàt
organized (adj)	ที่ถูกจัด	thêe thòok jàt
cancellation	การยกเลิก	gaan yók lêrk
to cancel (call off)	ยกเลิก	yók lêrk
report (official ~)	รายงาน	raai ngaan
patent	สิทธิบัตร	sìt-thí bàt
to patent (obtain patent)	จดสิทธิบัตร	jòt sìt-thí bàt
to plan (vt)	วางแผน	waang phǎen
bonus (money)	โบนัส	boh-nát
professional (adj)	ทางวิชาชีพ	thaang wí-chaa chêep
procedure	กระบวนการ	grà-buan gaan
to examine (contract, etc.)	ปรึกษาหารือ	bprèuk-sǎa hǎa-reu
calculation	การนับ	gaan náp
reputation	ความมีห	khwaam mee
	นามีตา	nâa mee dtaa
risk	ความเสี่ยง	khwaam sìang
to manage, to run	บริหาร	bor-rí-hǎan
information (report)	ขอมูล	khôr moon
property	ทรัพย์สิน	sáp sǐn
union	สหภาพ	sà-hà phâap
life insurance	การประกันชีวิต	gaan bprà-gan chee-wít
to insure (vt)	ประกันภัย	bprà-gan phai
insurance	การประกันภัย	gaan bprà-gan phai
auction (~ sale)	กูรขายเลหลัง	gaan khǎai lay-lǎng
to notify (inform)	แจง	jâeng
management (process)	การบริหาร	gaan bor-rí-hǎan
service (~ industry)	บริการ	bor-rí-gaan
forum	การประชุมฟอรั่ม	gaan bprà-chum for-râm
to function (vi)	ดำเนินการ	dam-nern gaan
stage (phase)	ขั้น	khân
legal (~ services)	ทางกฎหมาย	thaang gòt mǎai
lawyer (legal advisor)	ทนายความ	thá-naai khwaam

106. Production. Works

plant	โรงงาน	rohng ngaan
factory	โรงงาน	rohng ngaan
workshop	ห้องทำงาน	hôrng tham ngaan
works, production site	ที่ผลิต	thêe phà-lìt
industry (manufacturing)	อุตสาหกรรม	ùt-saa há-gam
industrial (adj)	ทางอุตสาหกรรม	thaang ùt-sǎa-hà-gam
heavy industry	อุตสาหกรรมหนัก	ùt-sǎa-hà-gam nàk

light industry	อุตสาหกรรมเบา	ùt-săa-hà-gam bao
products	ผลิตภัณฑ์	phà-lìt-dtà-phan
to produce (vt)	ผลิต	phà-lìt
raw materials	วัตถุดิบ	wát-thù dìp

foreman (construction ~)	คนคุมงาน	khon khum ngaan
workers team (crew)	ทีมคนงาน	theem khon ngaan
worker	คนงาน	khon ngaan

working day	วันทำงาน	wan tham ngaan
pause (rest break)	หยุดพัก	yùt phák
meeting	การประชุม	gaan bprà-chum
to discuss (vt)	หารือ	hăa-reu

plan	แผน	phăen
to fulfill the plan	ทำตามแผน	tham dtaam păen
rate of output	อัตราผลลัพธ์	àt-dtraa phŏn láp
quality	คุณภาพ	khun-ná-phâap
control (checking)	การควบคุม	gaan khûap khum
quality control	การควบคุม คุณภาพ	gaan khûap khum khun-ná-phâap

workplace safety	ความปลอดภัย ในที่ทำงาน	khwaam bplòrt phai nai thêe tham ngaan
discipline	วินัย	wí-nai
violation (of safety rules, etc.)	การละเมิด	gaan lá-mêrt
to violate (rules)	ละเมิด	lá-mêrt

strike	การประท้วง หยุดงาน	gaan bprà-thúang yùt ngaan
striker	ผู้ประท้วง หยุดงาน	phôo bprà-thúang yùt ngaan
to be on strike	ประท้วงหยุดงาน	bprà-thúang yùt ngaan
labor union	สหภาพแรงงาน	sà-hà-phâap raeng ngaan

to invent (machine, etc.)	ประดิษฐ์	bprà-dìt
invention	สิ่งประดิษฐ์	sìng bprà-dìt
research	การวิจัย	gaan wí-jai
to improve (make better)	ทำให้ดีขึ้น	tham hâi dee khêun
technology	เทคโนโลยี	thék-noh-loh-yee
technical drawing	ภาพราง ทางเทคนิค	phâap-râang thaang thék-nìk

load, cargo	ของบรรทุก	khŏrng ban-thúk
loader (person)	คนงานยกของ	khon ngaan yók khŏrng
to load (vehicle, etc.)	บรรทุก	ban-thúk
loading (process)	การบรรทุก	gaan ban-thúk
to unload (vi, vt)	ขนออก	khŏn òrk
unloading	การขนออก	gaan khŏn òrk
transportation	การขนส่ง	gaan khŏn sòng
transportation company	บริษัทขนส่ง	bor-rí-sàt khŏn sòng

to transport (vt)	ขนส่ง	khŏn sòng
freight car	ตู้รถไฟรถ	dtôo rót fai
tank (e.g., oil ~)	ถัง	thăng
truck	รถบรรทุก	rót ban-thúk
machine tool	เครื่องมือกล	khrêuang meu gon
mechanism	กลไก	gon-gai
industrial waste	ของเสียจาก โรงงาน	khŏrng sĭa jàak rohng ngaan
packing (process)	การทำหีบห่อ	gaan tham hèep hòr
to pack (vt)	แพ็คหีบหอ	pháek hèep hòr

107. Contract. Agreement

contract	สัญญา	săn-yaa
agreement	ขอตกลง	khŏr dtòk long
addendum	ภาคผนวก	phâak phà-nùak
to sign a contract	ลงนามในสัญญา	long naam nai săn-yaa
signature	ลายมือชื่อ	laai meu chêu
to sign (vt)	ลงนาม	long naam
seal (stamp)	ตราประทับ	dtraa bprà-tháp
subject of the contract	หัวข้อของสัญญา	hŭa khôr khŏrng săn-yaa
clause	ขอ	khôr
parties (in contract)	ฝ่าย	fàai
legal address	ที่อยูตามกฎหมาย	thêe yòo dtaam gòt măai
to violate the contract	การละเมิดสัญญา	gaan lá-mêrt săn-yaa
commitment (obligation)	พันธสัญญา	phan-thá-săn-yaa
responsibility	ความรับผิดชอบ	khwaam ráp phìt chôp
force majeure	เหตุสุดวิสัย	hàyt sùt wí-săi
dispute	ความขัดแยง	khwaam khàt yáeng
penalties	บทลงโทษ	bòt long thôht

108. Import & Export

import	การนำเข้า	gaan nam khâo
importer	ผู้นำเขา	phôo nam khâo
to import (vt)	นำเขา	nam khâo
import (as adj.)	นำเขา	nam khâo
export (exportation)	การส่งออก	gaan sòng òrk
exporter	ผู้สงออก	phôo sòng òrk
to export (vi, vt)	สงออก	sòng òrk
export (as adj.)	สงออก	sòng òrk
goods (merchandise)	สินคา	sĭn kháa

consignment, lot	สินค้าที่ส่งไป	sĭn kháa thêe sòng bpai
weight	น้ำหนัก	nám nàk
volume	ปริมาณ	bpà-rí-maan
cubic meter	ลูกบาศก์เมตร	lôok bàat máyt
manufacturer	ผู้ผลิต	phôo phà-lìt
transportation company	บริษัทขนส่ง	bor-rí-sàt khŏn sòng
container	ตู้คอนเทนเนอร์	dtôo khorn thay ná-ner
border	ชายแดน	chaai daen
customs	ด่านศุลกากร	dàan sŭn-lá-gaa-gon
customs duty	ภาษีศุลกากร	phaa-sĕe sŭn-lá-gaa-gon
customs officer	เจ้าหน้าที่ศุลกากร	jâo nâa-thêe sŭn-lá-gaa-gon
smuggling	การลักลอบ	gaan lák-lôrp
contraband	สินค้าที่	sĭn kháa thêe
(smuggled goods)	ผิดกฎหมาย	phìt gòt mǎai

109. Finances

stock (share)	หุ้น	hûn
bond (certificate)	ตราสารหนี้	dtraa sǎan nêe
promissory note	ตั๋วสัญญาใช้เงิน	dtǔa sǎn-yaa chái ngern
stock exchange	ตลาดหลักทรัพย์	dtà-làat làk sáp
stock price	ราคาหุ้น	raa-khaa hûn
to go down (become cheaper)	ถูกลง	thòok long
to go up (become more expensive)	แพงขึ้น	phaeng khêun
share	ปันผล	bpan phŏn
controlling interest	ส่วนได้เสียที่มีอำนาจควบคุม	sùan dâai sĭa têe mee am-nâat khûap khum
investment	การลงทุน	gaan long thun
to invest (vt)	ลงทุน	long thun
percent	เปอร์เซ็นต์	bper-sen
interest (on investment)	ดอกเบี้ย	dòrk bîa
profit	กำไร	gam-rai
profitable (adj)	ได้กำไร	dâai gam-rai
tax	ภาษี	phaa-sĕe
currency (foreign ~)	สกุลเงิน	sà-gun ngern
national (adj)	แห่งชาติ	hàeng châat
exchange (currency ~)	การแลกเปลี่ยน	gaan lâek bplìan
accountant	นักบัญชี	nák ban-chee
accounting	การทำบัญชี	gaan tham ban-chee

bankruptcy	การล้มละลาย	gaan lóm lá-laai
collapse, crash	การพังพินาศ	gaan phang phí-nâat
ruin	ความพินาศ	khwaam phí-nâat
to be ruined (financially)	ล้มละลาย	lóm lá-laai
inflation	เงินเฟ้อ	ngern fér
devaluation	การลดค่าเงิน	gaan lót khâa ngern

capital	เงินทุน	ngern thun
income	รายได้	raai dâai
turnover	การหมุนเวียน	gaan mǔn wian
resources	ทรัพยากร	sáp-pá-yaa-gon
monetary resources	แหล่งเงินทุน	làeng ngern thun

| overhead | ค่าใช้จ่าย | khâa chái jàai |
| to reduce (expenses) | ลด | lót |

110. Marketing

marketing	การตลาด	gaan dtà-làat
market	ตลาด	dtà-làat
market segment	ส่วนตลาด	sùan dtà-làat
product	ผลิตภัณฑ์	phà-lìt-dtà-phan
goods (merchandise)	สินค้า	sĭn kháa

brand	ยี่ห้อ	yêe hôr
trademark	เครื่องหมายการค้า	khrêuang mǎai gaan kháa
logotype	โลโก้	loh-gôh
logo	โลโก้	loh-gôh
demand	อุปสงค์	u-bpà-sǒng
supply	อุปทาน	u-bpà-thaan
need	ความต้องการ	khwaam dtôrng gaan
consumer	ผู้บริโภค	phôo bor-rí-phôhk

analysis	การวิเคราะห์	gaan wí-khrór
to analyze (vt)	วิเคราะห์	wí-khrór
positioning	การวางตำแหน่งผลิตภัณฑ์	gaan waang dtam-nàeng phà-lìt-dtà-phan
to position (vt)	วางตำแหน่งผลิตภัณฑ์	waang dtam-nàeng phà-lìt-dtà-phan
price	ราคา	raa-khaa
pricing policy	นโยบายการตั้งราคา	ná-yoh-baai gaan dtâng raa-khaa
price formation	การตั้งราคา	gaan dtâng raa-khaa

111. Advertising

| advertising | การโฆษณา | gaan khôht-sà-naa |
| to advertise (vt) | โฆษณา | khôht-sà-naa |

budget	งบประมาณ	ngóp bprà-maan
ad, advertisement	การโฆษณา	gaan khôht-sà-naa
TV advertising	การโฆษณา ทางทีวี	gaan khôht-sà-naa thaang thee wee
radio advertising	การโฆษณา ทางวิทยุ	gaan khôht-sà-naa thaang wít-thá-yú
outdoor advertising	การโฆษณา แบบกลางแจ้ง	gaan khôht-sà-naa bàep glaang jâeng
mass media	สื่อสารมวลชน	sèu sǎan muan chon
periodical (n)	หนังสือรายคาบ	nǎng-sěu raai khâap
image (public appearance)	ภาพลักษณ์	phâap-lák
slogan	คำขวัญ	kham khwǎn
motto (maxim)	คติพจน์	khá-dtì phót
campaign	การรณรงค์	gaan ron-ná-rorng
advertising campaign	การรณรงค์ โฆษณา	gaan ron-ná-rorng khôht-sà-naa
target group	กลุ่มเป้าหมาย	glùm bpâo-mǎai
business card	นามบัตร	naam bàt
leaflet (promotional ~)	ใบปลิว	bai bpliw
brochure (e.g., 12 pages ~)	โบรชัวร์	broh-chua
pamphlet	แผ่นพับ	phàen pháp
newsletter	จดหมายข่าว	jòt mǎai khàao
signboard (store sign, etc.)	ป้ายร้าน	bpâai ráan
poster	โปสเตอร์	bpòht-dtêr
billboard	กระดานปิดประกาศ โฆษณา	grà-daan bpìt bprà-gàat khôht-sà-naa

112. Banking

bank	ธนาคาร	thá-naa-khaan
branch (of bank, etc.)	สาขา	sǎa-khǎa
bank clerk, consultant	พนักงาน ธนาคาร	phá-nák ngaan thá-naa-khaan
manager (director)	ผู้จัดการ	phôo jàt gaan
bank account	บัญชีธนาคาร	ban-chee thá-naa-kaan
account number	หมายเลขบัญชี	mǎai lâyk ban-chee
checking account	กระแสรายวัน	grà-sǎe raai wan
savings account	บัญชีออมทรัพย์	ban-chee orm sáp
to open an account	เปิดบัญชี	bpèrt ban-chee
to close the account	ปิดบัญชี	bpìt ban-chee
to deposit into the account	ฝากเงินเข้าบัญชี	fàak ngern khâo ban-chee

to withdraw (vt)	ถอน	thŏrn
deposit	การฝาก	gaan fàak
to make a deposit	ฝาก	fàak
wire transfer	การโอนเงิน	gaan ohn ngern
to wire, to transfer	โอนเงิน	ohn ngern

| sum | จำนวนเงินรวม | jam-nuan ngern ruam |
| How much? | เทาไหร? | thâo rài |

| signature | ลายมือชื่อ | laai meu chêu |
| to sign (vt) | ลงนาม | long naam |

credit card	บัตรเครดิต	bàt khray-dìt
code (PIN code)	รหัส	rá-hàt
credit card number	หมายเลขบัตรเครดิต	mǎai lâyk bàt khray-dìt
ATM	เอทีเอ็ม	ay-thee-em

check	เช็ค	chék
to write a check	เขียนเช็ค	khǐan chék
checkbook	สมุดเช็ค	sà-mùt chék

loan (bank ~)	เงินกู้	ngern gôo
to apply for a loan	ขอสินเชื่อ	khŏr sǐn chêua
to get a loan	กู้เงิน	gôo ngern
to give a loan	ให้กู้เงิน	hâi gôo ngern
guarantee	การรับประกัน	gaan ráp bprà-gan

113. Telephone. Phone conversation

telephone	โทรศัพท์	thoh-rá-sàp
cell phone	มือถือ	meu thěu
answering machine	เครื่องพูดตอบ	khrêuang phôot dtòp

| to call (by phone) | โทรศัพท์ | thoh-rá-sàp |
| phone call | การโทรศัพท์ | gaan thoh-rá-sàp |

to dial a number	หมุนหมายเลขโทรศัพท์	mǔn mǎai lâyk thoh-rá-sàp
Hello!	สวัสดี!	sà-wàt-dee
to ask (vt)	ถาม	thǎam
to answer (vi, vt)	รับสาย	ráp sǎai

to hear (vt)	ได้ยิน	dǎai yin
well (adv)	ดี	dee
not well (adv)	ไม่ดี	mâi dee
noises (interference)	เสียงรบกวน	sǐang róp guan

receiver	ตัวรับสัญญาณ	dtua ráp sǎn-yaan
to pick up (~ the phone)	รับสาย	ráp sǎai
to hang up (~ the phone)	วางสาย	waang sǎai
busy (engaged)	ไม่วาง	mâi wâang

to ring (ab. phone)	ดัง	dang
telephone book	สมุดโทรศัพท์	sà-mùt thoh-rá-sàp
local (adj)	ในประเทศ	nai bprà-thâyt
local call	โทรในประเทศ	thoh nai bprà-thâyt
long distance (~ call)	ระยะไกล	rá-yá glai
long-distance call	โทรระยะไกล	thoh-rá-yá glai
international (adj)	ตางประเทศ	dtàang bprà-thâyt
international call	โทรตางประเทศ	thoh dtàang bprà-thâyt

114. Cell phone

cell phone	มือถือ	meu thěu
display	หนาจอ	nâa jor
button	ปุ่ม	bpùm
SIM card	ซิมการ์ด	sím gàat
battery	แบตเตอรี่	bàet-dter-rêe
to be dead (battery)	หมด	mòt
charger	ที่ชาร์จ	thêe châat
menu	เมนู	may-noo
settings	การตั้งคา	gaan dtâng khâa
tune (melody)	เสียงเพลง	sǐang phlayng
to select (vt)	เลือก	lêuak
calculator	เครื่องคิดเลข	khrêuang khít lâyk
voice mail	ขอความเสียง	khôr khwaam sǐang
alarm clock	นาฬิกาปลุก	naa-lí-gaa bplùk
contacts	รายชื่อผูติดตอ	raai chêu phôo dtìt dtòr
SMS (text message)	ŞMS	es-e-mes
subscriber	ผูสมัครรับ บริการ	phôo sà-màk ráp bor-rí-gaan

115. Stationery

ballpoint pen	ปากกาลูกลื่น	bpàak gaa lôok lêun
fountain pen	ปากกาหมึกซึม	bpàak gaa mèuk seum
pencil	ดินสอ	din-sǒr
highlighter	ปากกาเนน	bpàak gaa náyn
felt-tip pen	ปากกาเมจิค	bpàak gaa may jìk
notepad	สมุดจด	sà-mùt jòt
agenda (diary)	สมุดบันทึกรายวัน	sà-mùt ban-théuk raai wan
ruler	ไมบรรทัด	máai ban-thát
calculator	เครื่องคิดเลข	khrêuang khít lâyk

eraser	ยางลบ	yaang lóp
thumbtack	เป๊ก	bpáyk
paper clip	ลวดหนีบกระดาษ	lûat nèep grà-dàat

glue	กาว	gaao
stapler	ที่เย็บกระดาษ	thêe yép grà-dàat
hole punch	ที่เจาะรูกระดาษ	thêe jòr roo grà-dàat
pencil sharpener	ที่เหลาดินสอ	thêe lǎo din-sǒr

116. Various kinds of documents

account (report)	รายการ	raai gaan
agreement	ข้อตกลง	khôr dtòk long
application form	ใบสมัคร	bai sà-màk
authentic (adj)	แท้	tháe
badge (identity tag)	ป้ายชื่อ	bpâai chêu
business card	นามบัตร	naam bàt

certificate (~ of quality)	ใบรับรอง	bai ráp rorng
check (e.g., draw a ~)	เช็ค	chék
check (in restaurant)	คิดเงิน	khít ngern
constitution	รัฐธรรมนูญ	rát-thà-tham-má-noon

contract (agreement)	สัญญา	sǎn-yaa
copy	สำเนา	sǎm-nao
copy (of contract, etc.)	ฉบับ	chà-bàp

customs declaration	แบบฟอร์มการเสีย ภาษีศุลกากร	bàep form gaan sǐa phaa-sěe sǔn-lá-gaa-gon
document	เอกสาร	àyk sǎan
driver's license	ใบอนุญาตขับขี่	bai a-nú-yâat khàp khèe
addendum	ภาคผนวก	phâak phà-nùak
form	แบบฟอร์ม	bàep form

ID card (e.g., FBI ~)	บัตรประจำตัว	bàt bprà-jam dtua
inquiry (request)	คำร้องขอ	kham rórng khǒr
invitation card	บัตรเชิญ	bàt chern
invoice	ใบกำกับสินค้า	bai gam-gàp sǐn kháa

law	กฎหมาย	gòt mǎai
letter (mail)	จดหมาย	jòt mǎai
letterhead	แบบฟอร์ม	bàep form
list (of names, etc.)	รายชื่อ	raai chêu
manuscript	ต้นฉบับ	dtôn chà-bàp
newsletter	จุดหมายข่าว	jòt mǎai khàao
note (short letter)	ข้อความสั้นๆ	khôr khwaam sân sân

pass (for worker, visitor)	บัตรผ่าน	bàt phàan
passport	หนังสือเดินทาง	nǎng-sěu dern-thaang
permit	ใบอนุญาต	bai a-nú-yâat

résumé	ประวัติย่อ	bprà-wàt yôr
debt note, IOU	รายการหนี้	raai gaan nêe
receipt (for purchase)	ใบเสร็จ	bai sèt
sales slip, receipt	ใบเสร็จ	bai sèt
report (mil.)	รายงาน	raai ngaan

to show (ID, etc.)	แสดง	sà-daeng
to sign (vt)	ลงนาม	long naam
signature	ลายมือชื่อ	laai meu chêu
seal (stamp)	ตราประทับ	dtraa bprà-tháp
text	ขอความ	khôr khwaam
ticket (for entry)	ตั๋ว	dtŭa

| to cross out | ขีดฆ่า | khèet khâa |
| to fill out (~ a form) | กรอก | gròrk |

| waybill (shipping invoice) | รายการสินค้า ขนส่ง | raai gaan sĭn kháa khŏn sòng |
| will (testament) | พินัยกรรม | phí-nai-gam |

117. Kinds of business

accounting services	บริการทำบัญชี	bor-rí-gaan tham ban-chee
advertising	การโฆษณา	gaan khôht-sà-naa
advertising agency	บริษัทโฆษณา	bor-rí-sàt khôht-sà-naa
air-conditioners	เครื่องปรับอากาศ	khrêuang bpràp-aa-gàat
airline	สายการบิน	săai gaan bin

alcoholic beverages	เครื่องดื่ม แอลกอฮอล	khrêuang dèum aen-gor-hor
antiques (antique dealers)	ของเก่า	khŏrng gào
art gallery (contemporary ~)	หอศิลป์	hŏr sĭn
audit services	บริการตรวจ สอบบัญชี	bor-rí-gaan dtrùat sòrp ban-chee

banking industry	การธนาคาร	gaan thá-naa-khaan
bar	บาร์	baa
beauty parlor	ช่างเสริมสวย	châang sĕrm sŭay
bookstore	ร้านขายหนังสือ	ráan khăai năng-sĕu
brewery	โรงงานต้มเหล้า	rohng ngaan dtôm lăo
business center	ศูนย์ธุรกิจ	sŏon thú-rá gìt
business school	โรงเรียนธุรกิจ	rohng rian thú-rá gìt

casino	คาสิโน	khaa-sì-noh
construction	การก่อสร้าง	gaan gòr sâang
consulting	การปรึกษา	gaan bprèuk-săa

| dental clinic | คลินิกทันตกรรม | khlí-nìk than-ta-gam |
| design | การออกแบบ | gaan òrk bàep |

drugstore, pharmacy	ร้านขายยา	ráan khǎai yaa
dry cleaners	รานซักแหง	ráan sák hâeng
employment agency	สำนักงาน	sǎm-nák ngaan
	จัดหางาน	jàt hǎa ngaan

financial services	บริการด้าน	bor-rí-gaan dâan
	การเงิน	gaan ngern
food products	ผลิตภัณฑ์อาหาร	phà-lìt-dtà-phan aa hǎan
funeral home	บริษัทรับ	bor-rí-sàt ráp
	จัดงานศพ	jàt ngaan sòp
furniture (e.g., house ~)	เครื่องเรือน	khrêuang reuan
clothing, garment	เสื้อผา	sêua phâa
hotel	โรงแรม	rohng raem

ice-cream	ไอศกรีม	ai-sà-greem
industry (manufacturing)	อุตสาหกรรม	út-saa há-gam
insurance	การประกัน	gaan bprà-gan
Internet	อินเทอรเน็ต	in-thêr-nét
investments (finance)	การลงทุน	gaan long thun

jeweler	ช่างทำเครื่อง	châang tham khrêuang
	เพชรพลอย	phét phloi
jewelry	เครื่องเพชรพลอย	khrêuang phét phloi
laundry (shop)	โรงซักรีดผา	rohng sák rêet phâa
legal advisor	คนที่ปรึกษา	khon thêe bprèuk-sǎa
	ทางกฎหมาย	thaang gòt mǎai
light industry	อุตสาหกรรมเบา	ùt-sǎa-hà-gam bao

magazine	นิตยสาร	nít-dtà-yá-sǎan
mail order selling	การขายสินค้า	gaan khǎai sǐn kháa
	ทางไปรษณีย	thaang bprai-sà-nee
medicine	การแพทย	gaan phâet
movie theater	โรงภาพยนุตร	rohng phâap-phá-yon
museum	พิพิธภัณฑ	phí-phítha phan

news agency	สำนักข่าว	sǎm-nák khàao
newspaper	หนังสือพิมพ	nǎng-sěu phim
nightclub	ไนทคลับ	nai-khláp

oil (petroleum)	น้ำมัน	nám man
courier services	บริการจัดส่ง	bor-rí-gaan jàt sòng
pharmaceutics	เภสัชกรรม	phoy càt cha -gam
printing (industry)	สิ่งพิมพ	sìng phim
publishing house	สำนักพิมพ	sǎm-nák phim

radio (~ station)	วิทยุ	wít-thá-yú
real estate	อสังหาริมทรัพย	a-sǎng-hǎa-rim-má-sáp
restaurant	รานอาหาร	ráan aa-hǎan

security company	บริษัทรักษา	bor-rí-sàt rák-sǎa
	ความปลอดภัย	khwaam bplòrt phai
sports	กีฬา	gee-laa

stock exchange	ตลาดหลักทรัพย์	dtà-làat làk sáp
store	รานคา	ráan kháa
supermarket	ซูเปอร์มาร์เก็ต	soo-bper-maa-gèt
swimming pool (public ~)	สระว่ายน้ำ	sà wâai náam
tailor shop	ร้านตัดเสื้อ	ráan dtàt sêua
television	โทรทัศน์	thoh-rá-thát
theater	โรงละคร	rohng lá-khon
trade (commerce)	การค้าขาย	gaan kháa kǎai
transportation	การขนส่ง	gaan khǒn sòng
travel	การท่องเที่ยว	gaan thôrng thîeow
veterinarian	สัตวแพทย์	sàt phâet
warehouse	โกดังเก็บสินค้า	goh-dang gèp sǐn kháa
waste collection	การเก็บขยะ	gaan gèp khà-yà

Job. Business. Part 2

118. Show. Exhibition

exhibition, show	งานแสดง	ngaan sà-daeng
trade show	งานแสดงสินค้า	ngaan sà-daeng sĭn kháa
participation	การเข้าร่วม	gaan khâo rûam
to participate (vi)	เขาร่วมใน	khâo rûam nai
participant (exhibitor)	ผู้เขาร่วม	phôo khâo rûam
director	ผู้อำนวยการ	phôo am-nuay gaan
organizers' office	สำนักงานผู้จัด	săm-nák ngaan phôo jàt
organizer	ผู้จัด	phôo jàt
to organize (vt)	จัด	jàt
participation form	แบบฟอร์มลงทะเบียน	bàep form long thá-bian
to fill out (vt)	กรอก	gròrk
details	รายละเอียด	raai lá-ìat
information	ขอมูล	khôr moon
price (cost, rate)	ราคา	raa-khaa
including	รวมถึง	ruam thĕung
to include (vt)	รวม	ruam
to pay (vi, vt)	จ่าย	jàai
registration fee	คาลงทะเบียน	khâa long thá-bian
entrance	ทางเข้า	thaang khâo
pavilion, hall	ศาลา	săa-laa
to register (vt)	ลงทะเบียน	long thá-bian
badge (identity tag)	ป้ายชื่อ	bpâai chêu
booth, stand	บูธแสดงสินค้า	bòot sà-daeng sĭn kháa
to reserve, to book	จอง	jorng
display case	ตู้โบว์สินค้า	dtôo ohoh cĭn kháa
spotlight	ไฟรวมแสง	fai ruam săeng
	บนเวที	bon way-thee
design	การออกแบบ	gaan òrk bàep
to place (put, set)	วาง	waang
to be placed	ถูกตั้ง	thòok dtâng
distributor	ผู้จัดจำหน่าย	phôo jàt jam-nàai
supplier	ผู้จัดหา	phôo jàt hăa
to supply (vt)	จัดหา	jàt hăa
country	ประเทศ	bprà-thâyt

foreign (adj)	ต่างชาติ	dtàang châat
product	ผลิตภัณฑ์	phà-lìt-dtà-phan
association	สมาคม	sà-maa khom
conference hall	ห้องประชุม	hôrng bprà-chum
congress	การประชุม	gaan bprà-chum
contest (competition)	การแข่งขัน	gaan khàeng khǎn
visitor (attendee)	ผู้เข้าร่วม	phôo khâo rûam
to visit (attend)	เข้าร่วม	khâo rûam
customer	ลูกค้า	lôok kháa

119. Mass Media

newspaper	หนังสือพิมพ์	nǎng-sěu phim
magazine	นิตยสาร	nít-dtà-yá-sǎan
press (printed media)	สื่อสิ่งพิมพ์	sèu sìng phim
radio	วิทยุ	wít-thá-yú
radio station	สถานีวิทยุ	sà-thǎa-nee wít-thá-yú
television	โทรทัศน์	thoh-rá-thát
presenter, host	ผู้ประกาศข่าว	phôo bprà-gàat khàao
newscaster	ผู้ประกาศข่าว	phôo bprà-gàat khàao
commentator	ผู้อธิบาย	phôo à-thí-baai
journalist	นักข่าว	nák khàao
correspondent (reporter)	ผู้รายงานข่าว	phôo raai ngaan khàao
press photographer	ช่างภาพ	châang phâap
	หนังสือพิมพ์	nǎng-sěu phim
reporter	ผู้รายงาน	phôo raai ngaan
editor	บรรณาธิการ	ban-naa-thí-gaan
editor-in-chief	หัวหน้าบรรณาธิการ	hǔa nâa ban-naa-thí-gaan
to subscribe (to …)	รับ	ráp
subscription	การรับ	gaan ráp
subscriber	ผู้รับ	phôo ráp
to read (vi, vt)	อ่าน	àan
reader	ผู้อ่าน	phôo àan
circulation (of newspaper)	การเผยแพร่	gaan phǒie-phrâe
monthly (adj)	รายเดือน	raai deuan
weekly (adj)	รายสัปดาห์	raai sàp-daa
issue (edition)	ฉบับ	chà-bàp
new (~ issue)	ใหม่	mài
headline	ข่าวพาดหัว	khàao phâat hǔa
short article	บทความสั้นๆ	bòt khwaam sân sân
column (regular article)	คอลัมน์	khor lam
article	บทความ	bòt khwaam

page	หน้า	nâa
reportage, report	การรายงานข่าว	gaan raai ngaan khàao
event (happening)	เหตุการณ์	hàyt gaan
sensation (news)	ข่าวดัง	khàao dang
scandal	เรื่องอื้อฉาว	rêuang êu chǎao
scandalous (adj)	อื้อฉาว	êu chǎao
great (~ scandal)	ใหญ่	yài

show (e.g., cooking ~)	รายการ	raai gaan
interview	การสัมภาษณ์	gaan sǎm-phâat
live broadcast	ถ่ายทอดสด	thàai thôrt sòt
channel	ช่อง	chôrng

120. Agriculture

agriculture	เกษตรกูรรม	gà-sàyt-dtra -gam
peasant (masc.)	ชาวนาผู้ชาย	chaao naa phôo chaai
peasant (fem.)	ชาวนาผู้หญิง	chaao naa phôo yǐng
farmer	ชาวนา	chaao naa

tractor (farm ~)	รถแทร็คเตอร์	rót tráek-dtêr
combine, harvester	เครื่องเก็บเกี่ยว	khrêuang gèp gìeow

plow	คันไถ	khan thǎi
to plow (vi, vt)	ไถ	thǎi
plowland	ที่ดินที่ไถพรวน	thêe din thêe thǎi phruan
furrow (in field)	ร่องดิน	rôrng din

to sow (vi, vt)	หว่าน	wàan
seeder	เครื่องหว่านเมล็ด	khrêuang wàan má-lét
sowing (process)	การหว่าน	gaan wàan

scythe	เคียว	khieow
to mow, to scythe	ถาง	thǎang

spade (tool)	พลั่ว	phlûa
to till (vt)	ขุด	khùt

hoe	จอบ	jòrp
to hoe, to weed	ถาก	thàak
weed (plant)	วัชพืช	wát-chá-phêut

watering can	กระป๋องรดน้ำ	grà-bpǒrng rót náam
to water (plants)	รดน้ำ	rót náam
watering (act)	การรดน้ำ	gaan rót nám

pitchfork	ส้อมเสียบ	sôrm sìap
rake	คราด	khrâat
fertilizer	ปุ๋ย	bpǔi
to fertilize (vt)	ใส่ปุ๋ย	sài bpǔi

manure (fertilizer)	ปุ๋ยดอก	bpŭi khôrk
field	ทุ่งนา	thûng naa
meadow	ทุ่งหญ้า	thûng yâa
vegetable garden	สวนผัก	sŭan phàk
orchard (e.g., apple ~)	สวนผลไม้	sŭan phŏn-lá-máai
to graze (vt)	เล็มหญ้า	lem yâa
herder (herdsman)	คนเลี้ยงสัตว์	khon líang sàt
pasture	ทุ่งเลี้ยงสัตว์	thûng líang sàt
cattle breeding	การขยายพันธุ์สัตว์	gaan khà-yăai phan sàt
sheep farming	การขยายพันธุ์แกะ	gaan khà-yăai phan gàe
plantation	ที่เพาะปลูก	thêe phór bplòok
row (garden bed ~s)	แถว	thăe
hothouse	เรือนกระจกร้อน	reuan grà-jòk rón
drought (lack of rain)	ภัยแล้ง	phai láeng
dry (~ summer)	แลง	láeng
grain	ธัญพืช	than-yá-phêut
cereal crops	ผลผลิตธัญพืช	phŏn phà-lìt than-yá-phêut
to harvest, to gather	เก็บเกี่ยว	gèp gìeow
miller (person)	เจ้าของโรงโม่	jâo khŏrng rohng môh
mill (e.g., gristmill)	โรงสี	rohng sĕe
to grind (grain)	โม่	môh
flour	แป้ง	bpâeng
straw	ฟาง	faang

121. Building. Building process

construction site	สถานที่ก่อสร้าง	sà-thăan thêe gòr sâang
to build (vt)	สราง	sâang
construction worker	คนงานก่อสร้าง	khon ngaan gòr sâang
project	โครงการ	khrohng gaan
architect	สถาปนิก	sà-thăa-bpà-ník
worker	คนงาน	khon ngaan
foundation (of a building)	รากฐาน	râak thăan
roof	หลังคา	lăng khaa
foundation pile	เสาเข็ม	săo khĕm
wall	กำแพง	gam-phaeng
reinforcing bars	เหล็กเส้นเสริมแรง	lèk sên sĕrm raeng
scaffolding	นั่งราน	nâng ráan
concrete	คอนกรีต	khorn-grèet
granite	หินแกรนิต	hĭn grae-nít

stone	หิน	hĭn
brick	อิฐ	ìt
sand	ทราย	saai
cement	ปูนซีเมนต์	bpoon see-mayn
plaster (for walls)	พลาสเตอร์	phláat-dtêr
to plaster (vt)	ฉาบ	chàap
paint	สี	sĕe
to paint (~ a wall)	ทาสี	thaa sĕe
barrel	ถัง	thăng
crane	ปั้นจั่น	bpân jàn
to lift, to hoist (vt)	ยก	yók
to lower (vt)	ลด	lót
bulldozer	รถดันดิน	rót dan din
excavator	รถขุด	rót khùt
scoop, bucket	ช้อนขุด	chórn khùt
to dig (excavate)	ขุด	khùt
hard hat	หมวกนิรภัย	mùak ní-rá-phai

122. Science. Research. Scientists

science	วิทยาศาสตร์	wít-thá-yaa sàat
scientific (adj)	ทางวิทยาศาสตร์	thaang wít-thá-yaa sàat
scientist	นักวิทยาศาสตร	nák wít-thá-yaa sàat
theory	ทฤษฎี	thrít-sà-dee
axiom	สัจพจน์	sàt-jà-phót
analysis	การวิเคราะห์	gaan wí-khrór
to analyze (vt)	วิเคราะห์	wí-khrór
argument (strong ~)	ข้อโต้แย้ง	khôr dtôh yáeng
substance (matter)	สาร	săan
hypothesis	สมมุติฐาน	sŏm-mút thăan
dilemma	โจทย์	jòht
dissertation	ปริญญานิพนธ์	bpà-rin-yaa ní-phon
dogma	หลัก	làk
doctrine	หลักคำสอน	làk kham sŏrn
research	การวิจัย	gaan wí-jai
to research (vt)	วิจัย	wí-jai
tests (laboratory ~)	การควบคุม	gaan khûap khum
laboratory	ห้องทดลอง	hôrng thót lorng
method	วิธี	wí-thee
molecule	โมเลกุล	moh-lay-gun
monitoring	การเฝ้าสังเกต	gaan fâo săng-gàyt
discovery (act, event)	การค้นพบ	gaan khón phóp

postulate	สัจพจน์	sàt-jà-phót
principle	หลักการ	làk gaan
forecast	การคาดกวรณ์	gaan khâat gaan
to forecast (vt)	คาดการณ์	khâat gaan
synthesis	การสังเคราะห์	gaan sǎng-khrór
trend (tendency)	แนวโน้ม	naew nóhm
theorem	ทฤษฎีบท	thrít-sà-dee bòt
teachings	คำสอน	kham sŏrn
fact	ขอเท็จจริง	khôr thét jing
expedition	การสำรวจ	gaan sǎm-rùat
experiment	การทดลอง	gaan thót lorng
academician	นักวิชาการ	nák wí-chaa gaan
bachelor (e.g., ~ of Arts)	บัณฑิต	ban-dìt
doctor (PhD)	ดุษฎีบัณฑิต	dùt-sà-dee ban-dìt
Associate Professor	รองศาสตราจารย์	rorng sàat-sà-dtraa-jaan
Master (e.g., ~ of Arts)	มหาบัณฑิต	má-hǎa ban-dìt
professor	ศาสตราจารย์	sàat-sà-dtraa-jaan

Professions and occupations

123. Job search. Dismissal

job	งาน	ngaan
staff (work force)	พนักงาน	phá-nák ngaan
personnel	พนักงาน	phá-nák ngaan
career	อาชีพ	aa-chêep
prospects (chances)	โอกาส	oh-gàat
skills (mastery)	ทักษะ	thák-sà
selection (screening)	การคัดเลือก	gaan khát lêuak
employment agency	สำนักงาน	sǎm-nák ngaan
	จัดหางาน	jàt hǎa ngaan
résumé	ประวัติย่อ	bprà-wàt yôr
job interview	สัมภาษณ์งาน	sǎm-phâat ngaan
vacancy, opening	ตำแหน่งว่าง	dtam-nàeng wâang
salary, pay	เงินเดือน	ngern deuan
fixed salary	เงินเดือน	ngern deuan
pay, compensation	ค่าแรง	khâa raeng
position (job)	ตำแหน่ง	dtam-nàeng
duty (of employee)	หน้าที่	nâa thêe
range of duties	หน้าที่	nâa thêe
busy (I'm ~)	ไม่ว่าง	mâi wâang
to fire (dismiss)	ไล่ออก	lâi òrk
dismissal	การไล่ออก	gaan lâi òrk
unemployment	การว่างงาน	gaan wâang ngaan
unemployed (n)	คนว่างงาน	khon wâang ngaan
retirement	การเกษียณอายุ	gaan gà-sǐan aa-yú
to retire (from job)	เกษียณ	gà-sǐan

124. Business people

director	ผู้อำนวยการ	phôo am-nuay gaan
manager (director)	ผู้จัดการ	phôo jàt gaan
boss	หัวหน้า	hǔa-nâa
superior	ผู้บังคับบัญชา	phôo bang-kháp ban-chaa
superiors	คณะผู้บังคับ	khá-ná phôo bang-kháp
	บัญชา	ban-chaa

president	ประธานาธิปดี	bprà-thaa-naa-thí-bor-dee
chairman	ประธาน	bprà-thaan
deputy (substitute)	รอง	rorng
assistant	ผู้ช่วย	phôo chûay
secretary	เลขา	lay-khăa
personal assistant	ผู้ช่วยส่วน	phôo chûay sùan
	บุคคล	bùk-khon
businessman	นักธุรกิจ	nák thú-rá-gìt
entrepreneur	ผู้ประกอบการ	phôo bprà-gòp gaan
founder	ผู้ก่อตั้ง	phôo gòr dtâng
to found (vt)	ก่อตั้ง	gòr dtâng
incorporator	ผู้ก่อตั้ง	phôo gòr dtâng
partner	หุ้นส่วน	hûn sùan
stockholder	ผู้ถือหุ้น	phôo thěu hûn
millionaire	เศรษฐีเงินล้าน	sàyt-thěe ngern láan
billionaire	มหาเศรษฐี	má-hăa sàyt-thěe
owner, proprietor	เจ้าของ	jâo khŏrng
landowner	เจ้าของที่ดิน	jâo khŏrng thêe din
client	ลูกค้า	lôok kháa
regular client	ลูกค้าประจำ	lôok kháa bprà-jam
buyer (customer)	ลูกค้า	lôok kháa
visitor	ผู้เขาร่วม	phôo khâo rûam
professional (n)	ผู้เป็นมืออาชีพ	phôo bpen meu aa-chêep
expert	ผู้เชี่ยวชาญ	phôo chîeow-chaan
specialist	ผู้ชำนาญ	phôo cham-naan
	เฉพาะทาง	chà-phó thaang
banker	พนักงาน	phá-nák ngaan
	ธนาคาร	thá-naa-khaan
broker	นายหน้า	naai nâa
cashier, teller	แคชเชียร์	khâet chia
accountant	นักบัญชี	nák ban-chee
security guard	ยาม	yaam
investor	ผู้ลงทุน	phôo long thun
debtor	ลูกหนี้	lôok nêe
creditor	เจ้าหนี้	jâo nêe
borrower	ผู้ยืม	phôo yeum
importer	ผู้นำเข้า	phôo nam khâo
exporter	ผู้ส่งออก	phôo sòng òrk
manufacturer	ผู้ผลิต	phôo phà-lìt
distributor	ผู้จัดจำหน่าย	phôo jàt jam-nàai
middleman	คนกลาง	khon glaang

consultant	ที่ปรึกษา	thêe bprèuk-săa
sales representative	พนักงานขาย	phá-nák ngaan khăai
agent	ตัวแทน	dtua thaen
insurance agent	ตัวแทนประกัน	dtua thaen bprà-gan

125. Service professions

cook	ดูนครัว	khon khrua
chef (kitchen chef)	กุก	gúk
baker	ช่างอบขนมปัง	châang òp khà-nŏm bpang
bartender	บาร์เทนเดอร์	baa-thayn-dêr
waiter	พนักงานเสิร์ฟชาย	phá-nák ngaan sèrf chaai
waitress	พนักงานเสิร์ฟหญิง	phá-nák ngaan sèrf yĭng
lawyer, attorney	ทนายความ	thá-naai khwaam
lawyer (legal expert)	นักกฎหมาย	nák gòt măai
notary public	พนักงานจดทะเบียน	phá-nák ngaan jòt thá-bian
electrician	ช่างไฟฟ้า	châang fai-fáa
plumber	ช่างประปา	châang bprà-bpaa
carpenter	ช่างไม้	châang máai
masseur	หมอนวดชาย	mŏr nûat chaai
masseuse	หมอนวดหญิง	mŏr nûat yĭng
doctor	แพทย์	phâet
taxi driver	คนขับแท็กซี่	khon khàp tháek-sêe
driver	คนขับ	khon khàp
delivery man	คนส่งของ	khon sòng khŏrng
chambermaid	แม่บ้าน	mâe bâan
security guard	ยาม	yaam
flight attendant (fem.)	พนักงานต้อนรับ บนเครื่องบิน	phá-nák ngaan dtôrn ráp bon khrêuang bin
schoolteacher	อาจารย์	aa-jaan
librarian	บรรณารักษ์	ban-naa-rák
translator	นักแปล	nák bplae
interpreter	ล่าม	lâam
guide	มัคคุเทศก์	mák-khú-thâyt
hairdresser	ช่างทำผม	châang tham phŏm
mailman	บุรุษไปรษณีย์	bù-rùt bprai-sà-nee
salesman (store staff)	คนขายของ	khon khăai khŏrng
gardener	ชาวสวน	chaao sŭan
domestic servant	คนใช้	khon chái
maid (female servant)	สาวใช้	săao chái
cleaner (cleaning lady)	คนทำความสะอาด	khon tham khwaam sà-àat

126. Military professions and ranks

private	พลทหาร	phon-thá-hǎan
sergeant	สิบเอก	sìp àyk
lieutenant	ร้อยโท	rói thoh
captain	ร้อยเอก	rói àyk
major	พลตรี	phon-dtree
colonel	พันเอก	phan àyk
general	นายพล	naai phon
marshal	จอมพล	jorm phon
admiral	พลเรือเอก	phon reua àyk
military (n)	ทางทหาร	thaang thá-hǎan
soldier	ทหาร	thá-hǎan
officer	นายทหาร	naai thá-hǎan
commander	ผู้บัญชาการ	phôo ban-chaa gaan
border guard	ยามเฝ้าชายแดน	yaam fâo chaai daen
radio operator	พลวิทยุ	phon wít-thá-yú
scout (searcher)	ทหารพราน	thá-hǎan phraan
pioneer (sapper)	ทหารช่าง	thá-hǎan châang
marksman	พลแม่นปืน	phon mâen bpeun
navigator	ต้นหน	dtôn hǒn

127. Officials. Priests

king	กษัตริย์	gà-sàt
queen	ราชินี	raa-chí-nee
prince	เจ้าชาย	jâo chaai
princess	เจ้าหญิง	jâo yǐng
czar	ซาร์	saa
czarina	ซารีนา	saa-ree-naa
president	ประธานาธิบดี	bprà-thaa-naa-thí-bor-dee
Secretary (minister)	รัฐมนตรี	rát-thà-mon-dtree
prime minister	นายกรัฐมนตรี	naa-yók rát-thà-mon-dtree
senator	สมาชิกวุฒิสภา	sà-maa-chík wút-thí sà-phaa
diplomat	นักการทูต	nák gaan thôot
consul	กงสุล	gong-sǔn
ambassador	เอกอัครราชทูต	àyk-gà-àk-krá-râat-chá-tôot
counselor (diplomatic officer)	เจ้าหน้าที่การทูต	jâo nâa-thêe gaan thôot
official, functionary (civil servant)	ข้าราชการ	khâa râat-chá-gaan

prefect	เจ้าหน้าที่	jâo nâa-thêe
mayor	นายกเทศมนตรี	naa-yók thâyt-sà-mon-dtree
judge	ผู้พิพากษา	phôo phí-phâak-sǎa
prosecutor (e.g., district attorney)	อัยการ	ai-yá-gaan
missionary	ผู้สอนศาสนา	phôo sǒrn sàat-sà-nǎa
monk	พระ	phrá
abbot	เจ้าอาวาส	jâo aa-wâat
rabbi	พระในศาสนายิว	phrá nai sàat-sà-nǎa yiw
vizier	วีซีร์	wee see
shah	กษัตริย์อิหร่าน	gà-sàt i-ràan
sheikh	หัวหน้าเผ่าอาหรับ	hǔa nâa phào aa-ràp

128. Agricultural professions

beekeeper	คนเลี้ยงผึ้ง	khon líang phêung
herder, shepherd	คนเลี้ยงปศุสัตว์	khon líang bpà-sù-sàt
agronomist	นักปฐพีวิทยา	nák bpà-tà-phee wít-thá-yaa
cattle breeder	ผู้ขยายพันธุ์สัตว์	phôo khà-yǎai phan sàt
veterinarian	สัตวแพทย์	sàt phâet
farmer	ชาวนา	chaao naa
winemaker	ผู้ผลิตไวน์	phôo phà-lìt wai
zoologist	นักสัตววิทยา	nák sàt wít-thá-yaa
cowboy	โคบาล	khoh-baan

129. Art professions

actor	นักแสดงชาย	nák sà-daeng chaai
actress	นักแสดงหญิง	nák sà-daeng yǐng
singer (masc.)	นักร้องชาย	nák rórng chaai
singer (fem.)	นักร้องหญิง	nák rórng yǐng
dancer (masc.)	นักเต้นชาย	nák dtên chaai
dancer (fem.)	นักเต้นหญิง	nák dtên yǐng
performer (masc.)	นักแสดงชาย	nák sà-daeng chaai
performer (fem.)	นักแสดงหญิง	nák sà-daeng yǐng
musician	นักดนตรี	nák don-dtree
pianist	นักเปียโน	nák bpia noh
guitar player	ผู้เล่นกีตาร์	phôo lên gee-dtâa

conductor (orchestra ~)	ผู้ควบคุม วงดนตรี	phôo khûap khum wong don-dtree
composer	นักแต่งเพลง	nák dtàeng phlayng
impresario	ผู้ควบคุม การแสดง	phôo khûap khum gaan sà-daeng
film director	ผู้กำกับ ภาพยนตร์	phôo gam-gàp phâap-phá-yon
producer	ผู้อำนวยการสร้าง	phôo am-nuay gaan sâang
scriptwriter	คนเขียนบท ภาพยนตร์	khon khĭan bòt phâap-phá-yon
critic	นักวิจารณ์	nák wí-jaan
writer	นักเขียน	nák khĭan
poet	นักกวี	nák gà-wee
sculptor	ช่างสลัก	châang sà-làk
artist (painter)	ช่างวาดรูป	châang wâat rôop
juggler	นักมายากล โยนของ	nák maa-yaa gon yohn khŏrng
clown	ตัวตลก	dtua dtà-lòk
acrobat	นักกายกรรม	nák gaai-yá-gam
magician	นักเล่นกล	nák lên gon

130. Various professions

doctor	แพทย์	phâet
nurse	พยาบาล	phá-yaa-baan
psychiatrist	จิตแพทย์	jìt-dtà-phâet
dentist	ทันตแพทย์	than-dtà phâet
surgeon	ศัลยแพทย์	săn-yá-phâet
astronaut	นักบินอวกาศ	nák bin a-wá-gàat
astronomer	นักดาราศาสตร์	nák daa-raa sàat
pilot	นักบิน	nák bin
driver (of taxi, etc.)	คนขับ	khon khàp
engineer (train driver)	คนขับรถไฟ	khon khàp rót fai
mechanic	ช่างเครื่อง	châang khrêuang
miner	คนงานเหมือง	khon ngaan mĕuang
worker	คนงาน	khon ngaan
locksmith	ช่างโลหะ	châang loh-hà
joiner (carpenter)	ช่างไม้	châang máai
turner (lathe operator)	ช่างกลึง	châang gleung
construction worker	คนงานก่อสร้าง	khon ngaan gòr sâang
welder	ช่างเชื่อม	châang chêuam
professor (title)	ศาสตราจารย์	sàat-sà-dtraa-jaan
architect	สถาปนิก	sà-thăa-bpà-ník

historian	นักประวัติศาสตร์	nák bprà-wàt sàat
scientist	นักวิทยาศาสตร	nák wít-thá-yaa sàat
physicist	นักฟิสิกส	nák fí-sìk
chemist (scientist)	นักเคมี	nák khay-mee
archeologist	นักโบราณคดี	nák boh-raan-ná-khá-dee
geologist	นักธรณี	nák thor-rá-nee
	วิทยา	wít-thá-yaa
researcher (scientist)	ผู้วิจัย	phôo wí-jai
babysitter	พี่เลี้ยงเด็ก	phêe líang dèk
teacher, educator	อาจารย	aa-jaan
editor	บรรณาธิการ	ban-naa-thí-gaan
editor-in-chief	หัวหน้าบรรณาธิการ	hǔa nâa ban-naa-thí-gaan
correspondent	ผู้สื่อข่าว	phôo sèu khàao
typist (fem.)	พนักงานพิมพ์ดีด	phá-nák ngaan phim dèet
designer	นักออกแบบ	nák òrk bàep
computer expert	ผู้เชี่ยวชาญด้าน	pôo chîeow-chaan dâan
	คอมพิวเตอร	khorm-piw-dtêr
programmer	นักเขียนโปรแกรม	nák khĭan bproh-graem
engineer (designer)	วิศวกร	wít-sà-wá-gon
sailor	กะลาสี	gà-laa-sěe
seaman	คนเรือ	khon reua
rescuer	นักกู้ภัย	nák gôo phai
fireman	เจ้าหน้าที่ดับเพลิง	jâo nâa-thêe dàp phlerng
police officer	เจ้าหน้าที่ตำรวจ	jâo nâa-thêe dtam-rùat
watchman	คนยาม	khon yaam
detective	นักสืบ	nák sèup
customs officer	เจ้าหน้าที่	jâo nâa-thêe
	ศุลกากร	sǔn-lá-gaa-gon
bodyguard	ผู้คุ้มกัน	phôo khúm gan
prison guard	ผู้คุม	phôo khum
inspector	ผู้ตรวจการ	phôo dtrùat gaan
sportsman	นักกีฬา	nák gee-laa
trainer, coach	โค้ช	khóht
butcher	คนขายเนื้อ	khon khǎai néua
cobbler (shoe repairer)	คนซ่อมรองเท้า	khon sôrm rorng tháo
merchant	คนค้า	khon kháa
loader (person)	คนงานยกของ	khon ngaan yók khǒrng
fashion designer	นักออกแบบแฟชั่น	nák òrk bàep fae-chân
model (fem.)	นางแบบ	naang bàep

131. Occupations. Social status

schoolboy	นักเรียน	nák rian
student (college ~)	นักศึกษา	nák sèuk-săa
philosopher	นักปราชญ์	nák bpràat
economist	นักเศรษฐศาสตร์	nák sàyt-thà-sàat
inventor	นักประดิษฐ์	nák bprà-dìt
unemployed (n)	คนว่างงาน	khon wâang ngaan
retiree	ผู้เกษียณอายุ	phôo gà-sĭan aa-yú
spy, secret agent	สายลับ	săai láp
prisoner	นักโทษ	nák thôht
striker	คนนัดหยุดงาน	kon nát yùt ngaan
bureaucrat	อำมาตย์	am-màat
traveler (globetrotter)	นักเดินทาง	nák dern-thaang
gay, homosexual (n)	ผู้รักเพศเดียวกัน	phôo rák phâyt dieow gan
hacker	แฮ็กเกอร์	háek-gêr
hippie	ฮิปปี้	híp-bpêe
bandit	โจร	john
hit man, killer	นักฆ่า	nák khâa
drug addict	ผู้ติดยาเสพติด	phôo dtìt yaa-sàyp-dtìt
drug dealer	ผู้ค้ายาเสพติด	phôo kháa yaa-sàyp-dtìt
prostitute (fem.)	โสเภณี	sŏh-phay-nee
pimp	แมงดา	maeng-daa
sorcerer	พ่อมด	phôr mót
sorceress (evil ~)	แม่มด	mâe mót
pirate	โจรสลัด	john sà-làt
slave	ทาส	thâat
samurai	ซามูไร	saa-moo-rai
savage (primitive)	คนป่าเถื่อน	khon bpàa thèuan

Sports

132. Kinds of sports. Sportspersons

sportsman	นักกีฬา	nák gee-laa
kind of sports	ประเภทกีฬา	bprà-phâyt gee-laa
basketball	บาสเก็ตบอล	bàat-gèt-bon
basketball player	ผู้เล่นบาสเก็ตบอล	phôo lâyn bàat-gèt-bon
baseball	เบสบอล	bàyt-bon
baseball player	ผู้เล่นเบสบอล	phôo lâyn bàyt bon
soccer	ฟุตบอล	fút bon
soccer player	นักฟุตบอล	nák fút-bon
goalkeeper	ผู้รักษาประตู	phôo rák-sǎa bprà-dtoo
hockey	ฮอกกี้	hôk-gêe
hockey player	ผู้เล่นฮอกกี้	phôo lâyn hôk-gêe
volleyball	วอลเลย์บอล	won-lây-bon
volleyball player	ผู้เล่นวอลเลย์บอล	phôo lâyn won-lây-bon
boxing	การชกมวย	gaan chók muay
boxer	นักมวย	nák muay
wrestling	การมวยปล้ำ	gaan muay bplâm
wrestler	นักมวยปล้ำ	nák muay bplâm
karate	คาราเต้	khaa-raa-dtây
karate fighter	นักคาราเต้	nák khaa-raa-dtây
judo	ยูโด	yoo-doh
judo athlete	นักยูโด	nák yoo-doh
tennis	เทนนิส	then-nít
tennis player	นักเทนนิส	nák then-nít
swimming	กีฬาว่ายน้ำ	gee-laa wâai náam
swimmer	นักวายน้ำ	nák wâai náam
fencing	กีฬาฟันดาบ	gee-laa fan dàap
fencer	นักฟันดาบ	nák fan dàap
chess	หมากรุก	màak rúk
chess player	ผู้เล่นหมากรุก	phôo lên màak rúk

alpinism	การปีนเขา	gaan bpeen khǎo
alpinist	นักปีนเขา	nák bpeen khǎo
running	การวิ่ง	gaan wîng
runner	นักวิ่ง	nák wîng
athletics	กรีฑา	gree thaa
athlete	นักกรีฑา	nák gree thaa
horseback riding	กีฬาขี่ม้า	gee-laa khèe máa
horse rider	นักขี่มา	nák khèe máa
figure skating	สเก็ตลีลา	sà-gèt lee-laa
figure skater (masc.)	นักเสดง	nák sà-daeng
	สเก็ตลีลา	sà-gèt lee-laa
figure skater (fem.)	นักเสดง	nák sà-daeng
	สเก็ตลีลา	sà-gèt lee-laa
powerlifting	กีฬายกน้ำหนัก	gee-laa yók náam nàk
powerlifter	นักยกน้ำหนัก	nák yók nám nàk
car racing	การแข่งรถ	gaan khàeng rót
racer (driver)	นักแข่งรถ	nák khàeng rót
cycling	การแข่งจักรยาน	gaan khàeng jàk-grà-yaan
cyclist	นักแข่งจักรยาน	nák khàeng jàk-grà-yaan
broad jump	กีฬากระโดดไกล	gee-laa grà-dòht glai
pole vault	กีฬากระโดด	gee-laa grà dòht
	ค้ำถอ	khám thǒr
jumper	นักกระโดด	nák grà dòht

133. Kinds of sports. Miscellaneous

football	อเมริกันฟุตบอล	a-may-rí-gan fút bon
badminton	แบดมินตัน	bàet-min-dtân
biathlon	ไบแอธลอน	bpai-oht-lon
billiards	บิลเลียด	bin-lîat
bobsled	การขับเลื่อน	gaan khàp lêuan
	น้ำแข็ง	náam khǎeng
bodybuilding	การเพาะกาย	gaan phór gaai
water polo	กีฬาโปโลน้ำ	gee-laa bpoh loh nám
handball	แฮนด์บอล	haen-bon
golf	กอล์ฟ	góf
rowing, crew	การพายเรือ	gaan phaai reua
scuba diving	การดำน้ำ	gaan dam náam
cross-country skiing	การแข่งสกี	gaan khàeng sà-gee
	ตามเสนทาง	dtaam sên thaang

table tennis (ping-pong)	กีฬาปิงปอง	gee-laa bping-bpong
sailing	การแล่นเรือใบ	gaan lâen reua bai
rally racing	การแข่งแรลลี่	gaan khàeng rae lá-lêe
rugby	รักบี้	rák-bêe
snowboarding	สโน๊วบอร์ด	sà-nôh bòt
archery	การยิงธนู	gaan ying thá-noo

134. Gym

barbell	บาร์เบลล์	baa bayn
dumbbells	ที่ยกน้ำหนัก	thêe yók nám nàk
training machine	เครื่องออกกำลัง กาย	khrêuang òk gam-lang gaai
exercise bicycle	จักรยานออก กำลังกาย	jàk-grà-yaan òk gam-lang gaai
treadmill	ลู่วิ่งออกกำลังกาย	lôo wîng òk gam-lang gaai
horizontal bar	บาร์เดี่ยว	baa dìeow
parallel bars	บาร์คู่	baa khôo
vault (vaulting horse)	ม้าขวาง	máa khwăang
mat (exercise ~)	เสื่อออกกำลังกาย	sèua òrk gam-lang gaai
jump rope	กระโดดเชือก	grà dòht chêuak
aerobics	แอโรบิก	ae-roh-bìk
yoga	โยคะ	yoh-khá

135. Hockey

hockey	ฮอกกี้	hôk-gêe
hockey player	ผู้เล่นฮอกกี้	phôo lâyn hôk-gêe
to play hockey	เล่นฮอกกี้	lên hók-gêe
ice	น้ำแข็ง	nám khăeng
puck	ลูกฮอกกี้	lôok hók-gêe
hockey stick	ไม้ฮอกกี้	máai hók-gêe
ice skates	รองเท้าสเก็ต น้ำแข็ง	rorng tháo sà-gèt nám khăeng
board (ice hockey rink ~)	ลานสเก็ตน้ำแข็ง	laan sà-gèt nám khăeng
shot	การยิง	gaan ying
goaltender	ผู้รักษาประตู	phôo rák-săa bprà-dtoo
goal (score)	ประตู	bprà-dtoo
to score a goal	ทำประตู	tham bprà-dtoo
period	ช่วง	chûang
second period	ช่วงที่สอง	chûang thêe sŏrng

| substitutes bench | ซุ้มม้านั่ง | súm máa nâng |
| | ตัวสำรอง | dtua sǎm-rorng |

136. Soccer

soccer	ฟุตบอล	fút bon
soccer player	นักฟุตบอล	nák fút-bon
to play soccer	เล่นฟุตบอล	lên fút bon

major league	เมเจอร์ลีก	may-jer-lêek
soccer club	สโมสรฟุตบอล	sà-moh-sǒn fút-bon
coach	โค้ช	khóht
owner, proprietor	เจ้าของ	jâo khǒrng

team	ทีม	theem
team captain	หัวหน้าทีม	hǔa nâa theem
player	ผู้เล่น	phôo lên
substitute	ผู้เล่นสำรอง	phôo lên sǎm-rorng

forward	กองหน้า	gorng nâa
center forward	กองหน้าตัวเป้า	gorng nâa dtua bpâo
scorer	ผู้ทำประตู	phôo tham bprà-dtoo
defender, back	กองหลัง	gorng lǎng
midfielder, halfback	กองกลาง	gorng glaang

match	เกมการแข่ง	gaym gaan khàeng
to meet (vi, vt)	พบ	phóp
final	รอบสุดท้าย	rôrp sùt tháai
semi-final	รอบรองชนะเลิศ	rôrp rorng chá-ná lêrt
championship	ชิงแชมป์	ching chaem

period, half	ครึ่ง	khrêung
first period	ครึ่งแรก	khrêung râek
half-time	ช่วงพักครึ่ง	chûang phák khrêung

goal	ประตู	bprà-dtoo
goalkeeper	ผู้รักษาประตู	phôo rák-sǎa bprà-dtoo
goalpost	เสาประตู	sǎo bprà-dtoo
crossbar	คานประตู	khaan bprà-dtoo
net	ตาข่าย	dtaa khàai
to concede a goal	เสียประตู	sǐa bprà-dtoo

ball	บอล	bon
pass	การส่ง	gaan sòng
kick	การเตะ	gaan dtè
to kick (~ the ball)	เตะ	dtè
free kick (direct ~)	ฟรีคิก	free khík
corner kick	การเตะมุม	gaan dtè mum
attack	การบุก	gaan bùk
counterattack	การบุกสวนกลับ	gaan bùk sǔan glàp

combination	การผสมผสาน	gaan phà-sǒm phà-sǎan
referee	ผู้ตัดสิน	phôo dtàt sǐn
to blow the whistle	เป่านกหวีด	bpào nók wèet
whistle (sound)	เสียงนกหวีด	sǐang nók wèet
foul, misconduct	ฟาวล์	faao
to commit a foul	ทำฟาวล์	tham faao
to send off	ไล่ออก	lâi òrk
yellow card	ใบเหลือง	bai lěuang
red card	ใบแดง	bai daeng
disqualification	การตัดสิทธิ์	gaan dtàt sìt
to disqualify (vt)	ตัดสิทธิ์	dtàt sìt
penalty kick	ลูกโทษ	lôok thôht
wall	กำแพง	gam-phaeng
to score (vi, vt)	ทำประตู	tham bprà-dtoo
goal (score)	ประตู	bprà-dtoo
to score a goal	ทำประตู	tham bprà-dtoo
substitution	ตัวสำรอง	dtua sǎm-rorng
to replace (a player)	เปลี่ยนตัว	bplìan dtua
rules	กติกา	gà-dtì-gaa
tactics	ยุทธวิธี	yút-thá-wí-thee
stadium	สนาม	sà-nǎam
stand (bleachers)	อัฒจันทร์	àt-tá-jan
fan, supporter	แฟน	faen
to shout (vi)	ตะโกน	dtà-gohn
scoreboard	ป้ายคะแนน	bpâai khá-naen
score	คะแนน	khá-naen
defeat	ความพ่ายแพ้	khwaam phâai pháe
to lose (not win)	แพ้	pháe
tie	เสมอ	sà-měr
to tie (vi)	เสมอ	sà-měr
victory	ชัยชนะ	chai chá-ná
to win (vi, vt)	ชนะ	chá-ná
champion	แชมเปี้ยน	chaem-bpîan
best (adj)	ดีที่สุด	dee têe sùt
to congratulate (vt)	แสดงความยินดี	sà-daeng khwaam yin dee
commentator	ผู้อธิบาย	phôo à-thí-baai
to commentate (vt)	อธิบาย	à-thí-baai
broadcast	การออกอากาศ	gaan òrk aa-gàat

137. Alpine skiing

skis	สกี	sà-gee
to ski (vi)	เล่นสกี	lên sà-gee

mountain-ski resort	รีสอร์ทสำหรับ เลนสกีบนภูเขา	ree sòt săm-ràp lên sà-gee bon phoo khăo
ski lift	ลิฟต์สกี	líf sà-gee
ski poles	ไม้ค้ำสกี	máai khám sà-gee
slope	ทางลาด	thaang lâat
slalom	การเลนสกี	gaan lên sà-gee

138. Tennis. Golf

golf	กอล์ฟ	góf
golf club	กอล์ฟคลับ	góf khláp
golfer	นักกอล์ฟ	nák góf
hole	หลุม	lǔm
club	ไม้ตีกอล์ฟ	mái dtee góf
golf trolley	รถลากถุงกอล์ฟ	rót lâak thǔng góf
tennis	เทนนิส	then-nít
tennis court	สนามเทนนิส	sà-nǎam then-nít
serve	การเสิร์ฟ	gaan sèrf
to serve (vt)	เสิร์ฟ	sèrf
racket	ไม้ตีเทนนิส	mái dtee then-nít
net	ตาข่าย	dtaa khàai
ball	ลูกเทนนิส	lôok then-nít

139. Chess

chess	หมากรุก	màak rúk
chessmen	ตัวหมากรุก	dtua màak rúk
chess player	นักกีฬาหมากรุก	nák gee-laa màak rúk
chessboard	กระดานหมากรุก	grà-daan mǎak-grùk
chessman	ตัวหมากรุก	dtua màak rúk
White (white pieces)	ขาว	khǎao
Black (black pieces)	ดำ	dam
pawn	เบี้ย	bîa
bishop	บิชอป	bì-chôrp
knight	มา	máa
rook	เรือ	reua
queen	ควีน	khween
king	ขุน	khǔn
move	การเดิน	gaan dern
to move (vi, vt)	เดิน	dern
to sacrifice (vt)	สละ	sà-là
castling	การเข้าป้อม	gaan khâo bpôrm

| check | รุก | rúk |
| checkmate | รุกฆาต | rúk khâat |

chess tournament	การแข่งขัน	gaan khàeng khǎn
	หมากรุก	màak rúk
Grand Master	แกรนด์มาสเตอร์	graen maa-sà-dtêr
combination	การเดินหมาก	gaan dern màak
game (in chess)	เกม	gaym
checkers	หมากฮอส	màak-hórt

140. Boxing

boxing	การชกมวย	gaan chók muay
fight (bout)	ชกมวย	chók muay
boxing match	เกมการชกมวย	gaym gaan chók muay
round (in boxing)	ยก	yók

| ring | เวที | way-thee |
| gong | ฆอง | khórng |

punch	การต่อย	gaan dtòi
knockdown	การน็อค	gaan nórk
knockout	การน็อคเอาท์	gaan nórk ao
to knock out	น็อคเอาท	nórk ao

| boxing glove | นวมชกมวย | nuam chók muay |
| referee | กรรมการ | gam-má-gaan |

lightweight	ไลท์เวท	lai-wâyt
middleweight	มิดเดิ้ลเวท	mít dêrn wâyt
heavyweight	เฮฟวี่เวท	hay fá-wêe wâyt

141. Sports. Miscellaneous

Olympic Games	กีฬาโอลิมปิก	gee-laa oh-lim-bpìk
winner	ผู้ชนะ	phôo chá-ná
to be winning	ชนะ	chá-ná
to win (vi)	ชนะ	chá-ná

| leader | ผู้นำ | phôo nam |
| to lead (vi) | นำ | nam |

first place	อันดับที่หนึ่ง	an-dàp thêe nèung
second place	อันดับที่สอง	an-dàp thêe sŏrng
third place	อันดับที่สาม	an-dàp thêe sǎam

| medal | เหรียญรางวัล | rǐan raang-wan |
| trophy | ถ้วยรางวัล | thûay raang-wan |

prize cup (trophy)	เวท	wâyt
prize (in game)	รางวัล	raang-wan
main prize	รางวัลหลัก	raang-wan làk
record	สถิติ	sà-thì-dtì
to set a record	ทำสถิติ	tham sà-thì-dtì
final	รอบสุดท้าย	rôrp sùt tháai
final (adj)	สุดท้าย	sùt tháai
champion	แชมเปี้ยน	chaem-bpîan
championship	ชิงแชมป์	ching chaem
stadium	สนาม	sà-nǎam
stand (bleachers)	อัฒจันทร์	àt-tá-jan
fan, supporter	แฟน	faen
opponent, rival	คู่ต่อสู้	khôo dtòr sôo
start (start line)	เส้นเริ่ม	sên rêrm
finish line	เสนชัย	sên chai
defeat	ความพ่ายแพ้	khwaam phâai pháe
to lose (not win)	แพ้	pháe
referee	กรรมฏาร	gam-má-gaan
jury (judges)	คณะผู้ตัดสิน	khá-ná phôo dtàt sǐn
score	คะแนน	khá-naen
tie	เสมอ	sà-měr
to tie (vi)	ได้คะแนนเท่ากัน	dâai khá-naen thâo gan
point	แต้ม	dtâem
result (final score)	ผลลัพธ์	phǒn láp
period	ช่วง	chûang
half-time	ช่วงพักครึ่ง	chûang phák khrêung
doping	การใช้สารต้องห้ามทางการกีฬา	gaan chái sǎan dtôrng hâam thaang gaan gee-laa
to penalize (vt)	ทำโทษ	tham thôht
to disqualify (vt)	ตัดสิทธิ์	dtàt sìt
apparatus	อุปกรณ์	ù-bpà-gon
javelin	แหลน	lǎen
shot (metal ball)	ลูกเหล็ก	lôok lèk
ball (snooker, etc.)	ลูก	lôok
aim (target)	เล็งเป้า	leng bpâo
target	เป้านิ่ง	bpâo nîng
to shoot (vi)	ยิง	ying
accurate (~ shot)	แม่นยำ	mâen yam
trainer, coach	โค้ช	khóht
to train (sb)	ฝึก	fèuk

to train (vi)	ฝึกหัด	fèuk hàt
training	การฝึกหัด	gaan fèuk hàt
gym	โรงยิม	rohng-yim
exercise (physical)	การออกกำลัง	gaan òrk gam-lang
warm-up (athlete ~)	การอบอุ่นร่างกาย	gaan òp ùn râang gaai

Education

142. School

school	โรงเรียน	rohng rian
principal (headmaster)	อาจารย์ใหญ่	aa-jaan yài
pupil (boy)	นักเรียน	nák rian
pupil (girl)	นักเรียน	nák rian
schoolboy	เด็กนักเรียนชาย	dèk nák rian chaai
schoolgirl	เด็กนักเรียนหญิง	dèk nák rian yĭng
to teach (sb)	สอน	sŏrn
to learn (language, etc.)	เรียน	rian
to learn by heart	ทองจำ	thôrng jam
to learn (~ to count, etc.)	เรียน	rian
to be in school	ไปโรงเรียน	bpai rohng rian
to go to school	ไปโรงเรียน	bpai rohng rian
alphabet	ตัวอักษร	dtua àk-sŏn
subject (at school)	วิชา	wí-chaa
classroom	ห้องเรียน	hôrng rian
lesson	ชั่วโมงเรียน	chûa mohng rian
recess	ชวงพัก	chûang phák
school bell	สัญญาณหมดเรียน	săn-yaan mòt rian
school desk	โต๊ะนักเรียน	dtó nák rian
chalkboard	กระดานดำ	grà-daan dam
grade	เกรด	gràyt
good grade	เกรดดี	gràyt dee
bad grade	เกรดแย	gràyt yâe
to give a grade	ให้เกรด	hâi gràyt
mistake, error	ข้อผิดพลาด	khôr phìt phlâat
to make mistakes	ทำผิดพลาด	tham phìt phlâat
to correct (an error)	แก้ไข	gâe khăi
cheat sheet	โพย	phoi
homework	การบ้าน	gaan bâan
exercise (in education)	แบบฝึกหัด	bàep fèuk hàt
to be present	มาเรียน	maa rian
to be absent	ขาด	khàat
to miss school	ขาดเรียน	khàat rian

to punish (vt)	ลงโทษ	long thôht
punishment	การลงโทษ	gaan long thôht
conduct (behavior)	ความประพฤติ	khwaam bprà-préut
report card	สมุดพก	sà-mùt phók
pencil	ดินสอ	din-sŏr
eraser	ยางลบ	yaang lóp
chalk	ชอล์ค	chôrk
pencil case	กล่องดินสอ	glòrng din-sŏr
schoolbag	กระเป๋า	grà-bpǎo
pen	ปากกา	bpàak gaa
school notebook	สมุดจด	sà-mùt jòt
textbook	หนังสือเรียน	nǎng-sĕu rian
drafting compass	วงเวียน	wong wian
to make technical drawings	ร่างภาพ ทางเทคนิค	râang phâap thaang thék-nìk
technical drawing	ภาพร่าง ทางเทคนิค	phâap-râang thaang thék-nìk
poem	กลอน	glorn
by heart (adv)	โดยท่องจำ	doi thôrng jam
to learn by heart	ท่องจำ	thôrng jam
school vacation	เวลาปิดเทอม	way-laa bpìt therm
to be on vacation	หยุดปิดเทอม	yùt bpìt therm
to spend one's vacation	ใช้เวลาหยุดปิดเทอม	chái way-laa yùt bpìt therm
test (written math ~)	การทดสอบ	gaan thót sòrp
essay (composition)	ความเรียง	khwaam riang
dictation	การเขียนตาม คำบอก	gaan khĭan dtaam kam bòrk
exam (examination)	การสอบ	gaan sòrp
to take an exam	สอบไล่	sòrp lâi
experiment (e.g., chemistry ~)	การทดลอง	gaan thót lorng

143. College. University

academy	โรงเรียน	rohng rian
university	มหาวิทยาลัย	má-hăa wít-thá-yaa-lai
faculty (e.g., ~ of Medicine)	คณะ	khá-ná
student (masc.)	นักศึกษา	nák sèuk-săa
student (fem.)	นักศึกษา	nák sèuk-săa
lecturer (teacher)	อาจารย์	aa-jaan
lecture hall, room	ห้องบรรยาย	hôrng ban-yaai
graduate	บัณฑิต	ban-dìt

diploma	อนุปริญญา	a-nú bpà-rin-yaa
dissertation	ปริญญานิพนธ์	bpà-rin-yaa ní-phon
study (report)	การวิจัย	gaan wí-jai
laboratory	หองปฏิบัติการ	hôrng bpà-dtì-bàt gaan
lecture	การบรรยาย	gaan ban-yaai
coursemate	เพื่อนรวมชั้น	phêuan rûam chán
scholarship	ทุน	thun
academic degree	วุฒิการศึกษา	wút-thí gaan sèuk-săa

144. Sciences. Disciplines

mathematics	คณิตศาสตร์	khá-nít sàat
algebra	พีชคณิต	phee-chá-khá-nít
geometry	เรขาคณิต	ray-khăa khá-nít
astronomy	ดาราศาสตร์	daa-raa sàat
biology	ชีววิทยา	chee-wá-wít-thá-yaa
geography	ภูมิศาสตร	phoo-mí-sàat
geology	ธรณีวิทยา	thor-rá-nee wít-thá-yaa
history	ประวัติศาสตร์	bprà-wàt sàat
medicine	แพทยศาสตร์	phâet-tha-ya-sàat
pedagogy	ครุศาสตร	khrú sàat
law	ธรรมศาสตร	tham-ma -sàat
physics	ฟิสิกส์	fí-sìk
chemistry	เคมี	khay-mee
philosophy	ปรัชญา	bpràt-yaa
psychology	จิตวิทยา	jìt-wít-thá-yaa

145. Writing system. Orthography

grammar	ไวยากรณ์	wai-yaa-gon
vocabulary	คำศัพท	kham sàp
phonetics	การออกเสียง	gaan òrk sĭang
noun	นาม	naam
adjective	คำคุณศัพท์	kham khun-ná-sàp
verb	กริยา	grì-yaa
adverb	คำวิเศษณ	kham wí-sàyt
pronoun	คำสรรพนาม	kham sàp-phá-naam
interjection	คำอุทาน	kham u-thaan
preposition	คำบุพบท	kham bùp-phá-bòt
root	รากศัพท	râak sàp
ending	คำลงท้าย	kham long tháai

prefix	คำนำหน้า	kham nam nâa
syllable	พยางค์	phá-yaang
suffix	คำเสริมท้าย	kham sěrm tháai

| stress mark | เครื่องหมายเน้น | khrêuang mǎai náyn |
| apostrophe | อะพอสทรอฟี | à-phor-sòt-ror-fee |

period, dot	จุด	jùt
comma	จุลภาค	jun-lá-phâak
semicolon	อัฒภาค	àt-thá-phâak
colon	ทวิภาค	thá-wí phâak
ellipsis	การละไว้	gaan lá wái

| question mark | เครื่องหมายปรัศนี | khrêuang mǎai bpràt-nee |
| exclamation point | เครื่องหมาย อัศเจรีย์ | khrêuang mǎai àt-sà-jay-ree |

quotation marks	อัญประกาศ	an-yá-bprà-gàat
in quotation marks	ในอัญประกาศ	nai an-yá-bprà-gàat
parenthesis	วงเล็บ	wong lép
in parenthesis	ในวงเล็บ	nai wong lép

hyphen	ยัติภังค์	yát-dtì-phang
dash	ขีดคั่น	khèet khân
space (between words)	ช่องไฟ	chông fai

| letter | ตัวอักษร | dtua àk-sǒn |
| capital letter | อักษรตัวใหญ่ | àk-sǒn dtua yài |

| vowel (n) | สระ | sà-ra |
| consonant (n) | พยัญชนะ | phá-yan-chá-ná |

sentence	ประโยค	bprà-yòhk
subject	ภาคประธาน	phâak bprà-thaan
predicate	ภาคแสดง	phâak sà-daeng

line	บรรทัด	ban-thát
on a new line	ที่บรรทัดใหม่	têe ban-thát mài
paragraph	วรรค	wák

word	คำ	kham
group of words	กลุ่มคำ	glùm kham
expression	วลี	wá-lee
synonym	คำพ้องความหมาย	kham phóng khwaam mǎai
antonym	คำตรงกันข้าม	kham dtrorng gan khâam

rule	กฎ	gòt
exception	ข้อยกเว้น	khôr yok-wâyn
correct (adj)	ถูก	thòok

| conjugation | คอนจูเกชัน | khorn joo gay chan |
| declension | การกระจายคำ | gaan grà-jaai kham |

nominal case	การก	gaa-rók
question	คำถาม	kham thăam
to underline (vt)	ขีดเส้นใต้	khèet sên dtâi
dotted line	เส้นประ	sên bprà

146. Foreign languages

language	ภาษา	phaa-săa
foreign (adj)	ตางชาติ	dtàang châat
foreign language	ภาษาตางชาติ	phaa-săa dtàang châat
to study (vt)	เรียน	rian
to learn (language, etc.)	เรียน	rian

to read (vi, vt)	อาน	àan
to speak (vi, vt)	พูด	phôot
to understand (vt)	เขาใจ	khâo jai
to write (vt)	เขียน	khĭan

fast (adv)	รวดเร็ว	rûat reo
slowly (adv)	อยางชา	yàang cháa
fluently (adv)	อยางคลอง	yàang khlôrng

rules	กฎ	gòt
grammar	ไวยากรณ์	wai-yaa-gon
vocabulary	คำศัพท	kham sàp
phonetics	การออกเสียง	gaan òrk sĭang

textbook	หนังสือเรียน	năng-sĕu rian
dictionary	พจนานุกรม	phót-jà-naa-nú-grom
teach-yourself book	หนังสือแบบเรียน	năng-sĕu bàep rian
	ดวยตนเอง	dûay dton ayng
phrasebook	เฟรสบุก	frayt bùk

cassette, tape	เทปคาสเซ็ตต์	thâyp khaas-sét
videotape	วิดีโอ	wí-dee-oh
CD, compact disc	CD	see-dee
DVD	DVD	dee-wee-dee

alphabet	ตัวอักษร	dtua àk-sŏn
to spell (vt)	สะกด	sà-gòt
pronunciation	การออกเสียง	gaan òrk sĭang

accent	สำเนียง	săm-niang
with an accent	มีสำเนียง	mee săm-niang
without an accent	ไมมีสำเนียง	mâi mee săm-niang

word	คำ	kham
meaning	ความหมาย	khwaam măai
course (e.g., a French ~)	หลักสูตร	làk sòot
to sign up	สมัคร	sà-màk

teacher	อาจารย์	aa-jaan
translation (process)	การแปล	gaan bplae
translation (text, etc.)	คำแปล	kham bplae
translator	นักแปล	nák bplae
interpreter	ล่าม	lâam
polyglot	ผู้รู้หลายภาษา	phôo róo lăai paa-săa
memory	ความทรงจำ	khwaam song jam

147. Fairy tale characters

Santa Claus	ซานตาคลอส	saan-dtaa-khlôrt
Cinderella	ซินเดอเรลลา	sín-day-rayn-lâa
mermaid	เงือก	ngêuak
Neptune	เนปจูน	nâyp-joon
magician, wizard	พ่อมด	phôr mót
fairy	แม่มด	mâe mót
magic (adj)	วิเศษ	wí-sàyt
magic wand	ไม้กายสิทธิ์	mái gaai-yá-sìt
fairy tale	เทพนิยาย	thâyp ní-yaai
miracle	ปาฏิหาริย์	bpaa dtì-hăan
dwarf	คนแคระ	khon khráe
to turn into …	กลายเป็น…	glaai bpen...
ghost	ผี	phěe
phantom	ภูตผีปีศาจ	phôot phěe bpee-sàat
monster	สัตว์ประหลาด	sàt bprà-làat
dragon	มังกร	mang-gon
giant	ยักษ์	yák

148. Zodiac Signs

Aries	ราศีเมษ	raa-sěe mâyt
Taurus	ราศีพฤษภ	raa-sěe phréut-sòp
Gemini	ราศีมิถุน	raa-sěe me-thŭn
Cancer	ราศีกรกฎ	raa-sěe gor-rá-gòt
Leo	ราศีสิงห์	raa-sěe-sǐng
Virgo	ราศีกันย์	raa-sěe gan
Libra	ราศีตุล	raa-sěe dtun
Scorpio	ราศีพฤศจิก	raa-sěe phréut-sà-jìk
Sagittarius	ราศีธันว์	raa-sěe than
Capricorn	ราศีมังกร	raa-sěe mang-gon
Aquarius	ราศีกุมภ	raa-sěe gum
Pisces	ราศีมีน	raa-sěe meen
character	บุคลิก	bùk-khá-lík

character traits	ลักษณะบุคลิก	lák-sà-nà bùk-khá-lík
behavior	พฤติกรรม	phréut-dtì-gam
to tell fortunes	ทำนายชะตา	tham naai chá-dtaa
fortune-teller	หมอดู	mŏr doo
horoscope	ดวงชะตา	duang chá-dtaa

Arts

149. Theater

theater	โรงละุคร	rohng lá-khon
opera	โอเปรา	oh-bprào
operetta	ละครเพลง	lá-khon phlayng
ballet	บัลเลต	ban lây
theater poster	โปสเตอร์ละคร	bpòht-dtêr lá-khon
troupe (theatrical company)	คณะผูแสดง	khá-ná phôo sà-daeng
tour	การออกแสดง	gaan òrk sà-daeng
to be on tour	ออกแสดง	òrk sà-daeng
to rehearse (vi, vt)	ซอม	sórm
rehearsal	การซอม	gaan sórm
repertoire	รายการละคร	raai gaan lá-khon
performance	การแสดง	gaan sà-daeng
theatrical show	การแสดง	gaan sà-daeng
	มหรสพ	má-hǒr-rá-sòp
play	ละคร	lá-khon
ticket	ตั๋ว	dtǔa
box office (ticket booth)	ชองจำหน่ายตั๋ว	chôrng jam-nàai dtǔa
lobby, foyer	ล็อบบี้	lórp-bêe
coat check (cloakroom)	ที่รับฝากเสื้อโค้ท	thêe ráp fàak sêua khóht
coat check tag	ป้ายรับเสื้อ	bpâai ráp sêua
binoculars	กลองสองสองตา	glôrng sòrng sǒrng dtaa
usher	พนักงานที่นำ	phá-nák ngaan thêe nam
	ไปยังที่นั่ง	bpai yang thêe nâng
orchestra seats	ที่นั่งชั้นล่าง	thêe nâng chán lâang
balcony	ที่นั่งชั้นสอง	thêe nâng chán sǒrng
dress circle	ที่นั่งชนบน	thêe nâng chán bon
box	ที่นั่งพิเศษ	thêe nâng phí-sàyt
row	แถว	thǎe
seat	ที่นั่ง	thêe nâng
audience	ผูชม	phôo chom
spectator	ผูเขาชม	phôo khâo chom
to clap (vi, vt)	ปรบมือ	bpròp meu
applause	การปรบมือ	gaan bpròp meu
ovation	การปรบมือใหเกียรติ	gaan bpròp meu hâi gìat
stage	เวที	way-thee
curtain	ฉาก	chàak

| scenery | ฉาก | chàak |
| backstage | หลังเวที | lăng way-thee |

scene (e.g., the last ~)	ตอน	dtorn
act	องค์	ong
intermission	ช่วงหยุดพัก	chûang yùt phák

150. Cinema

| actor | นักแสดงชาย | nák sà-daeng chaai |
| actress | นักแสดงหญิง | nák sà-daeng yĭng |

movies (industry)	ภาพยนตร์	phâap-phá-yon
movie	หนัง	năng
episode	ตอน	dtorn

detective movie	หนังประโลมโลกสืบสวน	năng sèup sŭan
action movie	หนังแอ็คชั่น	năng áek-chân
adventure movie	หนังผจญภัย	năng phà-jon phai
sci-fi movie	หนังนิยาย วิทยาศาสตร์	năng ní-yaai wít-thá-yaa sàat
horror movie	หนังสยองขวัญ	năng sà-yŏrng khwăn

comedy movie	หนังตลก	năng dtà-lòk
melodrama	หนังประโลมโลก	năng bprà-lohm lôhk
drama	หนังดรามา	năng dràa maa

fictional movie	หนังเรื่องแต่ง	năng rêuang dtàeng
documentary	หนังสารคดี	năng săa-rá-khá-dee
cartoon	การ์ตูน	gaa-dtoon
silent movies	หนังเงียบ	năng ngîap

role (part)	บทบาท	bòt bàat
leading role	บทบาทนำ	bòt bàat nam
to play (vi, vt)	แสดง	sà-daeng

movie star	ดาราภาพยนตร์	daa-raa phâap-phá-yon
well-known (adj)	เป็นที่รู้จักดี	bpen thêe róo jàk dee
famous (adj)	ชื่อดัง	chêu dang
popular (adj)	ที่นิยม	thêe ní-yom

script (screenplay)	บท	bòt
scriptwriter	คนเขียนบท	khon khĭan bòt
movie director	ผู้กำกับ ภาพยนตร์	phôo gam-gàp phâap-phá-yon

producer	ผู้อำนวยการสร้าง	phôo am-nuay gaan sâang
assistant	ผู้ช่วย	phôo chûay
cameraman	ช่างกล้อง	châang glôrng
stuntman	นักแสดงแทน	nák sà-daeng thaen
double (stand-in)	นักแสดงแทน	nák sà-daeng thaen

to shoot a movie	ถ่ายทำภาพยนตร์	thàai tham phâap-phá-yon
audition, screen test	การคัดนักแสดง	gaan khát nák sà-daeng
shooting	การถ่ายทำ	gaan thàai tham
movie crew	กลุ่มคนถ่าย ภาพยนต	glùm khon thàai phâa-pha-yon
movie set	สถานที่ ถ่ายทำภาพยนตร์	sà-thăan thêe thàai tham phâap-phá-yon
camera	กล้อง	glôrng
movie theater	โรงภาพยนตร์	rohng phâap-phá-yon
screen (e.g., big ~)	หน้าจอ	nâa jor
to show a movie	ฉายภาพยนตร์	chăai phâap-phá-yon
soundtrack	เสียงซาวด์แทร็ก	sĭang saao tráek
special effects	เอฟเฟ็กต์พิเศษ	àyf-fék phí-sàyt
subtitles	ซับ	sáp
credits	เครดิต	khray-dìt
translation	การแปล	gaan bplae

151. Painting

art	ศิลปะ	sĭn-lá-bpà
fine arts	วิจิตรศิลป์	wí-jìt sĭn
art gallery	หอศิลป์	hŏr sĭn
art exhibition	การจัดแสดง ศิลปะ	gaan jàt sà-daeng sĭn-lá-bpà
painting (art)	จิตรกรรม	jìt-dtrà-gam
graphic art	เลขนศิลป์	lâyk-ná-sĭn
abstract art	ศิลปะนามธรรม	sĭn-lá-bpà naam-má-tham
impressionism	ลัทธิประทับใจ	lát-thí bprà-tháp jai
picture (painting)	ภาพ	phâap
drawing	ภาพวาด	phâap-wâat
poster	โปสเตอร์	bpòht-dtêr
illustration (picture)	ภาพประกอบ	phâap bprà-gòrp
miniature	รูปปั้นขนาดย่อ	rôop bpân khà-nàat yôr
copy (of painting, etc.)	สำเนา	săm-nao
reproduction	การทำซ้ำ	gaan tham sám
mosaic	โมเสก	moh-sàyk
stained glass window	หน้าต่างกระจกสี	nâa dtàang grà-jòk sĕe
fresco	ภาพผนัง	phâap phà-năng
engraving	การแกะลาย	gaan gàe laai
bust (sculpture)	รูปปั้นครึ่งตัว	rôop bpân khrêung dtua
sculpture	รูปปั้นแกะสลัก	rôop bpân gàe sà-làk
statue	รูปปั้น	rôop bpân
plaster of Paris	ปูนปลาสเตอร์	bpoon bpláat-dtêr

plaster (as adj)	ปูนปลาสเตอร์	bpoon bpláat-dtêr
portrait	ภาพเหมือน	phâap mĕuan
self-portrait	ภาพเหมือนของ ตนเอง	phâap mĕuan khŏrng dton ayng
landscape painting	ภาพภูมิทัศน์	phâap phoom-mi -thát
still life	ภาพหุ่นนิ่ง	phâap hùn nîng
caricature	ภาพล้อ	phâap-lór
sketch	ภาพสเก็ตช์	phâap sà-gèt
paint	สี	sĕe
watercolor paint	สีน้ำ	sĕe náam
oil (paint)	สีน้ำมัน	sĕe náam man
pencil	ดินสอ	din-sŏr
India ink	หมึกสีดำ	mèuk sĕe dam
charcoal	ถ่าน	thàan
to draw (vi, vt)	วาด	wâat
to paint (vi, vt)	ระบายสี	rá-baai sĕe
to pose (vi)	จัดท่า	jàt thâa
artist's model (masc.)	แบบภาพวาด	bàep phâap-wâat
artist's model (fem.)	แบบภาพวาด	bàep phâap-wâat
artist (painter)	ช่างวาดรูป	châang wâat rôop
work of art	งานศิลปะ	ngaan sĭn-lá-bpà
masterpiece	งานชิ้นเอก	ngaan chín àyk
studio (artist's workroom)	สตูดิโอ	sà-dtoo dì oh
canvas (cloth)	ผ้าใบ	phâa bai
easel	ขาตั้งกระดาน วาดรูป	khăa dtâng grà daan wâat rôop
palette	จานสี	jaan sĕe
frame (picture ~, etc.)	กรอบ	gròrp
restoration	การฟื้นฟู	gaan féun foo
to restore (vt)	ฟื้นฟู	féun foo

152. Literature & Poetry

literature	วรรณคดี	wan-ná-khá-dee
author (writer)	ผู้แต่ง	phôo dtàeng
pseudonym	นามปากกา	naam bpàak gaa
book	หนังสือ	năng-sĕu
volume	เล่ม	lêm
table of contents	สารบัญ	săa-rá-ban
page	หน้า	nâa
main character	ตัวละครหลัก	dtua lá-khon làk
autograph	ลายเซ็น	laai sen
short story	เรื่องสั้น	rêuang sân

story (novella)	เรื่องราว	rêuang raao
novel	นิยาย	ní-yaai
work (writing)	งานเขียน	ngaan khǐan
fable	นิทาน	ní-thaan
detective novel	นิยายสืบสวน	ní-yaai sèup sǔan
poem (verse)	กลอน	glorn
poetry	บทกลอน	bòt glorn
poem (epic, ballad)	บทกวี	bòt gà-wee
poet	นักกวี	nák gà-wee
fiction	เรื่องแต่ง	rêuang dtàeng
science fiction	นิยายวิทยาศาสตร์	ní-yaai wít-thá-yaa sàat
adventures	นิยายผจญภัย	ní-yaai phà-jon phai
educational literature	วรรณกรรม	wan-ná-gam
	การศึกษา	gaan sèuk-sǎa
children's literature	วรรณกรรมสำหรับเด็ก	wan-ná-gam sǎm-ràp dèk

153. Circus

circus	ละครสัตว์	lá-khon sàt
traveling circus	ละครสัตว์เล่รอน	lá-khon sàt lây rôrn
program	รายการการแสดง	raai gaan gaan sà-daeng
performance	การแสดง	gaan sà-daeng
act (circus ~)	การแสดง	gaan sà-daeng
circus ring	เวทีละครสัตว์	way-thee lá-kon sàt
pantomime (act)	ละครใบ้	lá-khon bâi
clown	ตัวตลก	dtua dtà-lòk
acrobat	นักกายกรรม	nák gaai-yá-gam
acrobatics	กายกรรม	gaai-yá-gam
gymnast	นักกายกรรม	nák gaai-yá-gam
acrobatic gymnastics	กายกรรม	gaai-yá-gam
somersault	การตีลังกา	gaan dtee lang-gaa
athlete (strongman)	นักกีฬา	nák gee-laa
tamer (e.g., lion ~)	ผู้ฝึกสัตว์	phôo fèuk sàt
rider (circus horse ~)	นักขี่	nák khèe
assistant	ผู้ช่วย	phôo chûay
stunt	ผาดโผน	phàat phǒhn
magic trick	มายากล	maa-yaa gon
conjurer, magician	นักมายากล	nák maa-yaa gon
juggler	นักมายากล	nák maa-yaa gon
	โยนของ	yohn khǒrng
to juggle (vi, vt)	โยนของ	yohn khǒrng
animal trainer	ผู้ฝึกสัตว์	phôo fèuk sàt

| animal training | การฝึกสัตว์ | gaan fèuk sàt |
| to train (animals) | ฝึก | fèuk |

154. Music. Pop music

music	ดนตรี	don-dtree
musician	นักดนตรี	nák don-dtree
musical instrument	เครื่องดนตรี	khrêuang don-dtree
to play ...	เล่น	lên

guitar	กีตาร์	gee-dtâa
violin	ไวโอลิน	wai-oh-lin
cello	เชลโล	chayn-lôh
double bass	ดับเบิลเบส	dàp-bern bàyt
harp	พิณ	phin

piano	เปียโน	bpia noh
grand piano	แกรนด์เปียโน	graen bpia-noh
organ	ออร์แกน	or-gaen

wind instruments	เครื่องเป่า	khrêuang bpào
oboe	โอโบ	oh-boh
saxophone	แซ็กโซโฟน	sáek-soh-fohn
clarinet	แคลริเน็ต	khlae-rí-nét
flute	ฟลูต	flút
trumpet	ทรัมเป็ต	thram-bpèt

| accordion | หีบเพลงชัก | hèep phlayng chák |
| drum | กลอง | glorng |

duo	คู่	khôo
trio	วงทริโอ	wong thrí-oh
quartet	กลุ่มที่มีสี่คน	glùm thêe mee sèe khon
choir	คณะประสานเสียง	khá-ná bprà-săan sĭang
orchestra	วงดุริยางค์	wong dù-rí-yaang

pop music	เพลงป๊อป	phlayng bpòp
rock music	เพลงร็อค	phlayng rók
rock group	วงร็อค	wong rórk
jazz	แจซ	jáet

| idol | ไอดอล | ai-dorn |
| admirer, fan | แฟน | faen |

concert	คอนเสิร์ต	khon-sèrt
symphony	ซิมโฟนี	sím-foh-nee
composition	การแต่งเพลง	gaan dtàeng phlayng
to compose (write)	แต่ง	dtàeng
singing (n)	การร้องเพลง	gaan róng playng
song	เพลง	phlayng

tune (melody)	เสียงเพลง	sĭang phlayng
rhythm	จังหวะ	jang wà
blues	บลูส์	bloo

sheet music	โน้ตเพลง	nóht phlayng
baton	ไม้สั้นของ	máai sân khŏrng
	วาทยากร	wâa-tha-yaa gon
bow	คันชอ	khan sor
string	สาย	săai
case (e.g., guitar ~)	กลอง	glòrng

Rest. Entertainment. Travel

155. Trip. Travel

tourism, travel	การท่องเที่ยว	gaan thôrng thîeow
tourist	นักท่องเที่ยว	nák thôrng thîeow
trip, voyage	การเดินทาง	gaan dern thaang
adventure	การผจญภัย	gaan phà-jon phai
trip, journey	การเดินทาง	gaan dern thaang
vacation	วันหยุดพักผ่อน	wan yùt phák phòrn
to be on vacation	หยุดพักผอน	yùt phák phòrn
rest	การพัก	gaan phák
train	รถไฟ	rót fai
by train	โดยรถไฟ	doi rót fai
airplane	เครื่องบิน	khrêuang bin
by airplane	โดยเครื่องบิน	doi khrêuang bin
by car	โดยรถยนต์	doi rót-yon
by ship	โดยเรือ	doi reua
luggage	สัมภาระ	sǎm-phaa-rá
suitcase	กระเป๋าเดินทาง	grà-bpǎo dern-thaang
luggage cart	รถขนสัมภาระ	rót khǒn sǎm-phaa-rá
passport	หนังสือเดินทาง	nǎng-sěu dern-thaang
visa	วีซา	wee-sâa
ticket	ตั๋ว	dtǔa
air ticket	ตั๋วเครื่องบิน	dtǔa khrêuang bin
guidebook	หนังสือแนะนำ	nǎng-sěu náe nam
map (tourist ~)	แผนที่	phǎen thêe
area (rural ~)	เขต	khàyt
place, site	สถานที่	sà-thǎan thêe
exotica (n)	สิ่งแปลกใหม่	sìng bplàek mài
exotic (adj)	ต่างแดน	dtàang daen
amazing (adj)	น่าประหลาดใจ	nâa bprà-làat jai
group	กลุ่ม	glùm
excursion, sightseeing tour	การเดินทาง ท่องเที่ยว	gaan dern taang thôrng thîeow
guide (person)	มัคคุเทศก์	mák-khú-thâyt

156. Hotel

hotel	โรงแรม	rohng raem
motel	โรงแรม	rohng raem
three-star (~ hotel)	สามดาว	sǎam daao
five-star	ห้าดาว	hâa daao
to stay (in a hotel, etc.)	พัก	phák
room	ห้อง	hôrng
single room	ห้องเดี่ยว	hôrng dìeow
double room	หองคู่	hôrng khôo
to book a room	จองห้อง	jorng hôrng
half board	พักครึ่งวัน	phák khrêung wan
full board	พักเต็มวัน	phák dtem wan
with bath	มีห้องอาบน้ำ	mee hôrng àap náam
with shower	มีฝักบัว	mee fàk bua
satellite television	โทรทัศน์ดาวเทียม	thoh-rá-thát daao thiam
air-conditioner	เครื่องปรับอากาศ	khrêuang bpràp-aa-gàat
towel	ผ้าเช็ดตัว	phâa chét dtua
key	กุญแจ	gun-jae
administrator	นักบริหาร	nák bor-rí-hǎan
chambermaid	แม่บ้าน	mâe bâan
porter, bellboy	พนักงาน ขนกระเป๋า	phá-nák ngaan khǒn grà-bpǎo
doorman	พนักงาน เปิดประตู	phá-nák ngaan bpèrt bprà-dtoo
restaurant	ร้านอาหาร	ráan aa-hǎan
pub, bar	บาร์	baa
breakfast	อาหารเช้า	aa-hǎan cháo
dinner	อาหารเย็น	aa-hǎan yen
buffet	บุฟเฟต์	bùf-fây
lobby	ล็อบบี้	lórp-bêe
elevator	ลิฟต	líf
DO NOT DISTURB	ห้ามรบกวน	hâam róp guan
NO SMOKING	หามสูบบุหรี่	hâam sòop bù rèe

157. Books. Reading

book	หนังสือ	nǎng-sěu
author	ผู้แต่ง	phôo dtàeng
writer	นักเขียน	nák khǐan
to write (~ a book)	เขียน	khǐan

reader	ผู้อ่าน	phôo àan
to read (vi, vt)	อ่าน	àan
reading (activity)	การอ่าน	gaan àan
silently (to oneself)	อย่างเงียบๆ	yàang ngîap ngîap
aloud (adv)	ออกเสียงดัง	òrk sĭang dang
to publish (vt)	ตีพิมพ์	dtee phim
publishing (process)	การตีพิมพ์	gaan dtee phim
publisher	ผู้พิมพ์	phôo phim
publishing house	สำนักพิมพ์	săm-nák phim
to come out (be released)	ออก	òrk
release (of a book)	การออก	gaan òrk
print run	จำนวน	jam-nuan
bookstore	ร้านหนังสือ	ráan năng-sĕu
library	ห้องสมุด	hôrng sà-mùt
story (novella)	เรื่องราว	rêuang raao
short story	เรื่องสั้น	rêuang sân
novel	นิยาย	ní-yaai
detective novel	นิยายสืบสวน	ní-yaai sèup sŭan
memoirs	บันทึกความทรงจำ	ban-théuk khwaam song jam
legend	ตำนาน	dtam naan
myth	นิทานปรัมปรา	ní-thaan bpram bpraa
poetry, poems	บทกวี	bòt gà-wee
autobiography	อัตชีวประวัติ	àt-chee-wá-bprà-wàt
selected works	งานที่ผ่านการคัดเลือก	ngaan thêe phàan gaan khát lêuak
science fiction	นิยายวิทยาศาสตร์	ní-yaai wít-thá-yaa sàat
title	ชื่อเรื่อง	chêu rêuang
introduction	บทนำ	bòt nam
title page	หน้าแรก	nâa râek
chapter	บท	bòt
extract	ข้อความที่คัดออกมา	khôr khwaam thêe khát òk maa
episode	ตอน	dtorn
plot (storyline)	เค้าเรื่อง	kháo rêuang
contents	เนื้อหา	néua hăa
table of contents	สารบัญ	săa-rá-ban
main character	ตัวละครหลัก	dtua lá-khon làk
volume	เล่ม	lêm
cover	ปก	bpòk
binding	สัน	săn

bookmark	ที่คั่นหนังสือ	thêe khân năng-sěu
page	หนา	nâa
to page through	เปิดผานๆ	bpèrt phàan phàan
margins	ระยะขอบ	rá-yá khòrp
annotation	ความเห็นประกอบ	khwaam hěn bprà-gòp
(marginal note, etc.)		
footnote	เชิงอรรถ	cherng àt-tha
text	บท	bòt
type, font	ตัวพิมพ์	dtua phim
misprint, typo	ความพิมพ์ผิด	khwaam phim phìt
translation	คำแปล	kham bplae
to translate (vt)	แปล	bplae
original (n)	ตนฉบับ	dtôn chà-bàp
famous (adj)	โด่งดัง	dòhng dang
unknown (not famous)	ไม่เป็นที่รู้จัก	mâi bpen thêe róo jàk
interesting (adj)	น่าสนใจ	nâa sŏn jai
bestseller	ขายดี	khăai dee
dictionary	พจนานุกรม	phót-jà-naa-nú-grom
textbook	หนังสือเรียน	năng-sěu rian
encyclopedia	สารานุกรม	săa-raa-nú-grom

158. Hunting. Fishing

hunting	การล่าสัตว์	gaan lâa sàt
to hunt (vi, vt)	ล่าสัตว์	lâa sàt
hunter	นักล่าสัตว์	nák lâa sàt
to shoot (vi)	ยิง	ying
rifle	ปืนไรเฟิล	bpeun rai-fern
bullet (shell)	กระสุนปืน	grà-sŭn bpeun
shot (lead balls)	กระสุน	grà-sŭn
steel trap	กับดักเหล็ก	gàp dàk lèk
snare (for birds, etc.)	กับดัก	gàp dàk
to fall into the steel trap	ติดกับดัก	dtìt gàp dàk
to lay a steel trap	วางกับดัก	waang gàp dàk
poacher	ผู้ลักลอบล่าสัตว์	phôo lák lôrp lâa sàt
game (in hunting)	สัตว์ที่ถูกล่า	sàt têe thòok lâa
hound dog	หมาล่าเนื้อ	măa lâa néua
safari	ซาฟารี	saa-faa-ree
mounted animal	สัตว์สตาฟ	sàt sà-dtàaf
fisherman, angler	คนประมง	khon bprà-mong
fishing (angling)	การจับปลา	gaan jàp bplaa
to fish (vi)	จับปลา	jàp bplaa

fishing rod	คันเบ็ด	khan bèt
fishing line	สายเบ็ด	sǎai bèt
hook	ตะขอ	dtà-khǒr
float, bobber	ทุน	thûn
bait	เหยื่อ	yèua
to cast a line	เหวี่ยงเบ็ด	wìang bèt
to bite (ab. fish)	งับเหยื่อ	ngáp yèua
catch (of fish)	ปลาจับ	bpla jàp
ice-hole	ช่องน้ำแข็ง	chôrng nám khǎeng
fishing net	แหจับปลา	hǎe jàp bplaa
boat	เรือ	reua
to net (to fish with a net)	จับปลาด้วยแห	jàp bplaa dûay hǎe
to cast[throw] the net	เหวี่ยงแห	wìang hǎe
to haul the net in	ลากอวน	lâak uan
to fall into the net	ติดแห	dtìt hǎe
whaler (person)	นักล่าปลาวาฬ	nák lâa bplaa waan
whaleboat	เรือล่าปลาวาฬ	reua lâa bplaa waan
harpoon	ฉมวก	chà-mùak

159. Games. Billiards

billiards	บิลเลียด	bin-lîat
billiard room, hall	ห้องบิลเลียด	hôrng bin-lîat
ball (snooker, etc.)	ลูก	lôok
to pocket a ball	แทงลูกลงหลุม	thaeng lôok long lǔm
cue	ไม้คิว	máai khiw
pocket	หลุม	lǔm

160. Games. Playing cards

diamonds	ข้าวหลามตัด	khâao lǎam dtàt
spades	โพดำ	phoh dam
hearts	โพแดง	phoh daeng
clubs	ดอกจิก	dòrk jìk
ace	เอส	àyt
king	คิง	king
queen	แหมม	màem
jack, knave	แจค	jáek
playing card	ไพ่	phâi
cards	ไพ่	phâi
trump	ไต๋	dtǎi
deck of cards	สำรับไพ่	sǎm-ráp phâi

point	แต้ม	dtâem
to deal (vi, vt)	แจกไพ่	jàek phâi
to shuffle (cards)	สับไพ่	sàp phâi
lead, turn (n)	ที	thee
cardsharp	คนโกงไพ่	khon gohng phâi

161. Casino. Roulette

casino	คาสิโน	khaa-sì-noh
roulette (game)	รูเล็ตต์	roo-lèt
bet	เดิมพัน	derm phan
to place bets	วางเดิมพัน	waang derm phan
red	แดง	daeng
black	ดำ	dam
to bet on red	เดิมพันสีแดง	derm phan sěe daeng
to bet on black	เดิมพันสีดำ	derm phan sěe dam
croupier (dealer)	เจ้ามือ	jâo meu
to spin the wheel	หมุนกงล้อ	mǔn gong lór
rules (of game)	กติกา	gà-dtì-gaa
chip	ชิป	chíp
to win (vi, vt)	ชนะ	chá-ná
win (winnings)	รางวัล	raang-wan
to lose (~ 100 dollars)	เสีย	sǐa
loss (losses)	เงินเสียพนัน	ngern sǐa phá-nan
player	ผู้เล่น	phôo lên
blackjack (card game)	แบล็คแจ๊ค	blàek-jáek
craps (dice game)	เกมลูกเต๋า	gaym lôok dtǎo
dice (a pair of ~)	เต๋า	dtǎo
slot machine	ตู้สล็อต	dtôo sà-lòrt

162. Rest. Games. Miscellaneous

to stroll (vi, vt)	เดินเล่น	dern lên
stroll (leisurely walk)	การเดินเล่น	gaan dern lên
car ride	การนั่งรถ	gaan nâng rót
adventure	การผจญภัย	gaan phà-jon phai
picnic	ปิคนิค	bpìk-ník
game (chess, etc.)	เกม	gaym
player	ผู้เล่น	phôo lên
game (one ~ of chess)	เกม	gaym
collector (e.g., philatelist)	นักสะสม	nák sà-sǒm
to collect (stamps, etc.)	สะสม	sà-sǒm

collection	การสะสม	gaan sà-sŏm
crossword puzzle	ปริศนาอักษรไขว้	bprìt-sà-năa àk-sŏn khwâi
racetrack	ลู่แข่ง	lôo khàeng
(horse racing venue)		
disco (discotheque)	ดิสโก้	dít-gôh
sauna	ซาวน่า	saao-nâa
lottery	สลากกินแบ่ง	sà-làak gin bàeng
camping trip	การเดินทาง	gaan dern thaang
	ตั้งแคมป์	dtâng-khaem
camp	แคมป์	khaem
tent (for camping)	เต็นท์	dtáyn
compass	เข็มทิศ	khĕm thít
camper	ผู้เดินทาง	phôo dern thaang
	ตั้งแคมป์	dtâng-khaem
to watch (movie, etc.)	ดู	doo
viewer	ผู้ชมทีวี	phôo chom thee wee
TV show (TV program)	รายการทีวี	raai gaan thee wee

163. Photography

camera (photo)	กล้อง	glôrng
photo, picture	ภาพถ่าย	phâap thài
photographer	ช่างถ่ายภาพ	châang thài phâap
photo studio	ห้องถ่ายภาพ	hôrng thài phâap
photo album	อัลบั้มภาพถ่าย	an-bâm phâap-thài
camera lens	เลนส์กล้อง	len glôrng
telephoto lens	เลนส์ถ่ายไกล	len thài glai
filter	ฟิลเตอร์	fin-dtêr
lens	เลนส์	len
optics (high-quality ~)	ออปติก	orp-dtìk
diaphragm (aperture)	รูรับแสง	roo ráp săeng
exposure time	เวลาในการ	way-laa nai gaan
(shutter speed)	ถ่ายภาพ	thài phâap
viewfinder	เครื่องจับภาพ	khrêuang jàp phâap
digital camera	กล้องดิจิตอล	glôrng dì-jì-dton
tripod	ขาตั้งกล้อง	khăa dtâng glông
flash	แฟลช	flâet
to photograph (vt)	ถ่ายภาพ	thài phâap
to take pictures	ถ่ายภาพ	thài phâap
to have one's picture taken	ได้รับการ	dâai ráp gaan
	ถ่ายภาพให้	thài phâap hâi
focus	โฟกัส	foh-gát

to focus	โฟกัส	foh-gát
sharp, in focus (adj)	คมชัด	khom chát
sharpness	ความคมชัด	khwaam khom chát
contrast	ความเปรียบต่าง	khwaam bprìap dtàang
contrast (as adj)	เปรียบต่าง	bprìap dtàang
picture (photo)	ภาพ	phâap
negative (n)	ภาพเนกาทีฟ	phâap nay gaa thêef
film (a roll of ~)	ฟิล์ม	fim
frame (still)	เฟรม	fraym
to print (photos)	พิมพ์	phim

164. Beach. Swimming

beach	ชายหาด	chaai hàat
sand	ทราย	saai
deserted (beach)	ร้าง	ráang
suntan	ผิวคล้ำแดด	phǐw khlám dàet
to get a tan	ตากแดด	dtàak dàet
tan (adj)	มีผิวคล้ำแดด	mee phǐw khlám dàet
sunscreen	ครีมกันแดด	khreem gan dàet
bikini	บิกินี่	bì-gì-nee
bathing suit	ชุดว่ายน้ำ	chút wâai náam
swim trunks	กางเกงว่ายน้ำ	gaang-gayng wâai náam
swimming pool	สระว่ายน้ำ	sà wâai náam
to swim (vi)	ว่ายน้ำ	wâai náam
shower	ฝักบัว	fàk bua
to change (one's clothes)	เปลี่ยนชุด	bplìan chút
towel	ผ้าเช็ดตัว	phâa chét dtua
boat	เรือ	reua
motorboat	เรือยนต์	reua yon
water ski	สกีน้ำ	sà-gee nám
paddle boat	เรือถีบ	reua thèep
surfing	การโต้คลื่น	gaan dtôh khlêun
surfer	นักโต้คลื่น	nák dtôh khlêun
scuba set	อุปกรณ์ดำน้ำ	u-bpà-gon dam náam
flippers (swim fins)	ตีนกบ	dteen gòp
mask (diving ~)	หน้ากากดำน้ำ	nâa gàak dam náam
diver	นักประดาน้ำ	nák bprà-daa náam
to dive (vi)	ดำน้ำ	dam náam
underwater (adv)	ใต้น้ำ	dtâi nám
beach umbrella	ร่มชายหาด	rôm chaai hàat
sunbed (lounger)	เตียงอาบแดด	dtiang àap dàet

sunglasses	แว่นกันแดด	wâen gan dàet
air mattress	ที่นอนเป่าลม	thêe non bpào lom
to play (amuse oneself)	เล่น	lên
to go for a swim	ไปว่ายน้ำ	bpai wâai náam
beach ball	บอล	bon
to inflate (vt)	เติมลม	dterm lom
inflatable, air (adj)	แบบเติมลม	bàep dterm lom
wave	คลื่น	khlêun
buoy (line of ~s)	ทุนลอย	thûn loi
to drown (ab. person)	จมน้ำ	jom náam
to save, to rescue	ช่วยชีวิต	chûay chee-wít
life vest	เสื้อชูชีพ	sêua choo chêep
to observe, to watch	สังเกตการณ์	sǎng-gàyt gaan
lifeguard	ไลฟ์การด	lai-gàat

TECHNICAL EQUIPMENT. TRANSPORTATION

Technical equipment

165. Computer

computer	คอมพิวเตอร์	khorm-phiw-dtêr
notebook, laptop	โน้ตบุ๊ค	nóht búk
to turn on	เปิด	bpèrt
to turn off	ปิด	bpìt
keyboard	แป้นพิมพ์	bpâen phim
key	ปุ่ม	bpùm
mouse	เมาส์	mao
mouse pad	แผ่นรองเมาส์	phàen rorng mao
button	ปุ่ม	bpùm
cursor	เคอร์เซอร์	khêr-sêr
monitor	จอมอนิเตอร์	jor mor-ní-dtêr
screen	หน้าจอ	nâa jor
hard disk	ฮาร์ดดิสก์	hâat-dìt
hard disk capacity	ความจุฮาร์ดดิสก์	kwaam jù hâat-dìt
memory	หน่วยความจำ	nùay khwaam jam
random access memory	หน่วยความจำเข้าถึงโดยสุ่ม	nùay khwaam jam khâo thěung doi sùm
file	ไฟล์	fai
folder	โฟลเดอร์	fohl-dêr
to open (vt)	เปิด	bpèrt
to close (vt)	ปิด	bpìt
to save (vt)	บันทึก	ban-théuk
to delete (vt)	ลบ	lóp
to copy (vt)	คัดลอก	khát lôrk
to sort (vt)	จัดเรียง	jàt riang
to transfer (copy)	ทำสำเนา	tham sǎm-nao
program	โปรแกรม	bproh-graem
software	ซอฟต์แวร์	sôf-wae
programmer	นักเขียนโปรแกรม	nák khǐan bproh-graem
to program (vt)	เขียนโปรแกรม	khǐan bproh-graem
hacker	แฮ็กเกอร์	háek-gêr

password	รหัสผ่าน	rá-hàt phàan
virus	ไวรัส	wai-rát
to find, to detect	ตรวจพบ	dtrùat phóp
byte	ไบท์	bai
megabyte	เมกะไบท์	may-gà-bai
data	ข้อมูล	khôr moon
database	ฐานข้อมูล	thăan khôr moon
cable (USB, etc.)	สายเคเบิล	săai khay-bêrn
to disconnect (vt)	ตัดการเชื่อมต่อ	dtàt gaan chêuam dtòr
to connect (sth to sth)	เชื่อมต่อ	chêuam dtòr

166. Internet. E-mail

Internet	อินเทอร์เน็ต	in-thêr-nét
browser	เบราวเซอร์	brao-sêr
search engine	โปรแกรมคนหา	bproh-graem khón hăa
provider	ผู้ให้บริการ	phôo hâi bor-rí-gaan
webmaster	เว็บมาสเตอร์	wép-mâat-dtêr
website	เว็บไซต์	wép sai
webpage	เว็บเพจ	wép phâyt
address (e-mail ~)	ที่อยู่	thêe yòo
address book	สมุดที่อยู่	sà-mùt thêe yòo
mailbox	กล่องจดหมายอีเมลล์	glòrng jòt măai ee-mayn
mail	จดหมาย	jòt măai
full (adj)	เต็ม	dtem
message	ข้อความ	khôr khwaam
incoming messages	ข้อความขาเข้า	khôr khwaam khăa khâo
outgoing messages	ข้อความขาออก	khôr khwaam khăa òrk
sender	ผู้ส่ง	phôo sòng
to send (vt)	ส่ง	sòng
sending (of mail)	การส่ง	gaan sòng
receiver	ผู้รับ	phôo ráp
to receive (vt)	รับ	ráp
correspondence	การติดต่อกัน	gaan dtìt dtòr gan
	ทางจดหมาย	thaang jòt măai
to correspond (vi)	ติดต่อกันทา	dtìt dtòr gan thaang
	งจดหมาย	jòt măai
file	ไฟล์	fai
to download (vt)	ดาวน์โหลด	daao lòht

to create (vt)	สร้าง	sâang
to delete (vt)	ลบ	lóp
deleted (adj)	ถูกลบ	thòok lóp
connection (ADSL, etc.)	การเชื่อมต่อ	gaan chêuam dtòr
speed	ความเร็ว	khwaam reo
modem	โมเด็ม	moh-dem
access	การเข้าถึง	gaan khâo thěung
port (e.g., input ~)	พอร์ท	phôt
connection (make a ~)	การเชื่อมต่อ	gaan chêuam dtòr
to connect to … (vi)	เชื่อมต่อกับ...	chêuam dtòr gàp...
to select (vt)	เลือก	lêuak
to search (for …)	คนหา	khón hǎa

<h2>167. Electricity</h2>

electricity	ไฟฟ้า	fai fáa
electric, electrical (adj)	ทางไฟฟ้า	thaang fai-fáa
electric power plant	โรงไฟฟ้า	rohng fai-fáa
energy	พลังงาน	phá-lang ngaan
electric power	กำลังไฟฟ้า	gam-lang fai-fáa
light bulb	หลอดไฟฟ้า	lòrt fai fáa
flashlight	ไฟฉาย	fai chǎai
street light	เสาไฟถนน	sǎo fai thà-nǒn
light	ไฟ	fai
to turn on	เปิด	bpèrt
to turn off	ปิด	bpìt
to turn off the light	ปิดไฟ	bpìt fai
to burn out (vi)	ขาด	khàat
short circuit	การลัดวงจร	gaan lát wong-jon
broken wire	สายขาด	sǎai khàat
contact (electrical ~)	สายตอกัน	sǎai dtòr gan
light switch	สวิตช์ไฟ	sà-wít fai
wall socket	เต้าเสียบปลั๊กไฟ	dtâo sìap bplák fai
plug	ปลั๊กไฟ	bplák fai
extension cord	สายพวงไฟ	sǎai phûang fai
fuse	ฟิวส์	fiw
cable, wire	สายไฟ	sǎai fai
wiring	การเดินสายไฟ	gaan dern sǎai fai
ampere	แอมแปร์	aem-bpae
amperage	กำลังไฟฟ้า	gam-lang fai-fáa
volt	โวลต์	wohn

voltage	แรงดันไฟฟ้า	raeng dan fai fáa
electrical device	เครื่องใช้ไฟฟ้า	khrêuang chái fai fáa
indicator	ตัวระบุ	dtua rá-bù
electrician	ช่างไฟฟ้า	châang fai-fáa
to solder (vt)	บัดกรี	bàt-gree
soldering iron	หัวแรงบัดกรี	hǔa ráeng bàt-gree
electric current	กระแสไฟฟ้า	grà-sǎe fai fáa

168. Tools

tool, instrument	เครื่องมือ	khrêuang meu
tools	เครื่องมือ	khrêuang meu
equipment (factory ~)	อุปกรณ์	ù-bpà-gon
hammer	ค้อน	khórn
screwdriver	ไขควง	khǎi khuang
ax	ขวาน	khwǎan
saw	เลื่อย	lêuay
to saw (vt)	เลื่อย	lêuay
plane (tool)	กบไสไม้	gòp sǎi máai
to plane (vt)	ไสกบ	sǎi gòp
soldering iron	หัวแรงบัดกรี	hǔa ráeng bàt-gree
to solder (vt)	บัดกรี	bàt-gree
file (tool)	ตะไบ	dtà-bai
carpenter pincers	คีม	kheem
lineman's pliers	คีมปอกสายไฟ	kheem bpòk sǎai fai
chisel	สิ่ว	sìw
drill bit	หัวสว่าน	hǔa sà-wàan
electric drill	สว่านไฟฟ้า	sà-wàan fai fáa
to drill (vi, vt)	เจาะ	jòr
knife	มีด	mêet
pocket knife	มีดพก	mêet phók
blade	ใบ	bai
sharp (blade, etc.)	คม	khom
dull, blunt (adj)	ทื่อ	thêu
to get blunt (dull)	ทำให้...ทื่อ	tham hâi...thêu
to sharpen (vt)	ลับคม	láp khom
bolt	สลักเกลียว	sà-làk glieow
nut	แหวนสกรู	wǎen sà-groo
thread (of a screw)	เกลียว	glieow
wood screw	สกรู	sà-groo
nail	ตะปู	dtà-bpoo
nailhead	หัวตะปู	hǔa dtà-bpoo

ruler (for measuring)	ไม้บรรทัด	máai ban-thát
tape measure	เทปวัดระยะทาง	thâyp wát rá-yá taang
spirit level	เครื่องวัดระดับน้ำ	khrêuang wát rá-dàp náam
magnifying glass	แว่นขยาย	wâen khà-yǎi
measuring instrument	เครื่องมือวัด	khrêuang meu wát
to measure (vt)	วัด	wát
scale	อัตรา	àt-dtraa
(of thermometer, etc.)		
readings	ค่ามิเตอร์	khâa mí-dtêr
compressor	เครื่องอัดอากาศ	khrêuang àt aa-gàat
microscope	กล้องจุลทัศน์	glôrng jun-la -thát
pump (e.g., water ~)	ปั๊ม	bpám
robot	หุ่นยนต์	hùn yon
laser	เลเซอร์	lay-sêr
wrench	ประแจ	bprà-jae
adhesive tape	เทปกาว	thâyp gaao
glue	กาว	gaao
sandpaper	กระดาษทราย	grà-dàat saai
spring	สปริง	sà-bpring
magnet	แม่เหล็ก	mâe lèk
gloves	ถุงมือ	thǔng meu
rope	เชือก	chêuak
cord	สาย	sǎai
wire (e.g., telephone ~)	สายไฟ	sǎai fai
cable	สายเคเบิล	sǎai khay-bêrn
sledgehammer	ค้อนขนาดใหญ่	khón khà-nàat yài
prybar	ชะแลง	chá-laeng
ladder	บันได	ban-dai
stepladder	กระได	grà-dai
to screw (tighten)	ขันเกลียวเข้า	khǎn glieow khâo
to unscrew (lid, filter, etc.)	ขันเกลียวออก	khǎn glieow òk
to tighten	ขันให้แน่น	khǎn hâi náen
(e.g., with a clamp)		
to glue, to stick	ติดกาว	dtìt gaao
to cut (vt)	ตัด	dtàt
malfunction (fault)	ความผิดพลาด	khwaam phìt phlâat
repair (mending)	การซ่อมแซม	gaan sôrm saem
to repair, to fix (vt)	ซ่อม	sôrm
to adjust (machine, etc.)	ปรับ	bpràp
to check (to examine)	ตรวจ	dtrùat
checking	การตรวจ	gaan dtrùat
readings	ค่ามิเตอร์	khâa mí-dtêr

reliable, solid (machine)	ไว้วงใจได้	wái waang jai dâai
complex (adj)	ซับซ้อน	sáp són
to rust (get rusted)	ขึ้นสนิม	khêun sà-nĭm
rusty, rusted (adj)	เป็นสนิม	bpen sà-nĭm
rust	สนิม	sà-nĭm

Transportation

169. Airplane

airplane	เครื่องบิน	khrêuang bin
air ticket	ตั๋วเครื่องบิน	dtŭa khrêuang bin
airline	สายการบิน	sǎai gaan bin
airport	สนามบิน	sà-nǎam bin
supersonic (adj)	ความเร็วเหนือเสียง	khwaam reo nĕua-sǐang
captain	กัปตัน	gàp dtan
crew	ลูกเรือ	lôok reua
pilot	นักบิน	nák bin
flight attendant (fem.)	พนักงวนต้อนรับ บนเครื่องบิน	phá-nák ngaan dtôrn ráp bon khrêuang bin
navigator	ต้นหน	dtôn hŏn
wings	ปีก	bpèek
tail	หาง	hǎang
cockpit	ห้องนักบิน	hôrng nák bin
engine	เครื่องยนต์	khrêuang yon
undercarriage (landing gear)	โครงส่วนล่าง ของเครื่องบิน	khrorng sùan lâang khŏrng khrêuang bin
turbine	กังหัน	gang-hăn
propeller	ใบพัด	bai phát
black box	กล่องดำ	glòrng dam
yoke (control column)	คันบังคับ	khan bang-kháp
fuel	เชื้อเพลิง	chéua phlerng
safety card	คู่มือความ ปลอดภัย	khôo meu khwaam bplòt phai
oxygen mask	หน้ากากอ็อกซิเจน	nâa gàak ók sí jayn
uniform	เครื่องแบบ	khrêuang bàep
life vest	เสื้อชูชีพ	sêua choo chêep
parachute	รมชูชีพ	rôm choo chêep
takeoff	การบินขึ้น	gaan bin khêun
to take off (vi)	บินขึ้น	bin khêun
runway	ทางวิ่งเครื่องบิน	thaang wîng khrêuang bin
visibility	ทัศนวิสัย	thát sá ná wí-sǎi
flight (act of flying)	การบิน	gaan bin
altitude	ความสูง	khwaam sŏong
air pocket	หลุมอากาศ	lŭm aa-gàat
seat	ที่นั่ง	thêe nâng

headphones	หูฟัง	hŏo fang
folding tray (tray table)	ถาดพับเก็บได้	thàat pháp gèp dâai
airplane window	หน้าต่างเครื่องบิน	nâa dtàang khrêuang bin
aisle	ทางเดิน	thaang dern

170. Train

train	รถไฟ	rót fai
commuter train	รถไฟชานเมือง	rót fai chaan meuang
express train	รถไฟด่วน	rót fai dùan
diesel locomotive	รถจักรดีเซล	rót jàk dee-sayn
steam locomotive	รถจักรไอน้ำ	rót jàk ai náam
passenger car	ตู้โดยสาร	dtôo doi săan
dining car	ตู้เสบียง	dtôo sà-biang
rails	รางรถไฟ	raang rót fai
railroad	ทางรถไฟ	thaang rót fai
railway tie	หมอนรองราง	mŏrn rorng raang
platform (railway ~)	ชานชลา	chaan-chá-laa
track (~ 1, 2, etc.)	ราง	raang
semaphore	ไฟสัญญาณรถไฟ	fai săn-yaan rót fai
station	สถานี	sà-thăa-nee
engineer (train driver)	คนขับรถไฟ	khon khàp rót fai
porter (of luggage)	พนักงาน ยกกระเป๋า	phá-nák ngaan yók grà-bpăo
car attendant	พนักงานรถไฟ	phá-nák ngaan rót fai
passenger	ผู้โดยสาร	phôo doi săan
conductor (ticket inspector)	พนักงานตรวจตั๋ว	phá-nák ngaan dtrùat dtŭa
corridor (in train)	ทางเดิน	thaang dern
emergency brake	เบรคฉุกเฉิน	bràyk chùk-chĕrn
compartment	ตู้นอน	dtôo norn
berth	เตียง	dtiang
upper berth	เตียงบน	dtiang bon
lower berth	เตียงล่าง	dtiang lâang
bed linen, bedding	ชุดเครื่องนอน	chút khrêuang norn
ticket	ตั๋ว	dtŭa
schedule	ตารางเวลา	dtaa-raang way-laa
information display	กระดานแสดงข้อมูล	grà daan sà-daeng khôr moon
to leave, to depart	ออกเดินทาง	òrk dern thaang
departure (of train)	การออกเดินทาง	gaan òrk dern thaang
to arrive (ab. train)	มาถึง	maa thĕung

arrival	การมาถึง	gaan maa thěung
to arrive by train	มาถึงโดยรถไฟ	maa thěung doi rót fai
to get on the train	ขึ้นรถไฟ	khêun rót fai
to get off the train	ลงจากรถไฟ	long jàak rót fai

| train wreck | รถไฟตกราง | rót fai dtòk raang |
| to derail (vi) | ตกราง | dtòk raang |

steam locomotive	หัวรถจักรไอน้ำ	hǔa rót jàk ai náam
stoker, fireman	คนควบคุมเตาไฟ	khon khûap khum dtao fai
firebox	เตาไฟ	dtao fai
coal	ถ่านหิน	thàan hǐn

171. Ship

| ship | เรือ | reua |
| vessel | เรือ | reua |

steamship	เรือจักรไอน้ำ	reua jàk ai náam
riverboat	เรือล่องแม่น้ำ	reua lông mâe náam
cruise ship	เรือเดินสมุทร	reua dern sà-mùt
cruiser	เรือลาดตระเวน	reua lâat dtrà-wayn

yacht	เรือยอชต์	reua yôt
tugboat	เรือลากจูง	reua lâak joong
barge	เรือบรรทุก	reua ban-thúk
ferry	เรือข้ามฟาก	reua khâam fâak

sailing ship	เรือใบ	reua bai
brigantine	เรือใบสอง	reua bai sǒrng
	เสากระโดง	sǎo grà-dohng

| ice breaker | เรือตัดน้ำแข็ง | reua dtàt náam khǎeng |
| submarine | เรือดำน้ำ | reua dam náam |

boat (flat-bottomed ~)	เรือพาย	reua phaai
dinghy	เรือบดเล็ก	reua bòt lék
lifeboat	เรือชูชีพ	reua choo chêep
motorboat	เรือยนต์	reua yon

captain	กัปตัน	gàp dtan
seaman	นาวิน	naa-win
sailor	คนเรือ	khon reua
crew	กะลาสี	gà-laa-sěe

boatswain	สรั่ง	sà-ràng
ship's boy	คนช่วยงาน	khon chûay ngaan
	ในเรือ	nai reua
cook	กุ๊ก	gúk
ship's doctor	แพทย์เรือ	phâet reua

deck	ดาดฟ้าเรือ	dàat-fáa reua
mast	เสากระโดงเรือ	săo grà-dohng reua
sail	ใบเรือ	bai reua

hold	ท้องเรือ	thórng-reua
bow (prow)	หัวเรือ	hŭa-reua
stern	ทวยเรือ	tháai reua
oar	ไม้พาย	máai phaai
screw propeller	ใบจักร	bai jàk

cabin	ห้องพัก	hôrng phák
wardroom	ห้องอาหาร	hôrng aa-hăan
engine room	หองเครื่องยนต์	hôrng khrêuang yon
bridge	สะพานเดินเรือ	sà-phaan dern reua
radio room	หองวิทยุ	hôrng wít-thá-yú
wave (radio)	คลื่นความถี่	khlêun khwaam thèe
logbook	สมุดบันทึก	sà-mùt ban-théuk

spyglass	กล้องส่องทางไกล	glôrng sòrng thaang glai
bell	ระฆัง	rá-khang
flag	ธง	thorng

| hawser (mooring ~) | เชือก | chêuak |
| knot (bowline, etc.) | ปม | bpom |

deckrails	ราว	raao
gangway	ไม้พาดให้	mái phâat hâi
	ขึ้นลงเรือ	khêun long reua

anchor	สมอ	sà-mŏr
to weigh anchor	ถอนสมอ	thŏrn sà-mŏr
to drop anchor	ทอดสมอ	thôrt sà-mŏr
anchor chain	โซ่สมอเรือ	sôh sà-mŏr reua

port (harbor)	ท่าเรือ	thâa reua
quay, wharf	ทา	thâa
to berth (moor)	จอดเทียบบุท่า	jòt thîap tâa
to cast off	ออกจากทา	òrk jàak tâa

trip, voyage	การเดินทาง	gaan dern thaang
cruise (sea trip)	การลองเรือ	gaan lôrng reua
course (route)	เสนทาง	sên thaang
route (itinerary)	เสนทาง	sên thaang

fairway	ร่องเรือเดิน	rông reua dern
(safe water channel)		
shallows	โขด	khòht
to run aground	เกยตื้น	goie dtêun

storm	พายุ	phaa-yú
signal	สัญญาณ	săn-yaan
to sink (vi)	ลม	lôm

Man overboard!	คนตกเรือ!	kon dtòk reua
SOS (distress signal)	SOS	es-o-es
ring buoy	หวงยาง	hùang yaang

172. Airport

airport	สนามบิน	sà-nǎam bin
airplane	เครื่องบิน	khrêuang bin
airline	สายการบิน	sǎai gaan bin
air traffic controller	เจาหนาที่ควบคุม จราจรทางอากาศ	jâo nâa-thêe khûap khum jà-raa-jon thaang aa-gàat

departure	การออกเดินทาง	gaan òrk dern thaang
arrival	การมาถึง	gaan maa thěung
to arrive (by plane)	มาถึง	maa thěung

| departure time | เวลาขาไป | way-laa khǎa bpai |
| arrival time | เวลามาถึง | way-laa maa thěung |

| to be delayed | ถูกเลื่อน | thòok lêuan |
| flight delay | เลื่อนเที่ยวบิน | lêuan thieow bin |

information board	กระดานแสดง ขอมูล	grà daan sà-daeng khôr moon
information	ขอมูล	khôr moon
to announce (vt)	ประกาศ	bprà-gàat
flight (e.g., next ~)	เที่ยวบิน	thîeow bin

| customs | ศุลกากร | sǔn-lá-gaa-gon |
| customs officer | เจาหนาที่ ศุลกากร | jâo nâa-thêe sǔn-lá-gaa-gon |

customs declaration	แบบฟอรมการเสีย ภาษีศุลกากร	bàep form gaan sǐa phaa-sěe sǔn-lá-gaa-gon
to fill out (vt)	กรอก	gròrk
to fill out the declaration	กรอกแบบฟอรม การเสียภาษี	gròrk bàep form gaan sǐa paa-sěe
passport control	จุดตรวจหนังสือ เดินทาง	jùt dtrùat nǎng-sěu dern-thaang

luggage	สัมภาระ	sǎm phaa-rá
hand luggage	กระเปาถือ	grà-bpǎo thěu
luggage cart	รถขนสัมภาระ	rót khǒn sǎm-phaa-rá

landing	การลงจอด	gaan long jòrt
landing strip	ลานบินลงจอด	laan bin long jòrt
to land (vi)	ลงจอด	long jòrt
airstair (passenger stair)	ทางขึ้นลง เครื่องบิน	thaang khêun long khrêuang bin
check-in	การเช็คอิน	gaan chék in

check-in counter	เคาน์เตอร์เช็คอิน	khao-dtêr chék in
to check-in (vi)	เช็คอิน	chék in
boarding pass	บัตรที่นั่ง	bàt thêe nâng
departure gate	ซองเขา	chôrng khâo

transit	การต่อเที่ยวบิน	gaan tòr thîeow bin
to wait (vt)	รอ	ror
departure lounge	หองผู้โดยสาร	hôrng phôo doi săan
	ขาออก	khăa òk
to see off	ไปส่ง	bpai sòng
to say goodbye	บอกลา	bòrk laa

173. Bicycle. Motorcycle

bicycle	รถจักรยาน	rót jàk-grà-yaan
scooter	สกูตเตอร์	sà-góot-dtêr
motorcycle, bike	รถมอเตอร์ไซค์	rót mor-dtêr-sai

to go by bicycle	ขี่จักรยาน	khèe jàk-grà-yaan
handlebars	พวงมาลัยรถ	phuang maa-lai rót
pedal	แป้นเหยียบ	bpâen yìap
brakes	เบรก	bràyk
bicycle seat (saddle)	ที่นั่งจักรยาน	thêe nâng jàk-grà-yaan

pump	ปั๊ม	bpám
luggage rack	ที่วางสัมภาระ	thêe waang săm-phaa-rá
front lamp	ไฟหนา	fai nâa
helmet	หมวกนิรภัย	mùak ní-rá-phai

wheel	ล้อ	lór
fender	บังโคลน	bang khlon
rim	ขอบลูอ	khòp lór
spoke	กานลอ	gâan lór

Cars

174. Types of cars

automobile, car	รถยนต์	rót yon
sports car	รถสปอร์ต	rót sà-bpòt
limousine	รถลีมูซีน	rót lee moo seen
off-road vehicle	รถเอสยูวี	rót àyt yoo wee
convertible (n)	รถยนต์เปิดประทุน	rót yon bpèrt bprà-thun
minibus	รถบัสเล็ก	rót bàt lék
ambulance	รถพยาบาล	rót phá-yaa-baan
snowplow	รถไถหิมะ	rót thăi hì-má
truck	รถบรรทุก	rót ban-thúk
tanker truck	รถบรรทุกน้ำมัน	rót ban-thúk nám man
van (small truck)	รถตู้	rót dtôo
road tractor (trailer truck)	รถลาก	rót lâak
trailer	รถพวง	rót phûang
comfortable (adj)	สะดวก	sà-dùak
used (adj)	มือสอง	meu sŏrng

175. Cars. Bodywork

hood	กระโปรงรถ	grà bprohng rót
fender	บังโคลน	bang khlon
roof	หลังคา	lăng khaa
windshield	กระจกหน้ารถ	grà-jòk nâa rót
rear-view mirror	กระจกมองหลัง	grà-jòk morng lăng
windshield washer	ที่ฉีดน้ำลวง กระจกหน้ารถ	thêe chèet nám láang grà-jòk nâa rót
windshield wipers	ที่ปัดล้างกระจก หน้ารถ	thêe bpàt láang grà jòk nâa rót
side window	กระจกข้าง	grà-jòk khâang
window lift (power window)	กระจกไฟฟ้า	grà-jòk fai-fáa
antenna	เสาอากาศ	săo aa-gàat
sunroof	หลังคารับแดด	lăng khaa ráp dàet
bumper	กันชน	gan chon
trunk	ท้ายรถ	tháai rót

roof luggage rack	ชั้นวางสัมภาระ	chán waang sǎm-phaa-rá
door	ประตู	bprà-dtoo
door handle	ที่เปิดประตู	thêe bpèrt bprà-dtoo
door lock	ล็อคประตูรถ	lók bprà-dtoo rót
license plate	ป้ายทะเบียน	bpâai thá-bian
muffler	ท่อไอเสีย	thôr ai sǐa
gas tank	ถังน้ำมัน	thǎng náam man
tailpipe	ท่อไอเสีย	thôr ai sǐa
gas, accelerator	เร่ง	râyng
pedal	แป้นเหยียบ	bpâen yìap
gas pedal	คันเร่ง	khan râyng
brake	เบรก	bràyk
brake pedal	แป้นเบรค	bpâen bràyk
to brake (use the brake)	เบรก	bràyk
parking brake	เบรกมือ	bràyk meu
clutch	คลัตช์	khlát
clutch pedal	แป้นคลัตช์	bpâen khlát
clutch disc	จวนคลัตช์	jaan khlát
shock absorber	โช๊คอัพ	chóhk-àp
wheel	ล้อ	lór
spare tire	ล้อสำรอง	lór sǎm-rorng
tire	ยางรถ	yaang rót
hubcap	ลอแม็ก	lór-máek
driving wheels	ล้อพวงมาลัย	lór phuang maa-lai
front-wheel drive (as adj)	ขับเคลื่อนล้อหน้า	khàp khlêuan lór nâa
rear-wheel drive (as adj)	ขับเคลื่อนล้อหลัง	khàp khlêuan lór lǎng
all-wheel drive (as adj)	ขับเคลื่อนสี่ล้อ	khàp khlêuan sèe lór
gearbox	กระปุกเกียร์	grà-bpùk gia
automatic (adj)	อัตโนมัติ	àt-noh-mát
mechanical (adj)	กลไก	gon-gai
gear shift	คันเกียร์	khan gia
headlight	ไฟหน้า	fai nâa
headlights	ไฟหน้า	fai nâa
low beam	ไฟต่ำ	fai dtàm
high beam	ไฟสูง	fai sǒong
brake light	ไฟเบรก	fai bràyk
parking lights	ไฟจอดรถ	fai jòt rót
hazard lights	ไฟฉุกเฉิน	fai chùk-chěrn
fog lights	ไฟตัดหมอก	fai dtàt mòk
turn signal	ไฟเลี้ยว	fai líeow
back-up light	ไฟรถถอย	fai rót thǒi

176. Cars. Passenger compartment

car inside (interior)	ภายในรถ	phaai nai rót
leather (as adj)	หนัง	năng
velour (as adj)	กำมะหยี่	gam-má-yèe
upholstery	เครื่องเบาะ	khrêuang bòr
instrument (gage)	อุปกรณ์	ù-bpà-gon
dashboard	แผงหน้าปัด	phăeng nâa bpàt
speedometer	มาตรวัดความเร็ว	mâat wát khwaam reo
needle (pointer)	เข็มชี้วัด	khĕm chée wát
odometer	มิเตอร์วัดระยะทาง	mí-dtêr wát rá-yá thaang
indicator (sensor)	มิเตอร์วัด	mí-dtêr wát
level	ระดับ	rá-dàp
warning light	ไฟเตือน	fai dteuan
steering wheel	พวงมาลัยรถ	phuang maa-lai rót
horn	แตร	dtrae
button	ปุ่ม	bpùm
switch	สวิตช์	sà-wít
seat	ที่นั่ง	thêe nâng
backrest	พนักพิง	phá-nák phing
headrest	ที่พิงศีรษะ	thêe phing sĕe-sà
seat belt	เข็มขัดนิรภัย	khĕm khàt ní-rá-phai
to fasten the belt	คาดเข็มขัดนิรภัย	khâat khĕm khàt ní-rá-phai
adjustment (of seats)	การปรับ	gaan bpràp
airbag	ถุงลมนิรภัย	thŭng lom ní-rá-phai
air-conditioner	เครื่องปรับอากาศ	khrêuang bpràp-aa-gàat
radio	วิทยุ	wít-thá-yú
CD player	เครื่องเล่น CD	khrêuang lên see-dee
to turn on	เปิด	bpèrt
antenna	เสาอากาศ	săo aa-gàat
glove box	ช่องเก็บของ	chôrng gèp khŏrng
	ข้างคนขับ	khâang khon khàp
ashtray	ที่เขี่ยบุหรี่	thêe khìa bù rèe

177. Cars. Engine

engine	เครื่องยนต์	khrêuang yon
motor	มอเตอร์	mor-dtêr
diesel (as adj)	ดีเซล	dee-sayn
gasoline (as adj)	น้ำมันเบนซิน	nám man bayn-sin
engine volume	ขนาดเครื่องยนต์	khà-nàat khrêuang yon
power	กำลัง	gam-lang

horsepower	แรงม้า	raeng máa
piston	ก้านลูกสูบ	gâan lôok sòop
cylinder	กระบอกสูบ	grà-bòrk sòop
valve	วาลว	waao

injector	หัวฉีด	hŭa chèet
generator (alternator)	เครื่องกำเนิดไฟฟ้า	khrêuang gam-nèrt fai fáa
carburetor	คาร์บูเรเตอร์	khaa-boo-ray-dtêr
motor oil	น้ำมันเครื่อง	nám man khrêuang

radiator	หม้อน้ำ	môr náam
coolant	สารทำความเย็น	săan tham khwaam yen
cooling fan	พัดลมระบาย	phát lom rá-baai
	ความรอน	khwaam rón

battery (accumulator)	แบตเตอรี่	bàet-dter-rêe
starter	มอเตอร์สตาร์ต	mor-dtêr sà-dtàat
ignition	การจุดระเบิด	gaan jùt rá-bèrt
spark plug	หัวเทียน	hŭa thian

terminal (of battery)	ขั้วแบตเตอรี่	khûa bàet-dter-rêe
positive terminal	ขั้วบวก	khûa bùak
negative terminal	ขั้วลบ	khûa lóp
fuse	ฟิวส์	fiw

air filter	เครื่องกรองอากาศ	khrêuang grorng aa-gàat
oil filter	ไส้กรองน้ำมัน	sâi grorng nám man
fuel filter	ไส้กรองน้ำมัน	sâi grorng nám man
	เชื้อเพลิง	chéua phlerng

178. Cars. Crash. Repair

car crash	อุบัติเหตุรถชน	u-bàt hàyt rót chon
traffic accident	อุบัติเหตุจราจร	u-bàt hàyt jà-raa-jon
to crash (into the wall, etc.)	ชน	chon

to get smashed up	ชนโครม	chon khrohm
damage	ความเสียหาย	khwaam sĭa hăai
intact (unscathed)	ไม่มีความเสียหาย	mâi mee khwaam sĭa hăai

breakdown	การเสีย	gaan sĭa
to break down (vi)	ตาย	dtaai
towrope	เชือกลากรถยนต์	chêuak lâak rót yon

puncture	ยางรั่ว	yaang rûa
to be flat	ทำให้ยางแบน	tham hâi yaang baen
to pump up	เติมลมยาง	dterm lom yaang
pressure	แรงดัน	raeng dan
to check (to examine)	ตรวจสอบ	dtrùat sòrp
repair	การซ่อม	gaan sôrm

auto repair shop	ร้านซ่อมรถยนต์	ráan sôrm rót yon
spare part	อะไหล่	a lài
part	ชิ้นส่วน	chín sùan
bolt (with nut)	สลักเกลียว	sà-làk glieow
screw (fastener)	สกรู	sà-groo
nut	แหวนสกรู	wǎen sà-groo
washer	แหวนเล็ก	wǎen lék
bearing (e.g., ball ~)	แบริง	bae-ring
tube	ท่อ	thôr
gasket (head ~)	ปะเก็น	bpà gen
cable, wire	สายไฟ	sǎai fai
jack	แม่แรง	mâe raeng
wrench	ประแจ	bprà-jae
hammer	ค้อน	khórn
pump	ปั้ม	bpám
screwdriver	ไขควง	khǎi khuang
fire extinguisher	ถังดับเพลิง	thǎng dàp phlerng
warning triangle	ป้ายเตือน	bpâai dteuan
to stall (vi)	มีเครื่องดับ	mee khrêuang dàp
stall (n)	การดับ	gaan dàp
to be broken	เสีย	sǐa
to overheat (vi)	ร้อนเกิน	rórn gern
to be clogged up	อุดตัน	ùt dtan
to freeze up (pipes, etc.)	เยือกแข็ง	yêuak khǎeng
to burst (vi, ab. tube)	แตก	dtàek
pressure	แรงดัน	raeng dan
level	ระดับ	rá-dàp
slack (~ belt)	ออน	òrn
dent	รอยบุบ	roi bùp
knocking noise (engine)	เสียงเครื่องยนต์ดับ	sǐang khrêuang yon dàp
crack	รอยแตก	roi dtàek
scratch	รอยขูด	roi khòot

179. Cars. Road

road	ถนน	thà-nǒn
highway	ทางหลวง	thaang lǔang
freeway	ทางด่วน	thaang dùan
direction (way)	ทิศทาง	thít thaang
distance	ระยะทาง	rá-yá thaang
bridge	สะพาน	sà-phaan
parking lot	ลานจอดรถ	laan jòrt rót

square	จัตุรัส	jàt-dtù-ràt
interchange	ทางแยกต่างระดับ	thaang yâek dtàang rá-dàp
tunnel	อุโมงค์	u-mohng
gas station	ปั้มน้ำมัน	bpám náam man
parking lot	ลานจอดรถ	laan jòrt rót
gas pump (fuel dispenser)	ที่เติมน้ำมัน	thêe dterm náam man
auto repair shop	ร้านซ่อมรถยนต์	ráan sôrm rót yon
to get gas (to fill up)	เติมน้ำมัน	dterm náam man
fuel	น้ำมันเชื้อเพลิง	nám man chéua phlerng
jerrycan	ถังน้ำมัน	thăng náam man
asphalt	ถนนลาดยาง	thà-nŏn lâat yaang
road markings	เครื่องหมายจราจร บนพื้นทาง	khrêuang măai jà-raa-jon bon phéun thaang
curb	ขอบถนน	khòrp thà-nŏn
guardrail	รั้วกั้น	rúa gân
ditch	คู	khoo
roadside (shoulder)	ข้างถนน	khâang thà-nŏn
lamppost	เสาไฟ	săo fai
to drive (a car)	ขับ	khàp
to turn (e.g., ~ left)	เลี้ยว	líeow
to make a U-turn	กลับรถ	glàp rót
reverse (~ gear)	ถอยรถ	thŏri rót
to honk (vi)	บีบแตร	bèep dtrae
honk (sound)	เสียงบีบแตร	sĭang bèep dtrae
to get stuck (in the mud, etc.)	ติด	dtìt
to spin the wheels	หมุนล้อ	mŭn lór
to cut, to turn off (vt)	ปิด	bpìt
speed	ความเร็ว	khwaam reo
to exceed the speed limit	ขับเร็วเกิน	khàp reo gern
to give a ticket	ให้ใบสั่ง	hâi bai sàng
traffic lights	ไฟสัญญาณจราจร	fai săn-yaan jà-raa-jon
driver's license	ใบขับขี่	bai khàp khèe
grade crossing	ทางข้ามรถไฟ	thaang khâam rót fai
intersection	สี่แยก	sèe yâek
crosswalk	ทางม้าลาย	thaang máa laai
bend, curve	ทางโค้ง	thaang khóhng
pedestrian zone	ถนนคนเดิน	thà-nŏn khon dern

180. Traffic signs

rules of the road	กฎจราจร	gòt jà-raa-jon
road sign (traffic sign)	ป้ายสัญญาณจราจร	bpâai săn-yaan jà-raa-jon
passing (overtaking)	การแซง	gaan saeng

curve	การโค้ง	gaan khóhng
U-turn	การกลับรถ	gaan glàp rót
traffic circle	วงเวียน	wong wian
No entry	ห้ามเข้า	hâam khâo
No vehicles allowed	ห้ามรถเข้า	hâam rót khâo
No passing	ห้ามแซง	hâam saeng
No parking	ห้ามจอดรถ	hâam jòrt rót
No stopping	หามหยุด	hâam yùt
dangerous bend	โค้งอันตราย	khóhng an-dtà-raai
steep descent	ทางลงลาดชัน	thaang long lâat chan
one-way traffic	การจราจร	gaan jà-raa-jon
	ทางเดียว	thaang dieow
crosswalk	ทางม้าลาย	thaang máa laai
slippery road	ทางลื่น	thaang lêun
YIELD	ให้ทาง	hâi taang

PEOPLE. LIFE EVENTS

Life events

celebration, holiday	วันหยุดเฉลิมฉลอง	wan yùt chà-lěrm chà-lǒng
national day	วันชาติ	wan châat
public holiday	วันหยุดนักขัตฤกษ์	wan yùt nák-kàt-rêrk
to commemorate (vt)	เฉลิมฉลอง	chà-lěrm chà-lǒrng
event (happening)	เหตุการณ์	hàyt gaan
event (organized activity)	งานอีเวนต์	ngaan ee wayn
banquet (party)	งานเลี้ยง	ngaan líang
reception (formal party)	งานเลี้ยง	ngaan líang
feast	งานฉลอง	ngaan chà-lǒrng
anniversary	วันครบรอบ	wan khróp rôrp
jubilee	วันครบรอบปี	wan khróp rôrp bpee
to celebrate (vt)	ฉลอง	chà-lǒrng
New Year	ปีใหม่	bpee mài
Happy New Year!	สวัสดีปีใหม่!	sà-wàt-dee bpee mài
Santa Claus	ซานตาคลอส	saan-dtaa-khlôrt
Christmas	คริสต์มาส	khrít-mâat
Merry Christmas!	สุขสันต์วันคริสต์มาส	sùk-sǎn wan khrít-mâat
Christmas tree	ต้นคริสต์มาส	dtôn khrít-mâat
fireworks (fireworks show)	ดอกไม้ไฟ	dòrk máai fai
wedding	งานแต่งงาน	ngaan dtàeng ngaan
groom	เจ้าบ่าว	jâo bàao
bride	เจ้าสาว	jâo sǎao
to invite (vt)	เชิญ	chern
invitation card	บัตรเชิญ	bàt chern
guest	แขก	khàek
to visit (~ your parents, etc.)	ไปเยี่ยม	bpai yîam
to meet the guests	ต้อนรับแขก	dton ráp khàek
gift, present	ของขวัญ	khǒrng khwǎn
to give (sth as present)	ให้	hâi
to receive gifts	รับของขวัญ	ráp khǒrng khwǎn

bouquet (of flowers)	ช่อดอกไม้	chôr dòrk máai
congratulations	คำแสดง ความยินดี	kham sà-daeng khwaam yin-dee
to congratulate (vt)	แสดงความยินดี	sà-daeng khwaam yin dee
greeting card	บัตรอวยพร	bàt uay phon
to send a postcard	ส่งโปสการ์ด	sòng bpòht-gàat
to get a postcard	รับโปสการ์ด	ráp bpòht-gàat
toast	ดื่มอวยพร	dèum uay phon
to offer (a drink, etc.)	เลี้ยงเครื่องดื่ม	líang khrêuang dèum
champagne	แชมเปญ	chaem-bpayn
to enjoy oneself	มีความสุข	mee khwaam sùk
merriment (gaiety)	ความรื่นเริง	khwaam rêun-rerng
joy (emotion)	ความสุขสันต์	khwaam sùk-săn
dance	การเต้น	gaan dtên
to dance (vi, vt)	เต้น	dtên
waltz	วอลทซ์	wɔːlts
tango	แทงโก	thaeng-gôh

182. Funerals. Burial

cemetery	สุสาน	sù-săan
grave, tomb	หลุมศพ	lŭm sòp
cross	ไม้กางเขน	mái gaang khăyn
gravestone	ป้ายหลุมศพ	bpâai lŭm sòp
fence	รั้ว	rúa
chapel	โรงสวด	rohng sùat
death	ความตาย	khwaam dtaai
to die (vi)	ตาย	dtaai
the deceased	ผู้เสียชีวิต	phôo sĭa chee-wít
mourning	การไว้อาลัย	gaan wái aa-lai
to bury (vt)	ฝังศพ	făng sòp
funeral home	บริษัทรับ จัดงานศพ	bor-rí-sàt ráp jàt ngaan sòp
funeral	งานศพ	ngaan sòp
wreath	พวงหรีด	phuang rèet
casket, coffin	โลงศพ	lohng sòp
hearse	รถขนศพ	rót khŏn sòp
shroud	ผ้าห่อศพ	phâa hòr sòp
funeral procession	พิธีศพ	phí-tee sòp
funerary urn	โกศ	gòht
crematory	เมรุ	mayn

obituary	ข่าวมรณกรรม	khàao mor-rá-ná-gam
to cry (weep)	ร้องไห้	rórng hâi
to sob (vi)	สะอื้น	sà-êun

183. War. Soldiers

platoon	หมวด	mùat
company	กองร้อย	gorng rói
regiment	กรม	grom
army	กองทัพ	gorng tháp
division	กองพล	gorng phon-la
section, squad	หมู่	mòo
host (army)	กองทัพ	gorng tháp
soldier	ทหาร	thá-hǎan
officer	นายทหาร	naai thá-hǎan
private	พลทหาร	phon-thá-hǎan
sergeant	สิบเอก	sìp àyk
lieutenant	ร้อยโท	rói thoh
captain	ร้อยเอก	rói àyk
major	พลตรี	phon-dtree
colonel	พันเอก	phan àyk
general	นายพล	naai phon
sailor	กะลาสี	gà-laa-sěe
captain	กัปตัน	gàp dtan
boatswain	สรั่งเรือ	sà-ràng reua
artilleryman	ทหารปืนใหญ่	thá-hǎan bpeun yài
paratrooper	พลรม	phon-rôm
pilot	นักบิน	nák bin
navigator	ต้นหน	dtôn hǒn
mechanic	ช่างเครื่อง	châang khrêuang
pioneer (sapper)	ทหารช่าง	thá-hǎan châang
parachutist	ทหารราบอากาศ	thá-hǎan râap aa-gàat
reconnaissance scout	ทหารพราน	thá-hǎan phraan
sniper	พลซุ่มยิง	phon sûm ying
patrol (group)	หน่วยลาดตระเวน	nùay lâat dtrà-wayn
to patrol (vt)	ลาดตระเวน	lâat dtrà-wayn
sentry, guard	ทหารยาม	tá-hǎan yaam
warrior	นักรบ	nák róp
patriot	ผู้รักชาติ	phôo rák châat
hero	วีรบุรุษ	wee-rá-bù-rùt
heroine	วีรสตรี	wee rá-sot dtree
traitor	ผู้ทรยศ	phôo thor-rá-yót

185

to betray (vt)	ทรยศ	thor-rá-yót
deserter	ทหารหนีทัพ	thá-hǎan nǐe tháp
to desert (vi)	หนีทัพ	nǐe tháp
mercenary	ทหารรับจ้าง	thá-hǎan ráp jâang
recruit	เกณฑ์ทหาร	gayn thá-hǎan
volunteer	อาสาสมัคร	aa-sǎa sà-màk
dead (n)	คนถูกฆ่า	khon thòok khâa
wounded (n)	ผู้ได้รับบาดเจ็บ	phôo dâai ráp bàat jèp
prisoner of war	เชลยศึก	chá-loie sèuk

184. War. Military actions. Part 1

war	สงคราม	sǒng-khraam
to be at war	ทำสงคราม	tham sǒng-khraam
civil war	สงคราม กลางเมือง	sǒng-khraam glaang-meuang
treacherously (adv)	ตลบตะแลง	dtà-lòp-dtà-laeng
declaration of war	การประกาศ สงคราม	gaan bprà-gàat sǒng-khraam
to declare (~ war)	ประกาศสงคราม	bprà-gàat sǒng-khraam
aggression	การรุกราน	gaan rúk-raan
to attack (invade)	บุกรุก	bùk rúk
to invade (vt)	บุกรุก	bùk rúk
invader	ผู้บุกรุก	phôo bùk rúk
conqueror	ผู้ยึดครอง	phôo yéut khrorng
defense	การป้องกัน	gaan bpôrng gan
to defend (a country, etc.)	ปกป้อง	bpòk bpôrng
to defend (against ...)	ป้องกัน	bpôrng gan
enemy	ศัตรู	sàt-dtroo
foe, adversary	ข้าศึก	khâa sèuk
enemy (as adj)	ศัตรู	sàt-dtroo
strategy	ยุทธศาสตร์	yút-thá-sàat
tactics	ยุทธวิธี	yút-thá-wí-thee
order	คำสั่ง	kham sàng
command (order)	คำบัญชาการ	kham ban-chaa gaan
to order (vt)	สั่ง	sàng
mission	ภารกิจ	phaa-rá-gìt
secret (adj)	อย่างลับ	yàang láp
battle, combat	การรบ	gaan róp
attack	การจู่โจม	gaan jòo johm
charge (assault)	การเข้าจู่โจม	gaan khâo jòo johm

to storm (vt)	บุกจู่โจม	bùk jòo johm
siege (to be under ~)	การโอบล้อมโจมตี	gaan òhp lóm johm dtee
offensive (n)	การโจมตี	gaan johm dtee
to go on the offensive	โจมตี	johm dtee
retreat	การถอย	gaan thǒi
to retreat (vi)	ถอย	thǒi
encirclement	การปิดล้อม	gaan bpìt lórm
to encircle (vt)	ปิดล้อม	bpìt lórm
bombing (by aircraft)	การทิ้งระเบิด	gaan thíng rá-bèrt
to drop a bomb	ทิ้งระเบิด	thíng rá-bèrt
to bomb (vt)	ทิ้งระเบิด	thíng rá-bèrt
explosion	การระเบิด	gaan rá-bèrt
shot	การยิง	gaan ying
to fire (~ a shot)	ยิง	ying
firing (burst of ~)	การยิง	gaan ying
to aim (to point a weapon)	เล็ง	leng
to point (a gun)	ชี้	chée
to hit (the target)	ถูกเป้าหมาย	thòok bpâo mǎai
to sink (~ a ship)	จม	jom
hole (in a ship)	รู	roo
to founder, to sink (vi)	จม	jom
front (war ~)	แนวหน้า	naew nâa
evacuation	การอพยพ	gaan òp-phá-yóp
to evacuate (vt)	อพยพ	òp-phá-yóp
trench	สนามเพลาะ	sà-nǎam phlór
barbwire	ลวดหนาม	lûat nǎam
barrier (anti tank ~)	สิ่งกีดขวาง	sìng gèet-khwǎang
watchtower	หอสังเกตการณ์	hǒr sǎng-gàyt gaan
military hospital	โรงพยาบาลทหาร	rohng phá-yaa-baan thá-hǎan
to wound (vt)	ทำให้บาดเจ็บ	tham hâi bàat jèp
wound	แผล	phlǎe
wounded (n)	ผู้ได้รับบาดเจ็บ	phôo dâai ráp bàat jèp
to be wounded	ได้รับบาดเจ็บ	dâai ráp bàat jèp
serious (wound)	รายแรง	ráai raeng

185. War. Military actions. Part 2

captivity	การเป็นเชลย	gaan bpen chá-loie
to take captive	จับเชลย	jàp chá-loie

to be held captive	เป็นเชลย	bpen chá-loie
to be taken captive	ถูกจับเป็นเชลย	thòok jàp bpen chá-loie
concentration camp	ค่ายกักกัน	khâai gàk gan
prisoner of war	เชลยศึก	chá-loie sèuk
to escape (vi)	หนี	něe
to betray (vt)	ทูรยศ	thor-rá-yót
betrayer	ผู้ทรยศ	phôo thor-rá-yót
betrayal	การทรยศ	gaan thor-rá-yót
to execute (by firing squad)	ประหาร	bprà-hǎan
execution (by firing squad)	การประหาร	gaan bprà-hǎan
equipment (military gear)	ชุดเสื้อผ้าทหาร	chút sêua phâa thá-hǎan
shoulder board	บ่ง	bâng
gas mask	หน้ากากกันแก๊ส	nâa gàak gan gàet
field radio	วิทยุสนาม	wít-thá-yú sà-nǎam
cipher, code	รหัส	rá-hàt
secrecy	ความลับ	khwaam láp
password	รหัสผ่าน	rá-hàt phàan
land mine	กับระเบิด	gàp rá-bèrt
to mine (road, etc.)	วางกับระเบิด	waang gàp rá-bèrt
minefield	เขตทุ่นระเบิด	khàyt thûn rá-bèrt
air-raid warning	สัญญาณเตือนภัยทางอากาศ	sǎn-yaan dteuan phai thaang aa-gàat
alarm (alert signal)	สัญญาณเตือนภัย	sǎn-yaan dteuan phai
signal	สัญญาณ	sǎn-yaan
signal flare	พลุสัญญาณ	phlú sǎn-yaan
headquarters	กองบัญชาการ	gorng ban-chaa gaan
reconnaissance	การลาดตระเวน	gaan lâat dtrà-wayn
situation	สถานการณ์	sà-thǎan gaan
report	การรายงาน	gaan raai ngaan
ambush	การซุ่มโจมตี	gaan sûm johm dtee
reinforcement (of army)	กำลังเสริม	gam-lang sěrm
target	เป้าหมาย	bpâo mǎai
proving ground	สถานที่ทดลอง	sà-tǎan thêe thót long
military exercise	การซ้อมรบ	gaan sórm róp
panic	ความตื่นตระหนก	khwaam dtèun dtrà-nòk
devastation	การทำลายล้าง	gaan tham-laai láang
destruction, ruins	ซาก	sâak
to destroy (vt)	ทำลาย	tham laai
to survive (vi, vt)	รอดชีวิต	rôt chee-wít
to disarm (vt)	ปลดอาวุธ	bplòt aa-wút

to handle (~ a gun)	ใช้	chái
Attention!	หยุด	yùt
At ease!	พัก	phák

feat, act of courage	การแสดงความ กล้าหาญ	gaan sà-daeng khwaam glâa hăan
oath (vow)	คำสาบาน	kham săa-baan
to swear (an oath)	สาบาน	săa baan

decoration (medal, etc.)	รางวัล	raang-wan
to award (give medal to)	มอบรางวัล	môrp raang-wan
medal	เหรียญรางวัล	rĭan raang-wan
order (e.g., ~ of Merit)	เครื่องอิสริยาภรณ์	khrêuang ìt-sà-rí-yaa-phon

victory	ชัยชนะ	chai chá-ná
defeat	ความพ่ายแพ้	khwaam phâai pháe
armistice	การพักรบ	gaan phák róp

standard (battle flag)	ธงรบ	thorng róp
glory (honor, fame)	ความรุ่งโรจน์	khwaam rûng-rôht
parade	ขบวนสวนสนาม	khà-buan sŭan sà-năam
to march (on parade)	เดินสวนสนาม	dern sŭan sà-năam

186. Weapons

weapons	อาวุธ	aa-wút
firearms	อาวุธปืน	aa-wút bpeun
cold weapons (knives, etc.)	อาวุธเย็น	aa-wút yen

chemical weapons	อาวุธเคมี	aa-wút khay-mee
nuclear (adj)	นิวเคลียร์	niw-khlia
nuclear weapons	อาวุธนิวเคลียร์	aa-wút niw-khlia

| bomb | ลูกระเบิด | lôok rá-bèrt |
| atomic bomb | ลูกระเบิด ปรมาณู | lôok rá-bèrt bpà-rá-maa-noo |

pistol (gun)	ปืนพก	bpeun phók
rifle	ปืนไรเฟิล	bpeun rai-fern
submachine gun	ปืนกลมือ	bpeun gon meu
machine gun	ปืนกล	bpeun gon

muzzle	ปากกระบอกปืน	bpàak bprà bòrk bpeun
barrel	ลำกล้อง	lam glôrng
caliber	ขนาดลำกล้อง	khà-nàat lam glôrng

trigger	ไกปืน	gai bpeun
sight (aiming device)	ศูนย์เล็ง	sŏon leng
magazine	แม็กกาซีน	máek-gaa-seen

butt (shoulder stock)	พานท้ายปืน	phaan tháai bpeun
hand grenade	ระเบิดมือ	rá-bèrt meu
explosive	วัตถุระเบิด	wát-thù rá-bèrt

bullet	ลูกกระสุน	lôok grà-sǔn
cartridge	ตลับกระสุน	dtà-làp grà-sǔn
charge	กระสุน	grà-sǔn
ammunition	อาวุธยุทธภัณฑ์	aa-wút yút-thá-phan

bomber (aircraft)	เครื่องบินทิ้งระเบิด	khrêuang bin thíng rá-bèrt
fighter	เครื่องบินขับไล่	khrêuang bin khàp lâi
helicopter	เฮลิคอปเตอร์	hay-lí-khôrp-dtêr

| anti-aircraft gun | ปืนต่อสู้ | bpeun dtòr sôo |
| | อากาศยาน | aa-gàat-sà-yaan |

| tank | รถถัง | rót thǎng |
| tank gun | ปืนรถถัง | bpeun rót thǎng |

artillery	ปืนใหญ่	bpeun yài
gun (cannon, howitzer)	ปืน	bpeun
to lay (a gun)	เล็งเป้าปืน	leng bpâo bpeun

shell (projectile)	กระสุน	grà-sǔn
mortar bomb	กระสุนปืนครก	grà-sǔn bpeun khrók
mortar	ปืนครก	bpeun khrók
splinter (shell fragment)	สะเก็ดระเบิด	sà-gèt rá-bèrt

submarine	เรือดำน้ำ	reua dam náam
torpedo	ตอร์ปิโด	dtor-bpì-doh
missile	ขีปนาวุธ	khěe-bpà-naa-wút

to load (gun)	ใส่กระสุน	sài grà-sǔn
to shoot (vi)	ยิง	ying
to point at (the cannon)	เล็ง	leng
bayonet	ดาบปลายปืน	dàap bplaai bpeun

rapier	เรเปียร์	ray-bpia
saber (e.g., cavalry ~)	ดาบโค้ง	dàap khóhng
spear (weapon)	หอก	hòrk
bow	ธนู	thá-noo
arrow	ลูกธนู	lôok-thá-noo
musket	ปืนคาบศิลา	bpeun khǎap sì-laa
crossbow	หน้าไม้	nâa máai

187. Ancient people

primitive (prehistoric)	แบบดั้งเดิม	bàep dâng derm
prehistoric (adj)	ยุคก่อนประวัติศาสตร์	yúk gòn bprà-wàt sàat
ancient (~ civilization)	โบราณ	boh-raan
Stone Age	ยุคหิน	yúk hǐn

| Bronze Age | ยุคสำริด | yúk sǎm-rít |
| Ice Age | ยุคน้ำแข็ง | yúk nám khǎeng |

tribe	เผ่า	phào
cannibal	ผู้ที่กินเนื้อคน	phôo thêe gin néua khon
hunter	นักล่าสัตว์	nák lâa sàt
to hunt (vi, vt)	ล่าสัตว์	lâa sàt
mammoth	ช้างแมมมอธ	cháang-maem-môt

cave	ถ้ำ	thâm
fire	ไฟ	fai
campfire	กองไฟ	gorng fai
cave painting	ภาพวาดในถ้ำ	phâap-wâat nai thâm

tool (e.g., stone ax)	เครื่องมือ	khrêuang meu
spear	หอก	hòrk
stone ax	ขวานหิน	khwǎan hǐn
to be at war	ทำสงคราม	tham sǒng-khraam
to domesticate (vt)	เชื่อง	chêuang

idol	เทวรูป	theu-rôop
to worship (vt)	บูชา	boo-chaa
superstition	ความเชื่อ	khwaam chêua
	งมงาย	ngom-ngaai
rite	พิธีกรรม	phí-thee gam

evolution	วิวัฒนาการ	wí-wát-thá-naa-gaan
development	การพัฒนา	gaan phát-thá-naa
disappearance (extinction)	การสูญพันธุ์	gaan sǒon phan
to adapt oneself	ปรับตัว	bpràp dtua

archeology	โบราณคดี	boh-raan khá-dee
archeologist	นักโบราณคดี	nák boh-raan-ná-khá-dee
archeological (adj)	ทางโบราณคดี	thaang boh-raan khá-dee

excavation site	แหล่งขุดค้น	làeng khùt khón
excavations	การขุดค้น	gaan khùt khón
find (object)	สิ่งที่คุนพบ	sìng thêe khón phóp
fragment	เศษชิ้นส่วน	sàyt chín sùan

188. Middle Ages

people (ethnic group)	ชาติพันธุ์	châat-dtì-phan
peoples	ชาุติพันธุ์	châat-dtì-phan
tribe	เผา	phào
tribes	เผา	phào

barbarians	อนารยชน	à-naa-rá-yá-chon
Gauls	ชาวโกล	chaao gloh
Goths	ชาวกอธ	chaao gòt

Slavs	ชาวสลาฟ	chaao sà-làaf
Vikings	ชาวไวกิ้ง	chaao wai-gîng
Romans	ชาวโรมัน	chaao roh-man
Roman (adj)	โรมัน	roh-man
Byzantines	ชาวไบแซนไทน์	chaao bai-saen-tpai
Byzantium	ไบแซนเทียม	bai-saen-thiam
Byzantine (adj)	ไบแซนไทน	bai-saen-thai
emperor	จักรพรรดิ	jàk-grà-phát
leader, chief (tribal ~)	ผู้นำ	phôo nam
powerful (~ king)	ทรงพลัง	song phá-lang
king	มูหากษัตริย์	má-hǎa gà-sàt
ruler (sovereign)	ผู้ปกครอง	phôo bpòk khrorng
knight	อัศวิน	àt-sà-win
feudal lord	เจ้าครองนคร	jâo khrorng ná-khon
feudal (adj)	ระบบศักดินา	rá-bòp sàk-gà-dì naa
vassal	เจ้าของที่ดิน	jâo khǒrng thêe din
duke	ดยุค	dà-yúk
earl	เอิร์ล	ern
baron	บารอน	baa-rorn
bishop	พระบิชอป	phrá bì-chôp
armor	เกราะ	gròr
shield	โล	lôh
sword	ดาบ	dàap
visor	กะบังหน้าของหมวก	gà-bang nâa khǒrng mùak
chainmail	เสื้อเกราะถัก	sêua gròr thàk
Crusade	สงครามครูเสด	sǒng-khraam khroo-sàyt
crusader	ผู้ทำสงคราม	phôo tham sǒng-kraam
	ศาสนา	sàat-sà-nǎa
territory	อาณาเขต	aa-naa khàyt
to attack (invade)	โจมตี	johm dtee
to conquer (vt)	ยึดครอง	yéut khrorng
to occupy (invade)	บุกยึด	bùk yéut
siege (to be under ~)	การโอบล้อมโจมตี	gaan òhp lóm johm dtee
besieged (adj)	ถูกล้อมกรอบ	thòok lóm gròp
to besiege (vt)	ล้อมโจมตี	lóm johm dtee
inquisition	การไต่สวน	gaan dtài sǔan
inquisitor	ผู้ไต่สวน	phôo dtài sǔan
torture	การทูรมาน	gaan thor-rá-maan
cruel (adj)	โหดร้าย	hòht ráai
heretic	ผู้นอกรีต	phôo nôrk rêet
heresy	ความนอกรีต	khwaam nôrk rêet
seafaring	การเดินเรือทะเล	gaan dern reua thá-lay

pirate	โจรสลัด	john sà-làt
piracy	การปล้นสะดม ในนานน้ำทะเล	gaan bplôn-sà-dom nai nâan náam thá-lay
boarding (attack)	การบุกขึ้นเรือ	gaan bùk khêun reua
loot, booty	ของที่ปล้น สะดมมา	khŏrng têe bplôn- sà-dom maa
treasures	สมบัติ	sŏm-bàt
discovery	การค้นพบ	gaan khón phóp
to discover (new land, etc.)	ค้นพบ	khón phóp
expedition	การสำรวจ	gaan săm-rùat
musketeer	ทหารถือ ปืนคาบศิลา	thá-hăan thĕu bpeun khâap sì-laa
cardinal	พระคาร์ดินัล	phrá khaa-dì-nan
heraldry	มุทราศาสตร์	mút-raa sàat
heraldic (adj)	ทางมุทราศาสตร์	thaang mút-raa sàat

189. Leader. Chief. Authorities

king	ราชา	raa-chaa
queen	ราชินี	raa-chí-nee
royal (adj)	เกี่ยวกับราชวงศ์	glìeow gàp râat-cha-wong
kingdom	ราชอาณาจักร	râat aa-naa jàk
prince	เจ้าชาย	jâo chaai
princess	เจ้าหญิง	jâo yĭng
president	ประธานาธิบดี	bprà-thaa-naa-thí-bor-dee
vice-president	รองประธา นาธิบดี	rorng bprà-thaa- naa-thí-bor-dee
senator	สมาชิกวุฒิสภา	sà-maa-chík wút-thí sà-phaa
monarch	กษัตริย์	gà-sàt
ruler (sovereign)	ผู้ปกครอง	phôo bpòk khrorng
dictator	เผด็จการ	phà-dèt gaan
tyrant	ทูรราช	thor-rá-râat
magnate	ผู้มีอิทธิ พลสูง	phôo mee ìt-thí phon sŏong
director	ผู้อำนวยการ	phôo am-nuay gaan
chief	หัวหน้า	hŭa-nâa
manager (director)	ผู้จัดการ	phôo jàt gaan
boss	หัวหน้า	hŭa-nâa
owner	เจ้าของ	jâo khŏrng
leader	ผู้นำ	phôo nam
head (~ of delegation)	หัวหน้า	hŭa-nâa
authorities	เจ้าหน้าที่	jâo nâa-thêe

superiors	ผู้บังคับบัญชา	phôo bang-kháp ban-chaa
governor	ผู้วาการ	phôo wâa gaan
consul	กงสุล	gong-sŭn
diplomat	นักการทูต	nák gaan thôot
mayor	นายกเทศ มนตรี	naa-yók thâyt-sà-mon-dtree
sheriff	นายอำเภอ	naai am-pher

emperor	จักรพรรดิ	jàk-grà-phát
tsar, czar	ซาร์	saa
pharaoh	ฟาโรห์	faa-roh
khan	ขาน	khàan

190. Road. Way. Directions

road	ถนน	thà-nŏn
way (direction)	ทิศทาง	thít thaang
freeway	ทางด่วน	thaang dùan
highway	ทางหลวง	thaang lŭang
interstate	ทางหลวงอินเตอร์สเตต	thaang lŭang in-dtèrt-dtàyt
main road	ถนนใหญ่	thà-nŏn yài
dirt road	ถนนลูกรัง	thà-nŏn loo-grang
pathway	ทางเดิน	thaang dern
footpath (troddenpath)	ทางเดิน	thaang dern
Where?	ที่ไหน?	thêe năi
Where (to)?	ที่ไหน?	thêe năi
From where?	จากที่ไหน?	jàak thêe năi
direction (way)	ทิศทาง	thít thaang
to point (~ the way)	ชี้	chée
to the left	ทางซ้าย	thaang sáai
to the right	ทางขวา	thaang khwăa
straight ahead (adv)	ตรงไป	dtrorng bpai
back (e.g., to turn ~)	กลับ	glàp
bend, curve	ทางโค้ง	thaang khóhng
to turn (e.g., ~ left)	เลี้ยว	líeow
to make a U-turn	กลับรถ	glàp rót
to be visible (mountains, castle, etc.)	มองเห็นได้	morng hĕn dâai
to appear (come into view)	ปรากฏ	bpraa-gòt
stop, halt (e.g., during a trip)	การหยุด	gaan yùt

to rest, to pause (vi)	พัก	phák
rest (pause)	การหยุดพัก	gaan yùt phák
to lose one's way	หลงทาง	lŏng thaang
to lead to ... (ab. road)	ไปสู่	bpai sòo
to come out (e.g., on the highway)	ออกมาถึง	òrk maa thĕung
stretch (of road)	ส่วน	sùan
asphalt	ถนนลาดยาง	thà-nŏn lâat yaang
curb	ขอบถนน	khòrp thà-nŏn
ditch	คูน้ำ	khoo náam
manhole	ฝาท่อระบายน้ำ	făa thôr rá-baai nám
roadside (shoulder)	ข้างถนน	khâang thà-nŏn
pit, pothole	หลุม	lŭm
to go (on foot)	ไป	bpai
to pass (overtake)	แซง	saeng
step (footstep)	ก้าวเดิน	gâao dern
on foot (adv)	เดินเท้า	dern tháo
to block (road)	กีดขวาง	gèet khwăang
boom gate	แขนกั้นรถ	khăen gân rót
dead end	ทางตัน	thaang dtan

191. Breaking the law. Criminals. Part 1

bandit	โจร	john
crime	อาชญากรรม	àat-yaa-gam
criminal (person)	อาชญากร	àat-yaa-gon
thief	ขโมย	khà-moi
to steal (vi, vt)	ขโมย	khà-moi
stealing (larceny)	การลักขโมย	gaan lák khà-moi
theft	การลักทรัพย์	gaan lák sáp
to kidnap (vt)	ลักพาตัว	lák phaa dtua
kidnapping	การลักพาตัว	gaan lák phaa dtua
kidnapper	ผู้ลักพาตัว	phôo lák phaa dtua
ransom	ค่าไถ่	khâa thài
to demand ransom	เรียกเงินค่าไถ่	rîak ngern khâa thài
to rob (vt)	ปล้น	bplôn
robbery	การปล้น	gaan bplôn
robber	ขโมยขโจร	khà-moi khà-john
to extort (vt)	รีดไถ	rêet thăi
extortionist	ผู้รีดไถ	phôo rêet thăi

extortion	การรีดไถ	gaan rêet thăi
to murder, to kill	ฆ่า	khâa
murder	ฆาตกรรม	khâat-dtà-gaam
murderer	ฆาตกร	khâat-dtà-gon
gunshot	การยิงปืน	gaan ying bpeun
to fire (~ a shot)	ยิง	ying
to shoot to death	ยิงให้ตาย	ying hâi dtaai
to shoot (vi)	ยิง	ying
shooting	การยิง	gaan ying
incident (fight, etc.)	เหตุการณ์	hàyt gaan
fight, brawl	การต่อสู้	gaan dtòr sôo
Help!	ขอช่วย	khŏr chûay
victim	เหยื่อ	yèua
to damage (vt)	ทำความเสียหาย	tham khwaam sĭa hăai
damage	ความเสียหาย	khwaam sĭa hăai
dead body, corpse	ศพ	sòp
grave (~ crime)	ร้ายแรง	ráai raeng
to attack (vt)	จู่โจม	jòo johm
to beat (to hit)	ตี	dtee
to beat up	ซ่อม	sórm
to take (rob of sth)	ปล้น	bplôn
to stab to death	แทงให้ตาย	thaeng hâi dtaai
to maim (vt)	ทำให้บาดเจ็บสาหัส	tham hâi bàat jèp săa hàt
to wound (vt)	บาด	bàat
blackmail	การกรรโชก	gaan-gan-chôhk
to blackmail (vt)	กรรโชก	gan-chôhk
blackmailer	ผู้ขู่กรรโชก	phôo khòo gan-chôhk
protection racket	การคุมครอง ผิดกฎหมาย	gaan khum khrorng phìt gòt măai
racketeer	ผู้ที่หาเงิน จากกิจกรรมที่ ผิดกฎหมาย	phôo thêe hăa ngern jàak gìt-jà-gam thêe phìt gòt măai
gangster	เหล่าร้าย	lào ráai
mafia, Mob	มาเฟีย	maa-fia
pickpocket	ขโมยล้วงกระเป๋า	khà-moi lúang grà-bpăo
burglar	ขโมยย่องเบา	khà-moi yông bao
smuggling	การลักลอบ	gaan lák-lôrp
smuggler	ผู้ลักลอบ	phôo lák lôrp
forgery	การปลอมแปลง	gaan bplorm bplaeng
to forge (counterfeit)	ปลอมแปลง	bplorm bplaeng
fake (forged)	ปลอม	bplorm

192. Breaking the law. Criminals. Part 2

rape	การข่มขืน	gaan khòm khĕun
to rape (vt)	ข่มขืน	khòm khĕun
rapist	โจรขุมขืน	john khòm khĕun
maniac	คนบ้า	khon bâa
prostitute (fem.)	โสเภณี	sŏh-phay-nee
prostitution	การค้าประเวณี	gaan kháa bprà-way-nee
pimp	แมงดา	maeng-daa
drug addict	ผู้ติดยาเสพติด	phôo dtìt yaa-sàyp-dtìt
drug dealer	พ่อค้ายาเสพติด	phôr kháa yaa-sàyp-dtìt
to blow up (bomb)	ระเบิด	rá-bèrt
explosion	การระเบิด	gaan rá-bèrt
to set fire	เผา	phăo
arsonist	ผู้ลอบวางเพลิง	phôo lôp waang phlerng
terrorism	การก่อการร้าย	gaan gòr gaan ráai
terrorist	ผู้ก่อการร้าย	phôo gòr gaan ráai
hostage	ตัวประกัน	dtua bprà-gan
to swindle (deceive)	ล่อลวง	lôr luang
swindle, deception	การล่อลวง	gaan lôr luang
swindler	นักต้มตุ๋น	nák dtôm dtŭn
to bribe (vt)	ติดสินบน	dtìt sĭn-bon
bribery	การติดสินบน	gaan dtìt sĭn-bon
bribe	สินบน	sĭn bon
poison	ยาพิษ	yaa phít
to poison (vt)	วางยาพิษ	waang-yaa phít
to poison oneself	กินยาตาย	gin yaa dtaai
suicide (act)	การฆ่าตัวตาย	gaan kháa dtua dtaai
suicide (person)	ผู้ฆ่าตัวตาย	phôo kháa dtua dtaai
to threaten (vt)	ขู่	khòo
threat	คำขู่	kham khòo
to make an attempt	พยายามฆ่า	phá-yaa-yaam khâa
attempt (attack)	การพยายามฆ่า	gaan phá-yaa-yaam khâa
to steal (a car)	จี้	jêe
to hijack (a plane)	จี้	jêe
revenge	การแก้แค้น	gaan gâe kháen
to avenge (get revenge)	แก้แค้น	gâe kháen
to torture (vt)	ทรมาณ	thon-maan
torture	การทรมาน	gaan thor-rá-maan

to torment (vt)	ทำทารุณ	tam taa-run
pirate	โจรสลัด	john sà-làt
hooligan	นักเลง	nák-layng
armed (adj)	มีอาวุธ	mee aa-wút
violence	ความรุนแรง	khwaam run raeng
illegal (unlawful)	ผิดกฎหมาย	phìt gòt mǎai
spying (espionage)	จารกรรม	jaa-rá-gam
to spy (vi)	ลวงความลับ	lúang khwaam láp

193. Police. Law. Part 1

justice	ยุติธรรม	yút-dtì-tham
court (see you in ~)	ศาล	sǎan
judge	ผู้พิพากษา	phôo phí-phâak-sǎa
jurors	ลูกขุน	lôok khǔn
jury trial	การไต่สวนคดี	gaan dtài sǔan khá-dee
	แบบมีลูกขุน	bàep mee lôok khǔn
to judge, to try (vt)	พิพากษา	phí-phâak-sǎa
lawyer, attorney	ทนายความ	thá-naai khwaam
defendant	จำเลย	jam loie
dock	คอกจำเลย	khôrk jam loie
charge	ข้อกล่าวหา	khôr glàao hǎa
accused	ถูกกลาวหา	thòok glàao hǎa
sentence	การลงโทษ	gaan long thôht
to sentence (vt)	พิพากษา	phí-phâak-sǎa
guilty (culprit)	ผู้กระทำ	phôo grà-tham
	ความผิด	khwaam phìt
to punish (vt)	ลงโทษ	long thôht
punishment	การลงโทษ	gaan long thôht
fine (penalty)	ปรับ	bpràp
life imprisonment	การจำคุก	gaan jam khúk
	ตลอดชีวิต	dtà-lòt chee-wít
death penalty	โทษประหาร	thôht-bprà-hǎan
electric chair	เก้าอี้ไฟฟ้า	gâo-êe fai-fáa
gallows	ตะแลงแกง	dtà-laeng-gaeng
to execute (vt)	ประหาร	bprà-hǎan
execution	การประหาร	gaan bprà-hǎan
prison, jail	คุก	khúk
cell	ห้องขัง	hôrng khǎng
escort (convoy)	ผู้ควบคุมตัว	phôo khûap khum dtua
prison guard	ผู้คุม	phôo khum

prisoner	นักโทษ	nák thôht
handcuffs	กุญแจมือ	gun-jae meu
to handcuff (vt)	ใสกุญแจมือ	sài gun-jae meu

prison break	การแหกคุก	gaan hàek khúk
to break out (vi)	แหก	hàek
to disappear (vi)	หายตัวไป	hǎai dtua bpai
to release (from prison)	ถูกปล่อยตัว	thòok bplòi dtua
amnesty	การนิรโทษกรรม	gaan ní-rá-thôht gam

police	ตำรวจ	dtam-rùat
police officer	เจ้าหน้าที่ตำรวจ	jâo nâa-thêe dtam-rùat
police station	สถานีตำรวจ	sà-thǎa-nee dtam-rùat
billy club	กระบองตำรวจ	grà-bong dtam-rùat
bullhorn	โทรโข่ง	toh-ra -khòhng

patrol car	รถลาดตระเวน	rót lâat dtrà-wayn
siren	หวอ	wǒr
to turn on the siren	เปิดหวอ	bpèrt wǒr
siren call	เสียงหวอ	sǐang wǒr

crime scene	ที่เกิดเหตุ	thêe gèrt hàyt
witness	พยาน	phá-yaan
freedom	อิสระ	ìt-sà-rà
accomplice	ผู้ร่วมกระทำผิด	phôo rûam grà-tham phìt
to flee (vi)	หนี	něe
trace (to leave a ~)	ร่องรอย	rông roi

194. Police. Law. Part 2

search (investigation)	การสืบสวน	gaan sèup sǔan
to look for ...	หาตัว	hǎa dtua
suspicion	ความสงสัย	khwaam sǒng-sǎi
suspicious (e.g., ~ vehicle)	น่าสงสัย	nâa sǒng-sǎi
to stop (cause to halt)	เรียกให้หยุด	rîak hâi yùt
to detain (keep in custody)	กักตัว	gàk dtua

case (lawsuit)	คดี	khá-dee
investigation	การสืบสวน	gaan sèup sǔan
detective	นักสืบ	nák sèup
investigator	นักสอบสวน	nák sòrp sǔan
hypothesis	สันนิษฐาน	sǎn-nít-thǎan

motive	เหตุจูงใจ	hàyt joong jai
interrogation	การสอบปากคำ	gaan sòp bpàak kham
to interrogate (vt)	สอบสวน	sòrp sǔan
to question (~ neighbors, etc.)	ไถ่ถาม	thài thǎam
check (identity ~)	การตรวจสอบ	gaan dtrùat sòp
round-up (raid)	การรวบตัว	gaan rûap dtua

search (~ warrant)	การตรวจค้น	gaan dtrùat khón
chase (pursuit)	การไล่ล่า	gaan lâi lâa
to pursue, to chase	ไล่ล่า	lâi lâa
to track (a criminal)	สืบ	sèup

arrest	การจับกุม	gaan jàp gum
to arrest (sb)	จับกุม	jàp gum
to catch (thief, etc.)	จับ	jàp
capture	การจับ	gaan jàp

document	เอกสาร	àyk săan
proof (evidence)	หลักฐาน	làk thăan
to prove (vt)	พิสูจน์	phí-sòot
footprint	รอยเท้า	roi tháo
fingerprints	รอยนิ้วมือ	roi níw meu
piece of evidence	หลักฐาน	làk thăan

alibi	ข้อแก้ตัว	khôr gâe dtua
innocent (not guilty)	พ้นผิด	phón phìt
injustice	ความอยุติธรรม	khwaam a-yút-dtì-tam
unjust, unfair (adj)	ไม่เป็นธรรม	mâi bpen-tham

criminal (adj)	อาชญากร	àat-yaa-gon
to confiscate (vt)	ยึด	yéut
drug (illegal substance)	ยาเสพติด	yaa sàyp dtìt
weapon, gun	อาวุธ	aa-wút
to disarm (vt)	ปลดอาวุธ	bplòt aa-wút
to order (command)	ออกคำสั่ง	òrk kham sàng
to disappear (vi)	หายตัวไป	hăai dtua bpai

law	กฎหมาย	gòt măai
legal, lawful (adj)	ตามกฎหมาย	dtaam gòt măai
illegal, illicit (adj)	ผิดกฎหมาย	phìt gòt măai

| responsibility (blame) | ความรับผิดชอบ | khwaam ráp phìt chôp |
| responsible (adj) | รับผิดชอบ | ráp phìt chôp |

NATURE

The Earth. Part 1

195. Outer space

space	อวกาศ	a-wá-gàat
space (as adj)	ทางอวกาศ	thang a-wá-gàat
outer space	อวกาศ	a-wá-gàat

world	โลก	lôhk
universe	จักรวาล	jàk-grà-waan
galaxy	ดาราจักร	daa-raa jàk

star	ดาว	daao
constellation	กลุ่มดาว	glùm daao
planet	ดาวเคราะห์	daao khrór
satellite	ดาวเทียม	daao thiam

meteorite	ดาวตก	daao dtòk
comet	ดาวหาง	daao hăang
asteroid	ดาวเคราะห์น้อย	daao khrór nói

orbit	วงโคจร	wong khoh-jon
to revolve (~ around the Earth)	เวียน	wian
atmosphere	บรรยากาศ	ban-yaa-gàat

the Sun	ดวงอาทิตย์	duang aa-thít
solar system	ระบบสุริยะ	rá-bòp sù-rí-yá
solar eclipse	สุริยุปราคา	sù-rí-yú-bpà-raa-kaa

the Earth	โลก	lôhk
the Moon	ดวงจันทร์	duang jan

Mars	ดาวอังคาร	daao ang-khaan
Venus	ดาวศุกร์	daao sùk
Jupiter	ดาวพฤหัส	daao phá-réu-hàt
Saturn	ดาวเสาร์	daao săo

Mercury	ดาวพุธ	daao phút
Uranus	ดาวยูเรนัส	daao-yoo-ray-nát
Neptune	ดาวเนปจูน	daao-nâyp-joon
Pluto	ดาวพลูโต	daao phloo-dtoh
Milky Way	ทางช้างเผือก	thaang cháang phèuak

Great Bear (Ursa Major)	กลุ่มดาวหมีใหญ่	glùm daao měe yài
North Star	ดาวเหนือ	daao něua
Martian	ชาวดาวอังคาร	chaao daao ang-khaan
extraterrestrial (n)	มนุษย์ต่างดาว	má-nút dtàang daao
alien	มนุษย์ต่างดาว	má-nút dtàang daao
flying saucer	จานบิน	jaan bin
spaceship	ยานอวกาศ	yaan a-wá-gàat
space station	สถานีอวกาศ	sà-thǎa-nee a-wá-gàat
blast-off	การปล่อยจรวด	gaan bplòi jà-rùat
engine	เครื่องยนต์	khrêuang yon
nozzle	ท่อไอพ่น	thôr ai phôn
fuel	เชื้อเพลิง	chéua phlerng
cockpit, flight deck	ที่นั่งคนขับ	thêe nâng khon khàp
antenna	เสาอากาศ	sǎo aa-gàat
porthole	ช่อง	chôrng
solar panel	อุปกรณ์พลังงานแสงอาทิตย์	ù-bpà-gon phá-lang ngaan sǎeng aa-thít
spacesuit	ชุดอวกาศ	chút a-wá-gàat
weightlessness	สภาพไร้น้ำหนัก	sà-phâap rái nám nàk
oxygen	อ็อกซิเจน	ók sí jayn
docking (in space)	การเทียบท่า	gaan thîap thâa
to dock (vi, vt)	เทียบทา	thîap thâa
observatory	หอดูดาว	hǒr doo daao
telescope	กล้องโทรทรรศน์	glôrng thoh-rá-thát
to observe (vt)	เฝ้าสังเกต	fâo sǎng-gàyt
to explore (vt)	สำรวจ	sǎm-rùat

196. The Earth

the Earth	โลก	lôhk
the globe (the Earth)	ลูกโลก	lôok lôhk
planet	ดาวเคราะห์	daao khrór
atmosphere	บรรยากาศ	ban-yaa-gàat
geography	ภูมิศาสตร์	phoo-mí-sàat
nature	ธรรมชาติ	tham-má-châat
globe (table ~)	ลูกโลก	lôok lôhk
map	แผนที่	phǎen thêe
atlas	หนังสือแผนที่โลก	nǎng-sěu phǎen thêe lôhk
Europe	ยุโรป	yú-ròhp
Asia	เอเชีย	ay-chia

| Africa | แอฟริกา | àef-rí-gaa |
| Australia | ออสเตรเลีย | òrt-dtray-lia |

America	อเมริกา	a-may-rí-gaa
North America	อเมริกาเหนือ	a-may-rí-gaa něua
South America	อเมริกาใต้	a-may-rí-gaa dtâi

| Antarctica | แอนตาร์กติกา | aen-dtàak-dtì-gaa |
| the Arctic | อาร์กติค | àak-dtìk |

197. Cardinal directions

north	เหนือ	něua
to the north	ทิศเหนือ	thít něua
in the north	ที่ภาคเหนือ	thêe phâak něua
northern (adj)	ทางเหนือ	thaang něua

south	ใต้	dtâi
to the south	ทิศใต้	thít dtâi
in the south	ที่ภาคใต้	thêe phâak dtâi
southern (adj)	ทางใต้	thaang dtâi

west	ตะวันตก	dtà-wan dtòk
to the west	ทิศตะวันตก	thít dtà-wan dtòk
in the west	ที่ภาคตะวันตก	thêe phâak dtà-wan dtòk
western (adj)	ทางตะวันตก	thaang dtà-wan dtòk

east	ตะวันออก	dtà-wan òrk
to the east	ทิศตะวันออก	thít dtà-wan òrk
in the east	ที่ภาคตะวันออก	thêe phâak dtà-wan òrk
eastern (adj)	ทางตะวันออก	thaang dtà-wan òrk

198. Sea. Ocean

sea	ทะเล	thá-lay
ocean	มหาสมุทร	má-hǎa sà-mùt
gulf (bay)	อ่าว	àao
straits	ช่องแคบ	chôrng khâep

| land (solid ground) | พื้นดิน | phéun din |
| continent (mainland) | ทวีป | thá-wêep |

island	เกาะ	gòr
peninsula	คาบสมุทร	khâap sà-mùt
archipelago	หมู่เกาะ	mòo gòr

| bay, cove | อ่าว | àao |
| harbor | ท่าเรือ | thâa reua |

lagoon	ลากูน	laa-goon
cape	แหลม	lăem
atoll	อะทอลล์	à-thorn
reef	แนวปะการัง	naew bpà-gaa-rang
coral	ปะการัง	bpà gaa-rang
coral reef	แนวปะการัง	naew bpà-gaa-rang
deep (adj)	ลึก	léuk
depth (deep water)	ความลึก	khwaam léuk
abyss	หุบเหวลึก	hùp wǎy léuk
trench (e.g., Mariana ~)	ร่องลึกก้นสมุทร	rông léuk gôn sà-mùt
current (Ocean ~)	กระแสน้ำ	grà-sǎe náam
to surround (bathe)	ล้อมรอบ	lórm rôrp
shore	ชายฝั่ง	chaai fàng
coast	ชายฝั่ง	chaai fàng
flow (flood tide)	น้ำขึ้น	náam khêun
ebb (ebb tide)	น้ำลง	náam long
shoal	หาดตื้น	hàat dtêun
bottom (~ of the sea)	ก้นทะเล	gôn thá-lay
wave	คลื่น	khlêun
crest (~ of a wave)	ม้วนคลื่น	múan khlêun
spume (sea foam)	ฟองคลื่น	forng khlêun
storm (sea storm)	พายุ	phaa-yú
hurricane	พายุเฮอร์ริเคน	phaa-yú her-rí-khayn
tsunami	คลื่นยักษ์	khlêun yák
calm (dead ~)	ภาวะไร้ลมพัด	phaa-wá rái lom phát
quiet, calm (adj)	สงบ	sà-ngòp
pole	ขั้วโลก	khûa lôhk
polar (adj)	ขั้วโลก	khûa lôhk
latitude	เส้นรุ้ง	sên rúng
longitude	เส้นแวง	sên waeng
parallel	เส้นขนาน	sên khà-nǎan
equator	เส้นศูนย์สูตร	sên sǒon sòot
sky	ท้องฟ้า	thórng fáa
horizon	ขอบฟ้า	khòrp fáa
air	อากาศ	aa-gàat
lighthouse	ประภาคาร	bprà-phaa-khaan
to dive (vi)	ดำ	dam
to sink (ab. boat)	จม	jom
treasures	สมบัติ	sǒm-bàt

199. Seas' and Oceans' names

Atlantic Ocean	มหาสมุทร แอตแลนติก	má-hǎa sà-mùt àet-laen-dtìk
Indian Ocean	มหาสมุทรอินเดีย	má-hǎa sà-mùt in-dia
Pacific Ocean	มหาสมุทรแปซิฟิก	má-hǎa sà-mùt bpae-sí-fík
Arctic Ocean	มหาสมุทรอาร์คติก	má-hǎa sà-mùt aa-ká-dtìk
Black Sea	ทะเลดำ	thá-lay dam
Red Sea	ทะเลแดง	thá-lay daeng
Yellow Sea	ทะเลเหลือง	thá-lay lěuang
White Sea	ทะเลขาว	thá-lay khǎao
Caspian Sea	ทะเลแคสเปียน	thá-lay khâet-bpian
Dead Sea	ทะเลเดดซี	thá-lay dàyt-see
Mediterranean Sea	ทะเลเมดิเตอร์เรเนียน	thá-lay may-dì-dtêr-ray-nian
Aegean Sea	ทะเลเอเจี้ยน	thá-lay ay-jîan
Adriatic Sea	ทะเลเอเดรียติก	thá-lay ay-day-ree-yá-dtìk
Arabian Sea	ทะเลอาหรับ	thá-lay aa-ràp
Sea of Japan	ทะเลญี่ปุ่น	thá-lay yêe-bpùn
Bering Sea	ทะเลเบริง	thá-lay bae-rîng
South China Sea	ทะเลจีนใต้	thá-lay jeen-dtâi
Coral Sea	ทะเลคอรัล	thá-lay khor-ran
Tasman Sea	ทะเลแทสมัน	thá-lay thâet man
Caribbean Sea	ทะเลแคริบเบียน	thá-lay khae-ríp-bian
Barents Sea	ทะเลบาเรนท์	thá-lay baa-rayn
Kara Sea	ทะเลคารา	thá-lay khaa-raa
North Sea	ทะเลเหนือ	thá-lay něua
Baltic Sea	ทะเลบอลติก	thá-lay bon-dtìk
Norwegian Sea	ทะเลนอรเวย์	thá-lay nor-rá-way

200. Mountains

mountain	ภูเขา	phoo khǎo
mountain range	ทิวเขา	thiw khǎo
mountain ridge	สันเขา	sǎn khǎo
summit, top	ยอดเขา	yôrt khǎo
peak	ยอด	yôrt
foot (~ of the mountain)	ตีนเขา	dteun khǎo
slope (mountainside)	ไหล่เขา	lài khǎo
volcano	ภูเขาไฟ	phoo khǎo fai
active volcano	ภูเขาไฟ มีพลัง	phoo khǎo fai mee phá-lang

dormant volcano	ภูเขาไฟ ที่ดับแลว	phoo khǎo fai thêe dàp láew
eruption	ภูเขาไฟระเบิด	phoo khǎo fai rá-bèrt
crater	ปลองภูเขาไฟ	bplòng phoo khǎo fai
magma	หินหนืด	hǐn nèut
lava	ลาวา	laa-waa
molten (~ lava)	หลอมเหลว	lǒrm lěo
canyon	หุบเขาลึก	hùp khǎo léuk
gorge	ชองเขา	chôrng khǎo
crevice	รอยแตกภูเขา	roi dtàek phoo khǎo
abyss (chasm)	หุบเหวลึก	hùp wǎy léuk
pass, col	ทางผาน	thaang phàan
plateau	ที่ราบสูง	thêe râap sǒong
cliff	หนาผา	nâa phǎa
hill	เนินเขา	nern khǎo
glacier	ธารน้ำแข็ง	thaan náam khǎeng
waterfall	น้ำตก	nám dtòk
geyser	น้ำพุรอน	nám phú rórn
lake	ทะเลสาบ	thá-lay sàap
plain	ที่ราบ	thêe râap
landscape	ภูมิทัศน์	phoom thát
echo	เสียงสะทอน	sǐang sà-thón
alpinist	นักปีนเขา	nák bpeen khǎo
rock climber	นักไตเขา	nák dtài khǎo
to conquer (in climbing)	ไตเขาถึงยอด	dtài khǎo thěung yôt
climb (an easy ~)	การปีนเขา	gaan bpeen khǎo

201. Mountains names

The Alps	เทือกเขาแอลป์	thêuak-khǎo-aen
Mont Blanc	ยอดเขามงบล็อง	yôt khǎo mong-bà-lǒng
The Pyrenees	เทือกเขาไพรีนีส	thêuak khǎo pai-ree-nêet
The Carpathians	เทือกเขา คารเพเทียน	thêuak khǎo khaa-phay-thian
The Ural Mountains	เทือกเขายูรัล	thêuak khǎo yoo-ran
The Caucasus Mountains	เทือกเขาคอเคซัส	thêuak khǎo khor-khay-sát
Mount Elbrus	ยอดเขาเอลบรุส	yôt khǎo ayn-brùt
The Altai Mountains	เทือกเขาอัลไต	thêuak khǎo an-dtai
The Tian Shan	เทือกเขาเทียนชาน	thêuak khǎo thian-chaan
The Pamir Mountains	เทือกเขาพาเมียร	thêuak khǎo paa-mia
The Himalayas	เทือกเขาหิมาลัย	thêuak khǎo hì-maa-lai
Mount Everest	ยอดเขาเอเวอเรสต์	yôt khǎo ay-wer-râyt
The Andes	เทือกเขาแอนดีส	thêuak-khǎo-aen-dèet
Mount Kilimanjaro	ยอดเขาคิลิมันจาโร	yôt khǎo khí-lí-man-jaa-roh

202. Rivers

river	แม่น้ำ	mâe náam
spring (natural source)	แหล่งน้ำแร่	làeng náam râe
riverbed (river channel)	เส้นทางแม่น้ำ	sên thaang mâe náam
basin (river valley)	ลุ่มน้ำ	lûm náam
to flow into ...	ไหลไปสู่...	lǎi bpai sòo...
tributary	สาขา	sǎa-khǎa
bank (of river)	ฝั่งแม่น้ำ	fàng mâe náam
current (stream)	กระแสน้ำ	grà-sǎe náam
downstream (adv)	ตามกระแสน้ำ	dtaam grà-sǎe náam
upstream (adv)	ทวนน้ำ	thuan náam
inundation	น้ำท่วม	nám thûam
flooding	น้ำท่วม	nám thûam
to overflow (vi)	เอ่อล้น	èr lón
to flood (vt)	ท่วม	thûam
shallow (shoal)	บริเวณน้ำตื้น	bor-rí-wayn nám dtêun
rapids	กระแสน้ำเชี่ยว	grà-sǎe nám-chîeow
dam	เขื่อน	khèuan
canal	คลอง	khlorng
reservoir (artificial lake)	ที่เก็บกักน้ำ	thêe gèp gàk náam
sluice, lock	ประตูระบายน้ำ	bprà-dtoo rá-baai náam
water body (pond, etc.)	พื้นน้ำ	phéun náam
swamp (marshland)	บึง	beung
bog, marsh	หวย	hûay
whirlpool	น้ำวน	nám won
stream (brook)	ลำธาร	lam thaan
drinking (ab. water)	น้ำดื่มได้	nám dèum dâai
fresh (~ water)	น้ำจืด	nám jèut
ice	น้ำแข็ง	nám khǎeng
to freeze over (ab. river, etc.)	แช่แข็ง	châe khǎeng

203. Rivers' names

Seine	แม่น้ำเซน	mâe náam sayn
Loire	แม่น้ำลัวร์	mâe-náam lua
Thames	แม่น้ำเทมส์	mâe-náam them
Rhine	แม่น้ำไรน์	mâe-náam rai
Danube	แม่น้ำดานูบ	mâe-náam daa-nôop

Volga	แม่น้ำวอลกา	mâe-náam won-gaa
Don	แม่น้ำดอน	mâe-náam don
Lena	แม่น้ำลีนา	mâe-náam lee-naa

Yellow River	แม่น้ำหวง	mâe-náam hŭang
Yangtze	แม่น้ำแยงซี	mâe-náam yaeng-see
Mekong	แม่น้ำโขง	mâe-náam khŏhng
Ganges	แม่น้ำคงคา	mâe-náam khong-khaa

Nile River	แม่น้ำไนล์	mâe-náam nai
Congo River	แม่น้ำคองโก	mâe-náam khong-goh
Okavango River	แม่น้ำ โอคาวังโก	mâe-náam oh-khaa wang goh
Zambezi River	แม่น้ำแซมบีซี	mâe-náam saem bee see
Limpopo River	แม่น้ำลิมโปโป	mâe-náam lim-bpoh-bpoh
Mississippi River	แม่น้ำ มิสซิสซิปปี	mâe-náam mít-sít-síp-bpee

204. Forest

| forest, wood | ป่าไม้ | bpàa máai |
| forest (as adj) | ป่า | bpàa |

thick forest	ป่าทึบ	bpàa théup
grove	ป่าละเมาะ	bpàa lá-mór
forest clearing	ทุ่งโล่ง	thûng lôhng

| thicket | ป่าละเมาะ | bpàa lá-mór |
| scrubland | ป่าละเมาะ | bpàa lá-mór |

| footpath (troddenpath) | ทางเดิน | thaang dern |
| gully | ร่องธาร | rông thaan |

tree	ต้นไม้	dtôn máai
leaf	ใบไม้	bai máai
leaves (foliage)	ใบไม้	bai máai

fall of leaves	ใบไม้ร่วง	bai máai rûang
to fall (ab. leaves)	ร่วง	rûang
top (of the tree)	ยอด	yôrt

branch	กิ่ง	gìng
bough	กานไม้	gâan mái
bud (on shrub, tree)	ยอดอ่อน	yôrt òrn
needle (of pine tree)	เข็ม	khĕm
pine cone	ลูกสน	lôok sŏn

tree hollow	โพรงไม้	phrohng máai
nest	รัง	rang
burrow (animal hole)	โพรง	phrohng

trunk	ลำต้น	lam dtôn
root	ราก	râak
bark	เปลือกไม้	bplèuak máai
moss	มอส	môt
to uproot (remove trees or tree stumps)	ถอนราก	thǒrn râak
to chop down	โค่น	khôhn
to deforest (vt)	ตัดไม้ทำลายป่า	dtàt mái tham laai bpàa
tree stump	ตอไม้	dtor máai
campfire	กองไฟ	gorng fai
forest fire	ไฟป่า	fai bpàa
to extinguish (vt)	ดับไฟ	dàp fai
forest ranger	เจ้าหน้าที่ดูแลป่า	jâo nâa-thêe doo lae bpàa
protection	การปกป้อง	gaan bpòk bpôrng
to protect (~ nature)	ปกป้อง	bpòk bpôrng
poacher	นักลอบล่าสัตว์	nák lôrp lâa sàt
steel trap	กับดักเหล็ก	gàp dàk lèk
to gather, to pick (vt)	เก็บ	gèp
to lose one's way	หลงทาง	lǒng thaang

205. Natural resources

natural resources	ทรัพยากรธรรมชาติ	sáp-pá-yaa-gon tham-má-châat
minerals	แร่	râe
deposits	ตะกอน	dtà-gorn
field (e.g., oilfield)	บ่อ	bòr
to mine (extract)	ขุดแร่	khùt râe
mining (extraction)	การขุดแร่	gaan khùt râe
ore	แร่	râe
mine (e.g., for coal)	เหมืองแร่	měuang râe
shaft (mine ~)	ช่องเหมือง	chôrng měuang
miner	คนงานเหมือง	khon ngaan měuang
gas (natural ~)	แก๊ส	gáet
gas pipeline	ท่อแก๊ส	thôr gáet
oil (petroleum)	น้ำมัน	nám man
oil pipeline	ท่อน้ำมัน	thôr náam man
oil well	บ่อน้ำมัน	bòr náam man
derrick (tower)	ปั้นจั่นขนาดใหญ่	bpân jàn khà-nàat yài
tanker	เรือบรรทุกน้ำมัน	reua ban-thúk nám man
sand	ทราย	saai
limestone	หินปูน	hǐn bpoon

gravel	กรวด	grùat
peat	พีต	phêet
clay	ดินเหนียว	din nïeow
coal	ถ่านหิน	thàan hĭn

iron (ore)	เหล็ก	lèk
gold	ทอง	thorng
silver	เงิน	ngern
nickel	นิเกิล	ní-gêrn
copper	ทองแดง	thorng daeng

zinc	สังกะสี	săng-gà-sĕe
manganese	แมงกานีส	maeng-gaa-nêet
mercury	ปรอท	bpa -ròrt
lead	ตะกั่ว	dtà-gùa

mineral	แร่	râe
crystal	ผลึก	phà-lèuk
marble	หินออน	hĭn òrn
uranium	ยูเรเนียม	yoo-ray-niam

The Earth. Part 2

206. Weather

weather	สภาพอากาศ	sà-phâap aa-gàat
weather forecast	พยากรณ์ สภาพอากาศ	phá-yaa-gon sà-phâap aa-gàat
temperature	อุณหภูมิ	un-hà-phoom
thermometer	ปรอทวัดอุณหภูมิ	bpà-ròrt wát un-hà-phoom
barometer	เครื่องวัดความดัน บรรยากาศ	khrêuang wát khwaam dan ban-yaa-gàat
humid (adj)	ชื้น	chéun
humidity	ความชื้น	khwaam chéun
heat (extreme ~)	ความร้อน	khwaam rórn
hot (torrid)	ร้อน	rórn
it's hot	มันร้อน	man rórn
it's warm	มันอุ่น	man ùn
warm (moderately hot)	อุ่น	ùn
it's cold	อากาศเย็น	aa-gàat yen
cold (adj)	เย็น	yen
sun	ดวงอาทิตย์	duang aa-thít
to shine (vi)	ส่องแสง	sòrng săeng
sunny (day)	มีแสงแดด	mee săeng dàet
to come up (vi)	ขึ้น	khêun
to set (vi)	ตก	dtòk
cloud	เมฆ	mâyk
cloudy (adj)	มีเมฆมาก	mee mâyk mâak
rain cloud	เมฆฝน	mâyk fŏn
somber (gloomy)	มืดครึ้ม	mêut khréum
rain	ฝน	fŏn
it's raining	ฝนตก	fŏn dtòk
rainy (~ day, weather)	ฝนตก	fŏn dtòk
to drizzle (vi)	ฝนปรอย	fòn bproi
pouring rain	ฝนตกหนัก	fŏn dtòk nàk
downpour	ฝนห่าใหญ่	fŏn hàa yài
heavy (e.g., ~ rain)	หนัก	nàk
puddle	หลุมน้ำ	lòm nám
to get wet (in rain)	เปียก	bpìak

fog (mist)	หมอก	mòrk
foggy	หมอกจัด	mòrk jàt
snow	หิมะ	hì-má
it's snowing	หิมะตก	hì-má dtòk

207. Severe weather. Natural disasters

thunderstorm	พายุฟ้าคะนอง	phaa-yú fáa khá-nong
lightning (~ strike)	ฟ้าผา	fáa phàa
to flash (vi)	แลบ	lâep
thunder	ฟ้าคะนอง	fáa khá-norng
to thunder (vi)	มีฟ้าคะนอง	mee fáa khá-norng
it's thundering	มีฟ้าร้อง	mee fáa rórng
hail	ลูกเห็บ	lôok hèp
it's hailing	มีลูกเห็บตก	mee lôok hèp dtòk
to flood (vt)	ท่วม	thûam
flood, inundation	น้ำท่วม	nám thûam
earthquake	แผ่นดินไหว	phàen din wǎi
tremor, shoke	ไหว	wǎi
epicenter	จุดเหนือศูนย์	jùt něua sǒon
	แผ่นดินไหว	phàen din wǎi
eruption	ภูเขาไฟระเบิด	phoo khǎo fai rá-bèrt
lava	ลาวา	laa-waa
twister	พายุหมุน	phaa-yú mǔn
tornado	พายุทอร์เนโด	phaa-yú thor-nay-doh
typhoon	พายุไต้ฝุ่น	phaa-yú dtâi fùn
hurricane	พายุเฮอร์ริเคน	phaa-yú her-rí-khayn
storm	พายุ	phaa-yú
tsunami	คลื่นสึนามิ	khlêun sèu-naa-mí
cyclone	พายุไซโคลน	phaa-yú sai-khlohn
bad weather	อากาศไม่ดี	aa-gàat mâi dee
fire (accident)	ไฟไหม	fai mâi
disaster	ความหายนะ	khwaam hǎa-yá-ná
meteorite	อุกกาบาต	ùk-gaa-bàat
avalanche	หิมะถล่ม	hì-má thà-lòm
snowslide	หิมะถลม	hì-má thà-lòm
blizzard	พายุหิมะ	phaa-yú hì-má
snowstorm	พายุหิมะ	phaa-yú hì-má

208. Noises. Sounds

silence (quiet)	ความเงียบ	khwaam ngîap
sound	เสียง	sĭang
noise	เสียงรบกวน	sĭang róp guan
to make noise	ทำเสียง	tam sĭang
noisy (adj)	หนวกหู	nùak hŏo
loudly (to speak, etc.)	เสียงดัง	sĭang dang
loud (voice, etc.)	ดัง	dang
constant (e.g., ~ noise)	ต่อเนื่อง	dtòr nêuang
cry, shout (n)	เสียงตะโกน	sĭang dtà-gohn
to cry, to shout (vi)	ตะโกน	dtà-gohn
whisper	เสียงกระซิบ	sĭang grà síp
to whisper (vi, vt)	กระซิบ	grà síp
barking (dog's ~)	เสียงเห่า	sĭang hào
to bark (vi)	เห่า	hào
groan (of pain, etc.)	เสียงคราง	sĭang khraang
to groan (vi)	คราง	khraang
cough	เสียงไอ	sĭang ai
to cough (vi)	ไอ	ai
whistle	เสียงผิวปาก	sĭang phĭw bpàak
to whistle (vi)	ผิวปาก	phĭw bpàak
knock (at the door)	เสียงเคาะ	sĭang khór
to knock (on the door)	เคาะ	khór
to crack (vi)	เปรี๊ยะ	bpría
crack (cracking sound)	เสียงเปรี๊ยะ	sĭang bpría
siren	เสียงสัญญาณเตือน	sĭang săn-yaan dteuan
whistle (factory ~, etc.)	เสียงนกหวีด	sĭang nók wèet
to whistle (ab. train)	เป่านกหวีด	bpào nók wèet
honk (car horn sound)	เสียงแตร	sĭang dtrae
to honk (vi)	บีบแตร	bèep dtrae

209. Winter

winter (n)	ฤดูหนาว	réu-doo năao
winter (as adj)	ฤดูหนาว	réu-doo năao
in winter	ช่วงฤดูหนาว	chûang réu-doo năao
snow	หิมะ	hì-má
it's snowing	มีหิมะตก	mee hì-má dtòk
snowfall	หิมะตก	hì-má dtòk
snowdrift	กองหิมะ	gong hì-má

snowflake	เกล็ดหิมะ	glèt hì-má
snowball	ก้อนหิมะ	gôn hì-má
snowman	ตุ๊กตาหิมะ	dtúk-gà-dtaa hì-má
icicle	แทงน้ำแข็ง	thâeng nám khǎeng
December	ธันวาคม	than-waa khom
January	มกราคม	mók-gà-raa khom
February	กุมภาพันธ์	gum-phaa phan
frost (severe ~, freezing cold)	ความหนาวๆ	kwaam nǎao nǎao
frosty (weather, air)	หนาวจัด	nǎao jàt
below zero (adv)	ต่ำกว่าศูนย์องศา	dtàm gwàa sǒon ong-sǎa
first frost	ลมหนาวแรก	lom nǎao râek
hoarfrost	น้ำค้างแข็ง	náam kháang khǎeng
cold (cold weather)	ความหนาว	khwaam nǎao
it's cold	อากาศหนาว	aa-gàat nǎao
fur coat	เสื้อโค้ทขนสัตว์	sêua khóht khǒn sàt
mittens	ถุงมือ	thǔng meu
to get sick	เป็นหวัด	bpen wàt
cold (illness)	หวัด	wàt
to catch a cold	เป็นหวัด	bpen wàt
ice	น้ำแข็ง	nám khǎeng
black ice	น้ำแข็งบาง บนพื้นถนน	nám khǎeng baang bon phéun thà-nǒn
to freeze over (ab. river, etc.)	แช่แข็ง	châe khǎeng
ice floe	แพน้ำแข็ง	phae nám khǎeng
skis	สกี	sà-gee
skier	นักสกี	nák sà-gee
to ski (vi)	เล่นสกี	lên sà-gee
to skate (vi)	เล่นสเก็ต	lên sà-gèt

Fauna

210. Mammals. Predators

predator	สัตว์กินเนื้อ	sàt gin néua
tiger	เสือ	sĕua
lion	สิงโต	sĭng dtoh
wolf	หมาป่า	măa bpàa
fox	หมาจิ้งจอก	măa jîng-jòk
jaguar	เสือจากัวร์	sĕua jaa-gua
leopard	เสือดาว	sĕua daao
cheetah	เสือชีตาห์	sĕua chee-dtaa
black panther	เสือดำ	sĕua dam
puma	สิงโตภูเขา	sĭng-dtoh phoo khăo
snow leopard	เสือดาวหิมะ	sĕua daao hì-má
lynx	แมวป่า	maew bpàa
coyote	โคโยตี้	khoh-yoh-dtêe
jackal	หมาจิ้งจอกทอง	măa jîng-jòk thorng
hyena	ไฮยีนา	hai-yee-naa

211. Wild animals

animal	สัตว์	sàt
beast (animal)	สัตว์	sàt
squirrel	กระรอก	grà rôk
hedgehog	เม่น	mâyn
hare	กระต่ายป่า	grà-dtàai bpàa
rabbit	กระต่าย	grà-dtàai
badger	แบดเจอร์	baet-jer
raccoon	แร็คคูน	ráek khoon
hamster	หนูแฮมสเตอร์	nŏo haem-sà-dtêr
marmot	มารมอต	maa-môt
mole	ตุ่น	dtùn
mouse	หนู	nŏo
rat	หนู	nŏo
bat	ค้างคาว	kháang khaao
ermine	เออร์มิน	er-min
sable	เซเบิล	say bern

marten	มาร์เทิน	maa thern
weasel	เพียงพอน	phiang phon
	สีน้ำตาล	sĕe nám dtaan
mink	เพียงพอน	phiang phorn
beaver	บีเวอร์	bee-wer
otter	นาก	nâak
horse	ม้า	máa
moose	กวางมูส	gwaang môot
deer	กวาง	gwaang
camel	อูฐ	òot
bison	วัวป่า	wua bpàa
wisent	วัวป่าออรอช	wua bpàa or rôt
buffalo	ควาย	khwaai
zebra	มาลาย	máa laai
antelope	แอนทีโลป	aen-thi-lòp
roe deer	กวางโรเดียร์	gwaang roh-dia
fallow deer	กวางแฟลโลว์	gwaang flae-loh
chamois	เลียงผา	liang-phăa
wild boar	หมูป่า	mŏo bpàa
whale	วาฬ	waan
seal	แมวน้ำ	maew náam
walrus	ช้างน้ำ	cháang náam
fur seal	แมวน้ำมีขน	maew náam mee khŏn
dolphin	โลมา	loh-maa
bear	หมี	mĕe
polar bear	หมีขั้วโลก	mĕe khûa lôhk
panda	หมีแพนด้า	mĕe phaen-dâa
monkey	ลิง	ling
chimpanzee	ลิงชิมแปนซี	ling chim-bpaen-see
orangutan	ลิงอุรังอุตัง	ling u-rang-u-dtang
gorilla	ลิงกอริลลา	ling gor-rin-lâa
macaque	ลิงแม็กแคก	ling mâk-khâk
gibbon	ชะนี	chá-nee
elephant	ช้าง	cháang
rhinoceros	แรด	râet
giraffe	ยีราฟ	yee-râaf
hippopotamus	ฮิปโปโปเตมัส	híp-bpoh-bpoh-dtay-mát
kangaroo	จิงโจ้	jing-jôh
koala (bear)	หมีโคอาล่า	mĕe khoh aa lâa
mongoose	พังพอน	phang phon
chinchilla	คินคิลลา	khin-khin laa
skunk	สกุ้งก	sà-gang
porcupine	เมน	mâyn

212. Domestic animals

cat	แมวตัวเมีย	maew dtua mia
tomcat	แมวตัวผู้	maew dtua phôo
dog	สุนัข	sù-nák
horse	ม้า	máa
stallion (male horse)	ม้าตัวผู้	máa dtua phôo
mare	มาตัวเมีย	máa dtua mia
cow	วัว	wua
bull	กระทิง	grà-thing
ox	วัว	wua
sheep (ewe)	แกะตัวเมีย	gàe dtua mia
ram	แกะตัวผู้	gàe dtua phôo
goat	แพะตัวเมีย	pháe dtua mia
billy goat, he-goat	แพะตัวผู้	pháe dtua phôo
donkey	ลา	laa
mule	ลอ	lôr
pig, hog	หมู	mǒo
piglet	ลูกหมู	lôok mǒo
rabbit	กระต่าย	grà-dtàai
hen (chicken)	ไก่ตัวเมีย	gài dtua mia
rooster	ไกตัวผู้	gài dtua phôo
duck	เป็ดตัวเมีย	bpèt dtua mia
drake	เป็ดตัวผู้	bpèt dtua phôo
goose	หาน	hàan
tom turkey, gobbler	ไก่งวงตัวผู้	gài nguang dtua phôo
turkey (hen)	ไกงวงตัวเมีย	gài nguang dtua mia
domestic animals	สัตว์เลี้ยง	sàt líang
tame (e.g., ~ hamster)	เลี้ยง	líang
to tame (vt)	เชื่อง	chêuang
to breed (vt)	ขยายพันธุ์	khà-yǎai phan
farm	ฟาร์ม	faam
poultry	สัตว์ปีก	sàt bpèek
cattle	วัวควาย	wua khwaai
herd (cattle)	ฝูง	fǒong
stable	คอกม้า	khôrk máa
pigpen	คอกหมู	khôrk mǒo
cowshed	คอกวัว	khôrk wua
rabbit hutch	คอกกระต่าย	khôrk grà-dtàai
hen house	เลาไก	láo gài

213. Dogs. Dog breeds

dog	สุนัข	sù-nák
sheepdog	สุนัขเลี้ยงแกะ	sù-nák líang gàe
German shepherd	เยอรมันเชฟเฟิร์ด	yer-rá-man chayf-fêrt
poodle	พูเดิ้ล	phoo dêrn
dachshund	ดัชชุน	dàt chun
bulldog	บูลด็อก	boon dòrk
boxer	ป๊อกเซอร์	bòk-sêr
mastiff	มัสตีฟ	mát-dtèef
Rottweiler	ร็อตไวเลอร์	rót-wai-ler
Doberman	โดเบอร์แมน	doh-ber-maen
basset	บาสเซ็ต	bàat-sét
bobtail	บ็อบเทล	bòp-thayn
Dalmatian	ดัลเมเชียน	dan-may-chian
cocker spaniel	ค็อกเกอรสเปเนียล	khórk-gêr sà-bpay-nian
Newfoundland	นิวฟาวน์ดฮาวน์ดแลนด์	niw-faao-dà-haao-dà-lǎen
Saint Bernard	เซนตเบอรนารด	sayn ber nâat
husky	ฮัสกี้	hát-gêe
Chow Chow	เชาเชา	chao chao
spitz	สูปิตซ	sà-bpìt
pug	ปั๊ก	bpák

214. Sounds made by animals

barking (n)	เสียงเห่า	sìang hào
to bark (vi)	เห่า	hào
to meow (vi)	ร้องเหมียว	rórng mǐeow
to purr (vi)	ทำเสียงคราง	tham sìang khraang
to moo (vi)	ร้องมอๆ	rórng mor mor
to bellow (bull)	ส่งเสียงคำราม	sòng sǐang kham-raam
to growl (vi)	โฮก	hôhk
howl (n)	เสียงหอน	sǐang hǒn
to howl (vi)	หอน	hǒrn
to whine (vi)	ครางหงิงๆ	khraang ngǐng ngǐng
to bleat (sheep)	ร้องแบะๆ	rórng bàe bàe
to oink, to grunt (pig)	ร้องอูดๆ	rórng ùut ùut
to squeal (vi)	ร้องเสียงแหลม	rórng sǐang lǎem
to croak (vi)	ร้องอบๆ	rórng ôp ôp
to buzz (insect)	หึ่ง	hèung
to chirp (crickets, grasshopper)	ทำเสียงจ๊อกแจ๊ก	tham sǐang jòrk jáek

215. Young animals

cub	ลูกสัตว์	lôok sàt
kitten	ลูกแมว	lôok maew
baby mouse	ลูกหนู	lôok nǒo
puppy	ลูกหมา	lôok mǎa
leveret	ลูกกระต่ายป่า	lôok grà-dtàai bpàa
baby rabbit	ลูกกระต่าย	lôok grà-dtàai
wolf cub	ลูกหมาป่า	lôok mǎa bpàa
fox cub	ลูกหมาจิ้งจอก	lôok mǎa jîng-jòk
bear cub	ลูกหมี	lôok měe
lion cub	ลูกสิงโต	lôok sǐng dtoh
tiger cub	ลูกเสือ	lôok sěua
elephant calf	ลูกช้าง	lôok cháang
piglet	ลูกหมู	lôok mǒo
calf (young cow, bull)	ลูกวัว	lôok wua
kid (young goat)	ลูกแพะ	lôok pháe
lamb	ลูกแกะ	lôok gàe
fawn (young deer)	ลูกกวาง	lôok gwaang
young camel	ลูกอูฐ	lôok òot
snakelet (baby snake)	ลูกงู	lôok ngoo
froglet (baby frog)	ลูกกบ	lôok gòp
baby bird	ลูกนก	lôok nók
chick (of chicken)	ลูกไก่	lôok gài
duckling	ลูกเป็ด	lôok bpèt

216. Birds

bird	นก	nók
pigeon	นกพิราบ	nók phí-râap
sparrow	นกกระจิบ	nók grà-jìp
tit (great tit)	นกติ๊ด	nók dtít
magpie	นกสาลิกา	nók sǎa-lí gaa
raven	นกอีกา	nók ee-gaa
crow	นกกา	nók gaa
jackdaw	นกจำพวกกา	nók jam phûak gaa
rook	นกการูค	nók gaa róok
duck	เป็ด	bpèt
goose	ห่าน	hàan
pheasant	ไก่ฟ้า	gài fáa
eagle	นกอินทรี	nók in-see
hawk	นกเหยี่ยว	nók yìeow

falcon	นกเหยี่ยว	nók yìeow
vulture	นกแร้ง	nók ráeng
condor (Andean ~)	นกแร้งขนาดใหญ่	nók ráeng kà-nàat yài
swan	นกหงส์	nók hŏng
crane	นกกระเรียน	nók grà rian
stork	นกกระสา	nók grà-săa
parrot	นกแก้ว	nók gâew
hummingbird	นกฮัมมิ่งเบิร์ด	nók ham-mîng-bèrt
peacock	นกยูง	nók yoong
ostrich	นกกระจอกเทศ	nók grà-jòrk-thâyt
heron	นกยาง	nók yaang
flamingo	นกฟลามิงโก	nók flaa-ming-goh
pelican	นกกระทุง	nók-grà-thung
nightingale	นกไนติงเกล	nók-nai-dting-gayn
swallow	นกนางแอ่น	nók naang-àen
thrush	นกเดินดง	nók dern dong
song thrush	นกเดินดง ร้องเพลง	nók dern dong rórng phlayng
blackbird	นกเดินดงสีดำ	nók-dern-dong sĕe dam
swift	นกแอ่น	nók àen
lark	นกลาร์ค	nók lâak
quail	นกคุ่ม	nók khûm
woodpecker	นกหัวขวาน	nók hŭa khwăan
cuckoo	นกดุเหว่า	nók dù hăy wâa
owl	นกฮูก	nók hôok
eagle owl	นกเค้าใหญ่	nók kháo yài
wood grouse	ไก่ป่า	gài bpàa
black grouse	ไก่ดำ	gài dam
partridge	นกกระทา	nók-grà-thaa
starling	นกกิ้งโครง	nók-gîng-khrohng
canary	นกขมิ้น	nók khà-mîn
hazel grouse	ไก่น้ำตาล	gài nám dtaan
chaffinch	นกจาบ	nók-jàap
bullfinch	นกบูลฟินช์	nók boon-fin
seagull	นกนางนวล	nók naang-nuan
albatross	นกอัลบาทรอส	nók an-baa-thrôt
penguin	นกเพนกวิน	nók phayn-gwin

217. Birds. Singing and sounds

| to sing (vi) | ร้องเพลง | rórng phlayng |
| to call (animal, bird) | ร้อง | rórng |

| to crow (rooster) | ร้องขัน | rórng khăn |
| cock-a-doodle-doo | เสียงขัน | sĭang khăn |

to cluck (hen)	ร้องกุ๊กๆ	rórng gúk gúk
to caw (crow call)	ร้องเสียงกาๆ	rórng sĭang gaa gaa
to quack (duck call)	ร้องกาบๆ	rórng gâap gâap
to cheep (vi)	ร้องเสียงจิ๊บ ๆ	rórng sĭang jíp jíp
to chirp, to twitter	ร้องจอกแจก	rórng jòk jáek

218. Fish. Marine animals

bream	ปลาบรีม	bplaa bpreem
carp	ปลาคาร์ป	bplaa khâap
perch	ปลาเพิร์ช	bplaa phêrt
catfish	ปลาดุก	bplaa-dùk
pike	ปลาไพค์	bplaa phai

| salmon | ปลาแชลมอน | bplaa saen-morn |
| sturgeon | ปลาสเตอร์เจียน | bpláa sà-dtêr jian |

| herring | ปลาเฮอร์ริง | bplaa her-ring |
| Atlantic salmon | ปลาแชลมอน แอตแลนติก | bplaa saen-mon àet-laen-dtìk |

| mackerel | ปลาซาบะ | bplaa saa-bà |
| flatfish | ปลาลิ้นหมา | bplaa lín-măa |

zander, pike perch	ปลาไพค์เพิร์ช	bplaa phái phert
cod	ปลาค็อด	bplaa khót
tuna	ปลาทูน่า	bplaa thoo-nâa
trout	ปลาเทราท์	bplaa thrau

eel	ปลาไหล	bplaa lăi
electric ray	ปลากระเบนไฟฟ้า	bplaa grà-bayn-fai-fáa
moray eel	ปลาไหลมอเรย์	bplaa lăi mor-ray
piranha	ปลาปิรันยา	bplaa bpì-ran-yâa

shark	ปลาฉลาม	bplaa chà-lăam
dolphin	โลมา	loh-maa
whale	วาฬ	waan

crab	ปู	bpoo
jellyfish	แมงกะพรุน	maeng gà-phrun
octopus	ปลาหมึก	bplaa mèuk

starfish	ปลาดาว	bplaa daao
sea urchin	หอยเม่น	hŏi mâyn
seahorse	ม้าน้ำ	máa nám

| oyster | หอยนางรม | hŏi naang rom |
| shrimp | กุ้ง | gûng |

| lobster | กุ้งมังกร | gûng mang-gon |
| spiny lobster | กุ้งมังกร | gûng mang-gon |

219. Amphibians. Reptiles

| snake | งู | ngoo |
| venomous (snake) | พิษ | phít |

viper	งูแมวเซา	ngoo maew sao
cobra	งูเห่า	ngoo hào
python	งูเหลือม	ngoo lĕuam
boa	งูโบอา	ngoo boh-aa

grass snake	งูเล็กที่ไม่เป็น อันตราย	ngoo lék thêe mâi bpen an-dtà-raai
rattle snake	งูหางกระดิ่ง	ngoo hăang grà-dìng
anaconda	งูอนาคอนดา	ngoo a -naa-khon-daa

lizard	กิ้งก่า	gîng-gàa
iguana	อีกัวนา	ee gua naa
monitor lizard	กิ้งกามอนิเตอร์	gîng-gàa mor-ní-dtêr
salamander	ซาลาแมนเดอร	saa-laa-maen-dêr
chameleon	กิ้งกาคามิเลียน	gîng-gàa khaa-mí-lian
scorpion	แมงป่อง	maeng bpòrng

turtle	เต่า	dtào
frog	กบ	gòp
toad	คางคก	khaang-kók
crocodile	จระเข้	jor-rá-khây

220. Insects

insect, bug	แมลง	má-laeng
butterfly	ผีเสื้อ	phĕe sêua
ant	มด	mót
fly	แมลงวัน	má-laeng wan
mosquito	ยุง	yung
beetle	แมลงปีกแข็ง	má-laeng bpèek khăeng

wasp	ตัวต่อ	dtòr
bee	ผึ้ง	phêung
bumblebee	ผึ้งบัมเบิลบี	phêung bam-bern bee
gadfly (botfly)	เหลือบ	lèuap

spider	แมงมุม	maeng mum
spiderweb	ใยแมงมุม	yai maeng mum
dragonfly	แมลงปอ	má-laeng bpor
grasshopper	ตั๊กแตน	dták-gà-dtaen

moth (night butterfly)	ผีเสื้อกลางคืน	phěe sêua glaang kheun
cockroach	แมลงสาบ	má-laeng sàap
tick	เห็บ	hèp
flea	หมัด	màt
midge	ริ้น	rín

locust	ตั๊กแตน	dták-gà-dtaen
snail	หอยทาก	hǒi thâak
cricket	จิ้งหรีด	jîng-rèet
lightning bug	หิ่งห้อย	hìng-hôi
ladybug	แมลงเต่าทอง	má-laeng dtào thorng
cockchafer	แมงอีนูน	maeng ee noon

leech	ปลิง	bpling
caterpillar	บุ้ง	bûng
earthworm	ไส้เดือน	sâi deuan
larva	ตัวอ่อน	dtua òrn

221. Animals. Body parts

beak	จงอยปาก	ja-ngoi bpàak
wings	ปีก	bpèek
foot (of bird)	เท้า	tháo
feathers (plumage)	ขนนก	khǒn nók
feather	ขนนก	khǒn nók
crest	ขนหัว	khǒn hǔa

gills	เหงือก	ngèuak
spawn	ไข่ปลา	khài-bplaa
larva	ตัวอ่อน	dtua òrn
fin	ครีบ	khrêep
scales (of fish, reptile)	เกล็ด	glèt

fang (canine)	เขี้ยว	khîeow
paw (e.g., cat's ~)	เท้า	tháo
muzzle (snout)	จมูกและปาก	jà-mòok láe bpàak
maw (mouth)	ปาก	bpàak

| tail | หาง | hǎang |
| whiskers | หนวด | nùat |

| hoof | กีบ | gèep |
| horn | เขา | khǎo |

carapace	กระดอง	grà dorng
shell (of mollusk)	เปลือก	bplèuak
eggshell	เปลือกไข่	bplèuak khài

| animal's hair (pelage) | ขน | khǒn |
| pelt (hide) | หนัง | nǎng |

222. Actions of animals

to fly (vi)	บิน	bin
to fly in circles	บินวน	bin-won
to fly away	บินไป	bin bpai
to flap (~ the wings)	กระพือ	grà-pheu
to peck (vi)	จิก	jìk
to sit on eggs	กกไข่	gòk khài
to hatch out (vi)	ฟักตัวออกจากไข่	fák dtua òrk jàak kài
to build a nest	สร้างรัง	sâang rang
to slither, to crawl	เลื้อย	léuay
to sting, to bite (insect)	ต่อย	dtòi
to bite (ab. animal)	กัด	gàt
to sniff (vt)	ดม	dom
to bark (vi)	เห่า	hào
to hiss (snake)	ออกเสียงฟ่อ	òrk sĭang fôr
to scare (vt)	ทำให้...กลัว	tham hâi...glua
to attack (vt)	จู่โจม	jòo johm
to gnaw (bone, etc.)	ขุบ	khòp
to scratch (with claws)	ข่วน	khùan
to hide (vi)	ซ่อน	sôrn
to play (kittens, etc.)	เล่น	lên
to hunt (vi, vt)	ล่า	lâa
to hibernate (vi)	จำศีล	jam sĕen
to go extinct	สูญพันธุ์	sŏon phan

223. Animals. Habitats

habitat	ที่อยู่อาศัย	thêe yòo aa-săi
migration	การอพยพ	gaan òp-phá-yóp
mountain	ภูเขา	phoo khăo
reef	แนวปะการัง	naew bpà-gaa-rang
cliff	หน้าผา	nâa phăa
forest	ป่า	bpàa
jungle	ป่าดิบชื้น	bpàa dìp chéun
savanna	สะวันนา	sà wan naa
tundra	ทันดรา	than-draa
steppe	ทุ่งหญ้าสเตปป์	thûng yâa sà-dtàyp
desert	ทะเลทราย	thá-lay saai
oasis	โอเอซิส	oh-ay-sít
sea	ทะเล	thá-lay

| lake | ทะเลสาบ | thá-lay sàap |
| ocean | มหาสมุทร | má-hǎa sà-mùt |

swamp (marshland)	บึง	beung
freshwater (adj)	น้ำจืด	nám jèut
pond	บ่อน้ำ	bòr náam
river	แม่น้ำ	mâe náam

den (bear's ~)	ถ้ำสัตว์	thâm sàt
nest	รัง	rang
tree hollow	โพรงไม้	phrohng máai
burrow (animal hole)	โพรง	phrohng
anthill	รังมด	rang mót

224. Animal care

| zoo | สวนสัตว์ | sǔan sàt |
| nature preserve | เขตสงวน ธรรมชาติ | khàyt sà-ngǔan tham-má-châat |

breeder (cattery, kennel, etc.)	ที่ขยายพันธุ์	thêe khà-yǎai phan
open-air cage	กรง	grorng
cage	กรง	grorng
doghouse (kennel)	บ้านสุนัข	baan sù-nák

dovecot	บ้านนกพิราบ	bâan nók phí-râap
aquarium (fish tank)	ตู้ปลา	dtôo bplaa
dolphinarium	บ่อโลมา	bòr loh-maa

to breed (animals)	ขยายพันธุ์	khà-yǎai phan
brood, litter	ลูกสัตว์	lôok sàt
to tame (vt)	เชื่อง	chêuang
to train (animals)	ฝึก	fèuk
feed (fodder, etc.)	อาหาร	aa-hǎan
to feed (vt)	ให้อาหาร	hâi aa-hǎan

pet store	ร้านสัตว์เลี้ยง	ráan sàt líang
muzzle (for dog)	ตะกร้อปาก	dtà-grôr bpàak
collar (e.g., dog ~)	ปลอกคอ	bplòrk kor
name (of animal)	ชื่อ	chêu
pedigree (of dog)	สายพันธุ์	sǎai phan

225. Animals. Miscellaneous

pack (wolves)	ฝูง	fǒong
flock (birds)	ฝูง	fǒong
shoal, school (fish)	ฝูง	fǒong

herd (horses)	ฝูง	fŏong
male (n)	ตัวผู้	dtua phôo
female (n)	ตัวเมีย	dtua mia
hungry (adj)	หิว	hĭw
wild (adj)	ป่า	bpàa
dangerous (adj)	อันตราย	an-dtà-raai

226. Horses

horse	ม้า	máa
breed (race)	พันธุ์	phan
foal	ลูกม้า	lôok máa
mare	มาตัวเมีย	máa dtua mia
mustang	ม้าป่า	máa bpàa
pony	ม้าพันธุ์เล็ก	máa phan lék
draft horse	มางาน	máa ngaan
mane	แผงคอ	phăeng khor
tail	หาง	hăang
hoof	กีบ	gèep
horseshoe	เกือก	gèuak
to shoe (vt)	ใส่เกือก	sài gèuak
blacksmith	ช่างเหล็ก	châang lèk
saddle	อานม้า	aan máa
stirrup	โกลน	glohn
bridle	บังเหียน	bang hĭan
reins	สายบังเหียน	săai bang hĭan
whip (for riding)	แส	sâe
rider	นักขี่ม้า	nák khèe máa
to saddle up (vt)	ใส่อานม้า	sài aan máa
to mount a horse	ขึ้นขี่มา	khêun khèe máa
gallop	การควบม้า	gaan khûap máa
to gallop (vi)	ควบม้า	khûap máa
trot (n)	การเหยาะย่ง	gaan yòr yâang
at a trot (adv)	แบบเหยาะย่าง	bàep yòr yâang
to go at a trot	เหยาะย่าง	yòr yâang
racehorse	ม้าแข่ง	máa khàeng
horse racing	การแข่งม้า	gaan khàeng máa
stable	คอกม้า	khôrk máa
to feed (vt)	ให้อาหาร	hâi aa-hăan
hay	หญ้าแหง	yâa hâeng

to water (animals)	ให้น้ำ	hâi nám
to wash (horse)	ทำความสะอาด	tham khwaam sà-àat
horse-drawn cart	รถเทียมม้า	rót thiam máa
to graze (vi)	เล็มหญ้า	lem yâa
to neigh (vi)	ร้องฮี่ๆ	rórng híí híí
to kick (to buck)	ถีบ	thèep

Flora

227. Trees

tree	ต้นไม้	dtôn máai
deciduous (adj)	ผลัดใบ	phlàt bai
coniferous (adj)	สน	sǒn
evergreen (adj)	ซึ่งเขียวชอุ่ม ตลอดปี	sêung khǐeow chá-ùm dtà-lòrt bpee
apple tree	ต้นแอปเปิ้ล	dtôn àep-bpêrn
pear tree	ต้นแพร	dtôn phae
sweet cherry tree	ต้นเชอร์รี่ป่า	dtôn cher-rêe bpàa
sour cherry tree	ต้นเชอร์รี่	dtôn cher-rêe
plum tree	ตนพลัม	dtôn phlam
birch	ต้นเบิร์ช	dtôn bèrt
oak	ต้นโอ๊ค	dtôn óhk
linden tree	ต้นไม้ดอกเหลือง	dtôn máai dòrk lěuang
aspen	ต้นแอสเพน	dtôn ae sà-phayn
maple	ตนเมเปิ้ล	dtôn may bpêrn
spruce	ต้นเฟอร์	dtôn fer
pine	ต้นเกี๊ยะ	dtôn gía
larch	ต้นลารช	dtôn lâat
fir tree	ต้นเฟอร์	dtôn fer
cedar	ตนซีดาร	dtôn-see-daa
poplar	ต้นปอปลาร์	dtôn bpor-bplaa
rowan	ต้นโรแวน	dtôn-roh-waen
willow	ต้นวิลโลว	dtôn win-loh
alder	ตนอัลเดอร	dtôn an-dêr
beech	ต้นบีช	dtôn bèet
elm	ต้นเอลม	dtôn elm
ash (tree)	ต้นแอช	dtôn aesh
chestnut	ตนเกาลัด	dtôn gao lát
magnolia	ต้นแมกโนเลีย	dtôn mâek-noh-lia
palm tree	ต้นปาลม	dtôn bpaam
cypress	ตนไซเปรส	dtôn-sai-bpràyt
mangrove	ต้นโกงกาง	dtôn gohng gaang
baobab	ต้นเบาบับ	dtôn bao-bàp
eucalyptus	ต้นยูคาลิปตัส	dtôn yoo-khaa-líp-dtàt
sequoia	ตนสนซีค้วยา	dtôn sǒn see kua yaa

228. Shrubs

bush	พุ่มไม้	phûm máai
shrub	ต้นไม้พุ่ม	dtôn máai phûm
grapevine	ต้นองุ่น	dtôn a-ngùn
vineyard	ไร่องุ่น	râi a-ngùn
raspberry bush	พุ่มราสเบอร์รี่	phûm râat-ber-rêe
blackcurrant bush	พุ่มแบล็คเคอร์แรนท์	phûm blàek-khêr-raen
redcurrant bush	พุ่มเรดเคอร์แรนท์	phûm râyt-khêr-raen
gooseberry bush	พุ่มกูสเบอร์รี่	phûm gòot-ber-rêe
acacia	ต้นอาเคเชีย	dtôn aa-khay-chia
barberry	ต้นบาร์เบอร์รี่	dtôn baa-ber-rêe
jasmine	มะลิ	má-lí
juniper	ต้นจูนิเปอร์	dtôn joo-ní-bper
rosebush	พุ่มกุหลาบ	phûm gù làap
dog rose	พุ่มด็อกโรส	phûm dòrk-rôht

229. Mushrooms

mushroom	เห็ด	hèt
edible mushroom	เห็ดกินได้	hèt gin dâai
poisonous mushroom	เห็ดมีพิษ	hèt mee pít
cap (of mushroom)	ดอกเห็ด	dòrk hèt
stipe (of mushroom)	ต้นเห็ด	dtôn hèt
cep (Boletus edulis)	เห็ดพอร์ชินี	hèt phor chí nee
orange-cap boletus	เห็ดพอร์ชินีดอกเหลือง	hèt phor chí nee dòrk lěuang
birch bolete	เห็ดตับเต่าที่ขึ้นบนต้นเบิรช	hèt dtàp dtào thêe khêun bon dtôn-bèrt
chanterelle	เห็ดก่อเหลือง	hèt gòr lěuang
russula	เห็ดตะไค	hèt dtà khai
morel	เห็ดมอเรล	hèt mor rayn
fly agaric	เห็ดพิษหมวกแดง	hèt phít mùak daeng
death cap	เห็ดระโงกหิน	hèt rá ngôhk hǐn

230. Fruits. Berries

fruit	ผลไม้	phǒn-lá-máai
fruits	ผลไม	phǒn-lá-máai
apple	แอปเปิ้ล	àep-bpêrn
pear	ลูกแพร	lôok phae

plum	พลัม	phlam
strawberry (garden ~)	สตรอว์เบอร์รี่	sà-dtror-ber-rêe
sour cherry	เชอร์รี่	cher-rêe
sweet cherry	เชอร์รี่ป่า	cher-rêe bpàa
grape	องุ่น	a-ngùn

raspberry	ราสเบอร์รี่	râat-ber-rêe
blackcurrant	แบล็คเคอร์แรนท์	blàek khêr-raen
redcurrant	เรดเคอร์แรนท	râyt-khêr-raen
gooseberry	กูสเบอร์รี่	gòot-ber-rêe
cranberry	แครนเบอร์รี่	khraen-ber-rêe

orange	ส้ม	sôm
mandarin	สมแมนดาริน	sôm maen daa rin
pineapple	สับปะรด	sàp-bpà-rót
banana	กล้วย	glûay
date	อินทผลัม	in-thá-phâ-lam

lemon	เลมอน	lay-mon
apricot	แอปริคอท	ae-bprì-khôrt
peach	ลูกทอ	lôok thór
kiwi	กีวี	gee wee
grapefruit	สมโอ	sôm oh

berry	เบอร์รี่	ber-rêe
berries	เบอร์รี่	ber-rêe
cowberry	คาวเบอร์รี่	khaao-ber-rêe
wild strawberry	สตรอวเบอร์รี่ป่า	sá-dtrorw ber-rêe bpàa
bilberry	บิลเบอร์รี่	bil-ber-rêe

231. Flowers. Plants

| flower | ดอกไม้ | dòrk máai |
| bouquet (of flowers) | ชอดอกไม้ | chôr dòrk máai |

rose (flower)	ดอกกุหลาบ	dòrk gù làap
tulip	ดอกทิวลิป	dòrk thiw-líp
carnation	ดอกคาร์เนชั่น	dòrk khaa-nay-chân
gladiolus	ดอกแกลดิโอลัส	dòrk gaen-dì-oh-lát

| cornflower | ดอกคอร์นฟลาวเวอร์ | dòrk khon-flaao-wer |
| harebell | ดอกระฆัง | dòrk rá-khang |

| dandelion | ดอกแดนดิไลออน | dòrk daen-dì-lai-on |
| camomile | ดอกคาโมมายล | dòrk khaa-moh maai |

aloe	ว่านหางจระเข้	wâan-hăang-jor-rá-khây
cactus	ตะบองเพชร	dtà-bong-phét
rubber plant, ficus	ตนเลียบ	dtôn lîap
lily	ดอกลิลี่	dòrk lí-lêe

geranium	ดอกเจอราเนียม	dòrk jer-raa-niam
hyacinth	ดอกไฮอะซินท์	dòrk hai-a-sin
mimosa	ดอกไมยราบ	dòrk mai râap
narcissus	ดอกนาร์ซิสซัส	dòrk naa-sít-sát
nasturtium	ดอกแนสเตอรชัม	dòrk nâet-dtêr-cham
orchid	ดอกกล้วยไม้	dòrk glûay máai
peony	ดอกโบตั๋น	dòrk boh-dtăn
violet	ดอกไวโอเล็ต	dòrk wai-oh-lét
pansy	ดอกแพนซี	dòrk phaen-see
forget-me-not	ดอกฟอร์เก็ตมีน็อต	dòrk for-gèt-mee-nót
daisy	ดอกเดซี	dòrk day see
poppy	ดอกป๊อปปี้	dòrk bpóp-bpêe
hemp	กัญชา	gan chaa
mint	สะระแหน่	sà-rá-nàe
lily of the valley	ดอกลิลลี่แห่ง หุบเขา	dòrk lí-lá-lêe hàeng hùp khăo
snowdrop	ดอกหยาดหิมะ	dòrk yàat hì-má
nettle	ตำแย	dtam-yae
sorrel	ซอรเรล	sor-rayn
water lily	บัว	bua
fern	เฟิร์น	fern
lichen	ไลเคน	lai-khayn
conservatory (greenhouse)	เรือนกระจก	reuan grà-jòk
lawn	สนามหญ้า	sà-năam yâa
flowerbed	สนามดอกไม้	sà-năam-dòrk-máai
plant	พืช	phêut
grass	หญ้า	yâa
blade of grass	ใบหญ้า	bai yâa
leaf	ใบไม้	bai máai
petal	กลีบดอก	glèep dòrk
stem	ลำต้น	lam dtôn
tuber	หัวใต้ดิน	hŭa dtâi din
young plant (shoot)	ต้นอ่อน	dtôn òrn
thorn	หนาม	năam
to blossom (vi)	บาน	baan
to fade, to wither	เหี่ยว	hìeow
smell (odor)	กลิ่น	glìn
to cut (flowers)	ตัด	dtàt
to pick (a flower)	เด็ด	dèt

232. Cereals, grains

grain	เมล็ด	má-lét
cereal crops	ธัญพืช	than-yá-phêut
ear (of barley, etc.)	รวงขาว	ruang khâao
wheat	ข้าวสาลี	khâao să-lee
rye	ขาวไรย์	khâao rai
oats	ข้าวโอ๊ต	khâao óht
millet	ข้าวฟ่าง	khâao fâang
barley	ขาวบาร์เลย์	khâao baa-lây
corn	ข้าวโพด	khâao-phôht
rice	ขาว	khâao
buckwheat	บัควีท	bàk-wêet
pea plant	ถั่วลันเตา	thùa-lan-dtao
kidney bean	ถั่วรูปไต	thùa rôop dtai
soy	ถั่วเหลือง	thùa lĕuang
lentil	ถั่วเลนทิล	thùa layn thin
beans (pulse crops)	ถั่ว	thùa

233. Vegetables. Greens

vegetables	ผัก	phàk
greens	ผักใบเขียว	phàk bai khĭeow
tomato	มะเขือเทศ	má-khĕua thâyt
cucumber	แตงกวา	dtaeng-gwaa
carrot	แครอท	khae-rót
potato	มันฝรั่ง	man fà-ràng
onion	หัวหอม	hŭa hŏrm
garlic	กระเทียม	grà-thiam
cabbage	กะหล่ำปลี	gà-làm bplee
cauliflower	ดอกกะหล่ำ	dòrk gà-làm
Brussels sprouts	กะหล่ำดาว	gà-làm-daao
broccoli	บร็อคโคลี่	bròrk-khoh-lêe
beet	บีท	beet
eggplant	มะเขือยาว	má-khĕua-yaao
zucchini	ชูกินี	soo-gi -nee
pumpkin	ฟักทอง	fák-thorng
turnip	หัวผักกาด	hŭa-phàk-gàat
parsley	ผักชีฝรั่ง	phàk chee fà-ràng
dill	ผักชีลาว	phàk-chee-laao
lettuce	ผักกาดหอม	phàk gàat hŏrm
celery	คื่นช่าย	khêun-châai

asparagus	หน่อไม้ฝรั่ง	nòr máai fà-ràng
spinach	ผักโขม	phàk khŏm
pea	ถั่วลันเตา	thùa-lan-dtao
beans	ถั่ว	thùa
corn (maize)	ข้าวโพด	khâao-phôht
kidney bean	ถั่วรูปไต	thùa rôop dtai
pepper	พริกหยวก	phrík-yùak
radish	หัวผักกาดแดง	hŭa-phàk-gàat daeng
artichoke	อาร์ติโชค	aa dtì chôhk

REGIONAL GEOGRAPHY

Countries. Nationalities

234. Western Europe

Europe	ยุโรป	yú-ròhp
European Union	สหภาพยุโรป	sà-hà phâap yú-ròhp
European (n)	คนยุโรป	khon yú-ròhp
European (adj)	ยุโรป	yú-ròhp

Austria	ประเทศออสเตรีย	bprà-thâyt òt-dtria
Austrian (masc.)	คนออสเตรีย	khon òt-dtria
Austrian (fem.)	คนออสเตรีย	khon òt-dtria
Austrian (adj)	ออสเตรีย	òrt-dtria

Great Britain	บริเตนใหญ่	brì-dtayn yài
England	ประเทศอังกฤษ	bprà-thâyt ang-grìt
British (masc.)	คนอังกฤษ	khon ang-grìt
British (fem.)	คนอังกฤษ	khon ang-grìt
English, British (adj)	อังกฤษ	ang-grìt

Belgium	ประเทศเบลเยียม	bprà-thâyt bayn-yiam
Belgian (masc.)	คนเบลเยียม	khon bayn-yiam
Belgian (fem.)	คนเบลเยียม	khon bayn-yiam
Belgian (adj)	เบลเยียม	bayn-yiam

Germany	ประเทศเยอรมนี	bprà-thâyt yer-rá-ma-nee
German (masc.)	คนเยอรมัน	khon yer-rá-man
German (fem.)	คนเยอรมัน	khon yer-rá-man
German (adj)	เยอรมัน	yer-rá-man

Netherlands	ประเทศเนเธอร์แลนด์	bprà-thâyt nay-ther-laen
Holland	ประเทศฮอลแลนด์	bprà-thâyt hon-laen
Dutch (masc.)	คนเนเธอร์แลนด์	khon nay-ther-laen
Dutch (fem.)	คนเนเธอร์แลนด์	khon nay-ther-laen
Dutch (adj)	เนเธอร์แลนด์	nay-ter-laen

Greece	ประเทศกรีซ	bprà-thâyt grèet
Greek (masc.)	คนกรีก	khon grèek
Greek (fem.)	คนกรีก	khon grèek
Greek (adj)	กรีซ	grèet

Denmark	ประเทศเดนมาร์ก	bprà-thâyt dayn-màak
Dane (masc.)	คนเดนมาร์ก	khon dayn-màak

Dane (fem.)	คนเดนมาร์ก	khon dayn-màak
Danish (adj)	เดนมารก	dayn-màak
Ireland	ประเทศไอร์แลนด์	bprà-thâyt ai-laen
Irish (masc.)	คนไอริช	khon ai-rít
Irish (fem.)	คนไอริช	khon ai-rít
Irish (adj)	ไอร์แลนด์	ai-laen
Iceland	ประเทศไอซ์แลนด์	bprà-thâyt ai-laen
Icelander (masc.)	คนไอซ์แลนด์	khon ai-laen
Icelander (fem.)	คนไอซ์แลนด์	khon ai-laen
Icelandic (adj)	ไอซ์แลนด์	ai-laen
Spain	ประเทศสเปน	bprà-thâyt sà-bpayn
Spaniard (masc.)	คนสเปน	khon sà-bpayn
Spaniard (fem.)	คนสเปน	khon sà-bpayn
Spanish (adj)	สเปน	sà-bpayn
Italy	ประเทศอิตาลี	bprà-thâyt i-dtaa-lee
Italian (masc.)	คนอิตาเลียน	khon i-dtaa-lian
Italian (fem.)	คนอิตาเลียน	khon i-dtaa-lian
Italian (adj)	อิตาลี	i-dtaa-lee
Cyprus	ประเทศไซปรัส	bprà-thâyt sai-bpràt
Cypriot (masc.)	คนไซปรัส	khon sai-bpràt
Cypriot (fem.)	คนไซปรัส	khon sai-bpràt
Cypriot (adj)	ไซปรัส	sai-bpràt
Malta	ประเทศมอลตา	bprà-thâyt mon-dtaa
Maltese (masc.)	คนมอลตา	khon mon-dtaa
Maltese (fem.)	คนมอลตา	khon mon-dtaa
Maltese (adj)	มอลตา	mon-dtâa
Norway	ประเทศนอร์เวย์	bprà-thâyt nor-way
Norwegian (masc.)	คนนอร์เวย์	khon nor-way
Norwegian (fem.)	คนนอร์เวย์	khon nor-way
Norwegian (adj)	นอร์เวย์	nor-way
Portugal	ประเทศโปรตุเกส	bprà-thâyt bproh-dtù-gàyt
Portuguese (masc.)	คนโปรตุเกส	khon bproh-dtù-gàyt
Portuguese (fem.)	คนโปรตุเกส	khon bproh-dtù-gàyt
Portuguese (adj)	โปรตุเกส	bproh-dtù-gàyt
Finland	ประเทศฟินแลนด์	bprà-thâyt fin-laen
Finn (masc.)	คนฟินแลนด์	khon fin-laen
Finn (fem.)	คนฟินแลนด์	khon fin-laen
Finnish (adj)	ฟินแลนด์	fin-laen
France	ประเทศฝรั่งเศส	bprà-thâyt fà-ràng-sàyt
French (masc.)	คนฝรั่งเศส	khon fà-ràng-sàyt
French (fem.)	คนฝรั่งเศส	khon fà-ràng-sàyt
French (adj)	ฝรั่งเศส	fà-ràng-sàyt

Sweden	ประเทศสวีเดน	bprà-thâyt sà-wĕe-dayn
Swede (masc.)	คนสวีเดน	khon sà-wĕe-dayn
Swede (fem.)	คนสวีเดน	khon sà-wĕe-dayn
Swedish (adj)	สวีเดน	sà-wĕe-dayn

Switzerland	ประเทศสวิตเซอร์แลนด์	bprà-thâyt sà-wìt-sêr-laen
Swiss (masc.)	คนสวิส	khon sà-wìt
Swiss (fem.)	คนสวิส	khon sà-wìt
Swiss (adj)	สวิส	sà-wìt

Scotland	ประเทศสก็อตแลนด์	bprà-thâyt sà-gòt-laen
Scottish (masc.)	คนสก็อต	khon sà-gòt
Scottish (fem.)	คนสก็อต	khon sà-gòt
Scottish (adj)	สก็อตแลนด์	sà-gòt-laen

Vatican	นครรัฐวาติกัน	ná-khon rát waa-dtì-gan
Liechtenstein	ประเทศลิกเตนสไตน์	bprà-thâyt lík-tay-ná-sà-dtai
Luxembourg	ประเทศลักเซมเบิร์ก	bprà-thâyt lák-saym-bèrk
Monaco	ประเทศโมนาโก	bprà-thâyt moh-naa-goh

235. Central and Eastern Europe

Albania	ประเทศแอลเบเนีย	bprà-thâyt aen-bay-nia
Albanian (masc.)	คนแอลเบเนีย	khon aen-bay-nia
Albanian (fem.)	คนแอลเบเนีย	khon aen-bay-nia
Albanian (adj)	แอลเบเนีย	aen-bay-nia

Bulgaria	ประเทศบัลแกเรีย	bprà-thâyt ban-gae-ria
Bulgarian (masc.)	คนบัลแกเรีย	khon ban-gae-ria
Bulgarian (fem.)	คนบัลแกเรีย	khon ban-gae-ria
Bulgarian (adj)	บัลแกเรีย	ban-gae-ria

Hungary	ประเทศฮังการี	bprà-thâyt hang-gaa-ree
Hungarian (masc.)	คนฮังการี	khon hang-gaa-ree
Hungarian (fem.)	คนฮังการี	khon hang-gaa-ree
Hungarian (adj)	ฮังการี	hang-gaa-ree

Latvia	ประเทศลัตเวีย	bprà-thâyt lát-wia
Latvian (masc.)	คนลัตเวีย	khon lát-wia
Latvian (fem.)	คนลัตเวีย	khon lát-wia
Latvian (adj)	ลัตเวีย	lát-wia

Lithuania	ประเทศลิทัวเนีย	bprà-thâyt lí-thua-nia
Lithuanian (masc.)	คนลิทัวเนีย	khon lí-thua-nia
Lithuanian (fem.)	คนลิทัวเนีย	khon lí-thua-nia
Lithuanian (adj)	ลิทัวเนีย	lí-thua-nia

| Poland | ประเทศโปแลนด์ | bprà-thâyt bpoh-laen |
| Pole (masc.) | คนโปแลนด | khon bpoh-laen |

Pole (fem.)	คนโปแลนด์	khon bpoh-laen
Polish (adj)	โปแลนด์	bpoh-laen

Romania	ประเทศโรมาเนีย	bprà-thâyt roh-maa-nia
Romanian (masc.)	คนโรมาเนีย	khon roh-maa-nia
Romanian (fem.)	คนโรมาเนีย	khon roh-maa-nia
Romanian (adj)	โรมาเนีย	roh-maa-nia

Serbia	ประเทศเซอร์เบีย	bprà-thâyt sêr-bia
Serbian (masc.)	คนเซอร์เบีย	khon sêr-bia
Serbian (fem.)	คนเซอร์เบีย	khon sêr-bia
Serbian (adj)	เซอรเบีย	sêr-bia

Slovakia	ประเทศสโลวาเกีย	bprà-thâyt sà-loh-waa-gia
Slovak (masc.)	คนสโลวาเกีย	khon sà-loh-waa-gia
Slovak (fem.)	คนสโลวาเกีย	khon sà-loh-waa-gia
Slovak (adj)	สโลวาเกีย	sà-loh-waa-gia

Croatia	ประเทศโครเอเชีย	bprà-thâyt khroh-ay-chia
Croatian (masc.)	คนโครเอเชีย	khon khroh-ay-chia
Croatian (fem.)	คนโครเอเชีย	khon khroh-ay-chia
Croatian (adj)	โครเอเชีย	khroh-ay-chia

Czech Republic	ประเทศเช็กเกีย	bprà-thâyt chék-gia
Czech (masc.)	คนเช็ก	khon chék
Czech (fem.)	คนเช็ก	khon chék
Czech (adj)	เช็กเกีย	chék-gia

Estonia	ประเทศเอสโตเนีย	bprà-thâyt àyt-dtoh-nia
Estonian (masc.)	คนเอสโตเนีย	khon àyt-dtoh-nia
Estonian (fem.)	คนเอสโตเนีย	khon àyt-dtoh-nia
Estonian (adj)	เอสโตเนีย	àyt-dtoh-nia

Bosnia and Herzegovina	ประเทศบอสเนีย และเฮอรเซโกวีนา	bprà-thâyt bòt-nia láe her-say-goh-wí-naa
Macedonia (Republic of ~)	ประเทศมาซิโดเนีย	bprà-thâyt maa-sí-doh-nia
Slovenia	ประเทศสโลวีเนีย	bprà-thâyt sà-loh-wee-nia
Montenegro	ประเทศ มอนเตเนโกร	bprà-thâyt mon-dtay-nay-groh

236. Former USSR countries

Azerbaijan	ประเทศอาเซอร์ไบจาน	bprà-thâyt aa-sêr-bai-jaan
Azerbaijani (masc.)	คนอาเซอร์ไบจาน	khon aa-sêr-bai-jaan
Azerbaijani (fem.)	คนอาเซอร์ไบจาน	khon aa-sêr-bai-jaan
Azerbaijani, Azeri (adj)	อาเซอรไบจาน	aa-sêr-bai-jaan

Armenia	ประเทศอารเมเนีย	bprà-thâyt aa-may-nia
Armenian (masc.)	คนอารเมเนีย	khon aa-may-nia
Armenian (fem.)	คนอารเมเนีย	khon aa-may-nia

Armenian (adj)	อาร์เมเนีย	aa-may-nia
Belarus	ประเทศเบลารุส	bprà-thâyt blao-rút
Belarusian (masc.)	คนเบลารุส	khon blao-rút
Belarusian (fem.)	คนเบลารุส	khon blao-rút
Belarusian (adj)	เบลารุส	blao-rút
Georgia	ประเทศจอร์เจีย	bprà-thâyt jor-jia
Georgian (masc.)	คนจอร์เจีย	khon jor-jia
Georgian (fem.)	คนจอร์เจีย	khon jor-jia
Georgian (adj)	จอร์เจีย	jor-jia
Kazakhstan	ประเทศ คาซัคสถาน	bprà-thâyt khaa-sák--à-thǎan
Kazakh (masc.)	คนคาซัคสถาน	khon khaa-sák-sà-thǎan
Kazakh (fem.)	คนคาซัคสถาน	khon khaa-sák-sà-thǎan
Kazakh (adj)	คาซัคสถาน	khaa-sák-sà-thǎan
Kirghizia	ประเทศ คีร์กีซสถาน	bprà-thâyt khee-gèet--à-thǎan
Kirghiz (masc.)	คนคีร์กีซสถาน	khon khee-gèet-sà-thǎan
Kirghiz (fem.)	คนคีร์กีซสถาน	khon khee-gèet-sà-thǎan
Kirghiz (adj)	คีร์กีซสถาน	khee-gèet-sà-thǎan
Moldova, Moldavia	ประเทศมอลโดวา	bprà-thâyt mon-doh-waa
Moldavian (masc.)	คนมอลโดวา	khon mon-doh-waa
Moldavian (fem.)	คนมอลโดวา	khon mon-doh-waa
Moldavian (adj)	มอลโดวา	mon-doh-waa
Russia	ประเทศรัสเซีย	bprà-thâyt rát-sia
Russian (masc.)	คนรัสเซีย	khon rát-sia
Russian (fem.)	คนรัสเซีย	khon rát-sia
Russian (adj)	รัสเซีย	rát-sia
Tajikistan	ประเทศทาจิกิสถาน	bprà-thâyt thaa-jì-gìt-thǎan
Tajik (masc.)	คนทาจิกิสถาน	khon thaa-jì-gìt-thǎan
Tajik (fem.)	คนทาจิกิสถาน	khon thaa-jì-gìt-thǎan
Tajik (adj)	ทาจิกิสถาน	thaa-jì-gìt-thǎan
Turkmenistan	ประเทศ เติร์กเมนิสถาน	bprà-thâyt dtèrk-may-nít-thǎan
Turkmen (masc.)	คนเติร์กเมนิสถาน	khon dtèrk-may-nít-thǎan
Turkmen (fem.)	คนเติร์กเมนิสถาน	khon dtèrk-may-nít-thǎan
Turkmenian (adj)	เติร์กเมนิสถาน	dtèrk-may-nít-thǎan
Uzbekistan	ประเทศอุซเบกิสถาน	bprà-thâyt ùt-bay-gìt-thǎan
Uzbek (masc.)	คนอุซเบกิสถาน	khon ùt-bay-gìt-thǎan
Uzbek (fem.)	คนอุซเบกิสถาน	khon ùt-bay-gìt-thǎan
Uzbek (adj)	อุซเบกิสถาน	ùt-bay-gìt-thǎan
Ukraine	ประเทศยูเครน	bprà-thâyt yoo-khrayn
Ukrainian (masc.)	คนยูเครน	khon yoo-khrayn
Ukrainian (fem.)	คนยูเครน	khon yoo-khrayn
Ukrainian (adj)	ยูเครน	yoo-khrayn

237. Asia

| Asia | เอเชีย | ay-chia |
| Asian (adj) | เอเชีย | ay-chia |

Vietnam	ประเทศเวียดนาม	bprà-thâyt wîat-naam
Vietnamese (masc.)	คนเวียดนาม	khon wîat-naam
Vietnamese (fem.)	คนเวียดนาม	khon wîat-naam
Vietnamese (adj)	เวียดนาม	wîat-naam

India	ประเทศอินเดีย	bprà-thâyt in-dia
Indian (masc.)	คนอินเดีย	khon in-dia
Indian (fem.)	คนอินเดีย	khon in-dia
Indian (adj)	อินเดีย	in-dia

Israel	ประเทศอิสราเอล	bprà-thâyt ìt-sà-rǎa-ayn
Israeli (masc.)	คนอิสราเอล	khon ìt-sà-rǎa-ayn
Israeli (fem.)	คนอิสราเอล	khon ìt-sà-rǎa-ayn
Israeli (adj)	อิสราเอล	ìt-sà-rǎa-ayn

Jew (n)	คนยิว	khon yiw
Jewess (n)	คนยิว	khon yiw
Jewish (adj)	ยิว	yiw

China	ประเทศจีน	bprà-thâyt jeen
Chinese (masc.)	คนจีน	khon jeen
Chinese (fem.)	คนจีน	khon jeen
Chinese (adj)	จีน	jeen

Korean (masc.)	คนเกาหลี	khon gao-lěe
Korean (fem.)	คนเกาหลี	khon gao-lěe
Korean (adj)	เกาหลี	gao-lěe

Lebanon	ประเทศเลบานอน	bprà-thâyt lay-baa-non
Lebanese (masc.)	คนเลบานอน	khon lay-baa-non
Lebanese (fem.)	คนเลบานอน	khon lay-baa-non
Lebanese (adj)	เลบานอน	lay-baa-non

Mongolia	ประเทศมองโกเลีย	bprà-thâyt mong-goh-lia
Mongolian (masc.)	คนมองโกล	khon mong-gloh
Mongolian (fem.)	คนมองโกล	khon mong-gloh
Mongolian (adj)	มองโกเลีย	mong-goh-lia

Malaysia	ประเทศมาเลเซีย	bprà-thâyt maa-lay-sia
Malaysian (masc.)	คนมาเลย์	khon maa-lây
Malaysian (fem.)	คนมาเลย์	khon maa-lây
Malaysian (adj)	มาเลเซีย	maa-lay-sia

| Pakistan | ประเทศ
ปากีสถาน | bprà-thâyt
bpaa-gèet-thǎan |
| Pakistani (masc.) | คนปากีสถาน | khon bpaa-gèet-thǎan |

Pakistani (fem.)	คนปากีสถาน	khon bpaa-gèet-thăan
Pakistani (adj)	ปากีสถาน	bpaa-gèet-thăan
Saudi Arabia	ประเทศ ซาอุดีอาระเบีย	bprà-thâyt saa-u-dì aa-ra--bia
Arab (masc.)	คนอาหรับ	khon aa-ràp
Arab (fem.)	คนอาหรับ	khon aa-ràp
Arab, Arabic (adj)	อาหรับ	aa-ràp
Thailand	ประเทศไทย	bprà-tâyt thai
Thai (masc.)	คนไทย	khon thai
Thai (fem.)	คนไทย	khon thai
Thai (adj)	ไทย	thai
Taiwan	ไต้หวัน	dtâi-wăn
Taiwanese (masc.)	คนไต้หวัน	khon dtâi-wăn
Taiwanese (fem.)	คนไต้หวัน	khon dtâi-wăn
Taiwanese (adj)	ไต้หวัน	dtâi-wăn
Turkey	ประเทศตุรกี	bprà-thâyt dtù-rá-gee
Turk (masc.)	คนเติร์ก	khon dtèrk
Turk (fem.)	คนเติร์ก	khon dtèrk
Turkish (adj)	ตุรกี	dtù-rá-gee
Japan	ประเทศญี่ปุ่น	bprà-thâyt yêe-bpùn
Japanese (masc.)	คนญี่ปุ่น	khon yêe-bpùn
Japanese (fem.)	คนญี่ปุ่น	khon yêe-bpùn
Japanese (adj)	ญี่ปุ่น	yêe-bpùn
Afghanistan	ประเทศอัฟกานิสถาน	bprà-thâyt àf-gaa-nít-thăan
Bangladesh	ประเทศ บังคลาเทศ	bprà-thâyt bang-khlaa-thâyt
Indonesia	ประเทศอินโดนีเซีย	bprà-thâyt in-doh-nee-sia
Jordan	ประเทศจอรแดน	bprà-thâyt jor-daen
Iraq	ประเทศอิรัก	bprà-thâyt i-rák
Iran	ประเทศอิหราน	bprà-thâyt i-ràan
Cambodia	ประเทศกัมพูชา	bprà-thâyt gam-phoo-chaa
Kuwait	ประเทศคูเวต	bprà-thâyt khoo-wâyt
Laos	ประเทศลาว	bprà-thâyt laao
Myanmar	ประเทศเมียนมาร์	bprà-thâyt mian-maa
Nepal	ประเทศเนปาล	bprà-thâyt nay-bpaan
United Arab Emirates	สหรัฐอาหรับเอมิเรตส์	sà-hà-rát aa-ràp ay-mí-râyt
Syria	ประเทศซีเรีย	bprà-thâyt see-ria
Palestine	ปาเลสไตน์	bpaa-lâyt-dtai
South Korea	เกาหลีใต้	gao-lĕe dtâi
North Korea	เกาหลีเหนือ	gao-lĕe nĕua

238. North America

United States of America	สหรัฐอเมริกา	sà-hà-rát a-may-rí-gaa
American (masc.)	คนอเมริกา	khon a-may-rí-gaa
American (fem.)	คนอเมริกา	khon a-may-rí-gaa
American (adj)	อเมริกา	a-may-rí-gaa
Canada	ประเทศแคนาดา	bprà-thâyt khae-naa-daa
Canadian (masc.)	คนแคนาดา	khon khae-naa-daa
Canadian (fem.)	คนแคนาดา	khon khae-naa-daa
Canadian (adj)	แคนาดา	khae-naa-daa
Mexico	ประเทศเม็กซิโก	bprà-thâyt mék-sí-goh
Mexican (masc.)	คนเม็กซิโก	khon mék-sí-goh
Mexican (fem.)	คนเม็กซิโก	khon mék-sí-goh
Mexican (adj)	เม็กซิโก	mék-sí-goh

239. Central and South America

Argentina	ประเทศอาร์เจนตินา	bprà-thâyt aa-jayn-dtì-naa
Argentinian (masc.)	คนอาร์เจนตินา	khon aa-jayn-dtì-naa
Argentinian (fem.)	คนอาร์เจนตินา	khon aa-jayn-dtì-naa
Argentinian (adj)	อาร์เจนตินา	aa-jayn-dtì-naa
Brazil	ประเทศบราซิล	bprà-thâyt braa-sin
Brazilian (masc.)	คนบราซิล	khon braa-sin
Brazilian (fem.)	คนบราซิล	khon braa-sin
Brazilian (adj)	บราซิล	braa-sin
Colombia	ประเทศโคลัมเบีย	bprà-thâyt khoh-lam-bia
Colombian (masc.)	คนโคลัมเบีย	khon khoh-lam-bia
Colombian (fem.)	คนโคลัมเบีย	khon khoh-lam-bia
Colombian (adj)	โคลัมเบีย	khoh-lam-bia
Cuba	ประเทศคิวบา	bprà-thâyt khiw-baa
Cuban (masc.)	คนคิวบา	khon khiw-baa
Cuban (fem.)	คนคิวบา	khon khiw-baa
Cuban (adj)	คิวบา	khiw-baa
Chile	ประเทศชิลี	bprà-thâyt chí-lee
Chilean (masc.)	คนชิลี	khon chí-lee
Chilean (fem.)	คนชิลี	khon chí-lee
Chilean (adj)	ชิลี	chí-lee
Bolivia	ประเทศโบลิเวีย	bprà-thâyt boh-lí-wia
Venezuela	ประเทศเวเนซุเอลา	bprà-thâyt way-nay-sú-ay-laa
Paraguay	ประเทศปารากวัย	bprà-thâyt bpaa-raa-gwai
Peru	ประเทศเปรู	bprà-thâyt bpay-roo

Suriname	ประเทศซูรินาม	bprà-thâyt soo-rí-naam
Uruguay	ประเทศอุรุกวัย	bprà-thâyt u-rúk-wai
Ecuador	ประเทศเอกวาดอร์	bprà-thâyt ay-gwaa-dor
The Bahamas	ประเทศบาฮามาส	bprà-thâyt baa-haa-mâat
Haiti	ประเทศเฮติ	bprà-thâyt hay-dtì
Dominican Republic	สาธารณรัฐ โดมินิกัน	sǎa-thaa-rá-ná rát doh-mí-ní-gan
Panama	ประเทศปานามา	bprà-thâyt bpaa-naa-maa
Jamaica	ประเทศจาเมกา	bprà-thâyt jaa-may-gaa

240. Africa

Egypt	ประเทศ อียิปต์	bprà-thâyt bprà-thâyt ee-yíp
Egyptian (masc.)	คนอียิปต์	khon ee-yíp
Egyptian (fem.)	คนอียิปต์	khon ee-yíp
Egyptian (adj)	อียิปต์	ee-yíp
Morocco	ประเทศมอร็อคโค	bprà-thâyt mor-rók-khoh
Moroccan (masc.)	คนมอร็อคโค	khon mor-rók-khoh
Moroccan (fem.)	คนมอร็อคโค	khon mor-rók-khoh
Moroccan (adj)	มอร็อคโค	mor-rók-khoh
Tunisia	ประเทศตูนิเซีย	bprà-thâyt dtoo-ní-sia
Tunisian (masc.)	คนตูนีเซีย	khon dtoo-ní-sia
Tunisian (fem.)	คนตูนีเซีย	khon dtoo-ní-sia
Tunisian (adj)	ตูนีเซีย	dtoo-ní-sia
Ghana	ประเทศกานา	bprà-thâyt gaa-naa
Zanzibar	ประเทศแซนซิบาร์	bprà-thâyt saen-sí-baa
Kenya	ประเทศเคนยา	bprà-thâyt khayn-yâa
Libya	ประเทศลิเบีย	bprà-thâyt lí-bia
Madagascar	ประเทศ มาดากัสการ์	bprà-thâyt maa-daa-gàt-gaa
Namibia	ประเทศนามิเบีย	bprà-thâyt naa-mí-bia
Senegal	ประเทศเซเนกัล	bprà-thâyt say-nay-gan
Tanzania	ประเทศแทนซาเนีย	bprà-thâyt thaen-saa-nia
South Africa	ประเทศแอฟริกาใต้	bprà-thâyt àef-rí-gaa dtâi
African (masc.)	คนแอฟริกา	khon àef-rí-gaa
African (fem.)	คนแอฟริกา	khon àef-rí-gaa
African (adj)	แอฟริกา	àef-rí-gaa

241. Australia. Oceania

| Australia | ประเทศออสเตรเลีย | bprà-thâyt òt-dtray-lia |
| Australian (masc.) | คนออสเตรเลีย | khon òt-dtray-lia |

Australian (fem.)	คนออสเตรเลีย	khon òt-dtray-lia
Australian (adj)	ออสเตรเลีย	òt-dtray-lia
New Zealand	ประเทศนิวซีแลนด์	bprà-thâyt niw-see-laen
New Zealander (masc.)	คนนิวซีแลนด์	khon niw-see-laen
New Zealander (fem.)	คนนิวซีแลนด์	khon niw-see-laen
New Zealand (as adj)	นิวซีแลนด์	niw-see-laen
Tasmania	ประเทศแทสเมเนีย	bprà-thâyt thâet-may-nia
French Polynesia	เฟรนช์โปลินีเซีย	frayn-bpoh-lí-nee-sia

242. Cities

Amsterdam	อัมสเตอร์ดัม	am-sà-dtêr-dam
Ankara	อังคารา	ang-khaa-raa
Athens	เอเธนส์	ay-thayn
Baghdad	แบกแดด	bàek-dàet
Bangkok	กรุงเทพฯ	grung thâyp
Barcelona	บาร์เซโลนา	baa-say-loh-naa
Beijing	ปักกิ่ง	bpàk-gìng
Beirut	เบรุต	bay-rút
Berlin	เบอร์ลิน	ber-lin
Mumbai (Bombay)	มุมไบ	mum-bai
Bonn	บอนน์	bon
Bordeaux	บอร์โด	bor doh
Bratislava	บราติสลาวา	braa-dtìt-laa-waa
Brussels	บรัสเซล	bràt-sayn
Bucharest	บูคาเรสต์	boo-khaa-râyt
Budapest	บูดาเปส	boo-daa-bpàyt
Cairo	ไคโร	khai-roh
Kolkata (Calcutta)	คัลคัตตา	khan-khát-dtaa
Chicago	ชิคาโก	chí-khaa-goh
Copenhagen	โคเปนเฮเกน	khoh-bpayn-hay-gayn
Dar-es-Salaam	ดาร์เอสซาลาม	daa àyt saa laam
Delhi	เดลี	day-lee
Dubai	ดูไบ	doo-bai
Dublin	ดับลิน	dàp-lin
Düsseldorf	ดุสเซลดอร์ฟ	dùt-sayn-dòf
Florence	ฟลอเรนซ์	flor-rayn
Frankfurt	แฟรงค์เฟิร์ท	fraeng-fêrt
Geneva	เจนีวา	jay-nee-waa
The Hague	เดอะเฮก	dùh hêyk
Hamburg	แฮมเบิร์ก	haem-bèrk
Hanoi	ฮานอย	haa-noi

Havana	ฮาวานา	haa waa-naa
Helsinki	เฮลซิงกิ	hayn-sing-gì
Hiroshima	ฮิโรชิมา	hí-roh-chí-mâa
Hong Kong	ฮองกง	hôrng-gong
Istanbul	อิสตันบูล	ìt-dtan-boon
Jerusalem	เยรูซาเลม	yay-roo-saa-laym
Kyiv	เคียฟ	khîaf
Kuala Lumpur	กัวลาลัมเปอร์	gua-laa lam-bper
Lisbon	ลิสบอน	lít-bon
London	ลอนดอน	lon-don
Los Angeles	ลอสแองเจลิส	lôt-aeng-jay-lít
Lyons	ลียง	lee-yong
Madrid	มาดริด	maa-drìt
Marseille	มารกเซย	màak-soie
Mexico City	เม็กซิโกซิตี้	mék-sí-goh sí-dtêe
Miami	ไมอามี่	mai-aa-mêe
Montreal	มอนทรีออล	mon-three-on
Moscow	มอสโกว	mor-sà-goh
Munich	มิวนิค	miw-ník
Nairobi	ไนโรบี	nai-roh-bee
Naples	เนเปิลสู่	nay-bpern
New York	นิวยอรค	niw-yôk
Nice	นิซ	nít
Oslo	ออสโล	òrt-loh
Ottawa	อ็อตตาวา	òt-dtaa-waa
Paris	ปารีส	bpaa-rêet
Prague	ปราก	bpràak
Rio de Janeiro	ริโอเอจาเนโร	rí-oh-ay jaa-nay-roh
Rome	โรม	rohm
Saint Petersburg	เซนต์ปิเตอร์สเบิร์ก	sayn bpì-dtèrt-bèrk
Seoul	โซล	sohn
Shanghai	เซี่ยงไฮ้	sîang-hái
Singapore	สิงคโปร์	sǐng-khá-bpoh
Stockholm	สต็อกโฮล์ม	sà-dtòk-hohm
Sydney	ซิดนีย์	sít-nee
Taipei	ไทเป	thai-bpay
Tokyo	โตเกียว	dtoh-gieow
Toronto	โตรอนโต	dtoh-ron-dtoh
Venice	เวนิส	way-nít
Vienna	เวียนนา	wian-naa
Warsaw	วอรซอว	wor-sor
Washington	วอชิงตัน	wor ching dtan

243. Politics. Government. Part 1

politics	การเมือง	gaan meuang
political (adj)	ทางการเมือง	thang gaan meuang
politician	นักการเมือง	nák gaan meuang
state (country)	รัฐ	rát
citizen	พลเมือง	phon-lá-meuang
citizenship	สัญชาติ	săn-châat
national emblem	ตราประจำชาติ	dtraa bprà-jam châat
national anthem	เพลงชาติ	phlayng châat
government	รัฐบาล	rát-thà-baan
head of state	ผู้นำประเทศ	phôo nam bprà-thâyt
parliament	รัฐสภา	rát-thà-sà-phaa
party	พรรคการเมือง	phák gaan meuang
capitalism	ทุนนิยม	thun ní-yom
capitalist (adj)	แบบทุนนิยม	bàep thun ní-yom
socialism	สังคมนิยม	săng-khom ní-yom
socialist (adj)	แบบสังคมนิยม	bàep săng-khom ní-yom
communism	ลัทธิคอมมิวนิสต์	lát-thí khom-miw-nít
communist (adj)	แบบคอมมิวนิสต์	bàep khom-miw-nít
communist (n)	คนคอมมิวนิสต์	khon khom-miw-nít
democracy	ประชาธิปไตย	bprà-chaa-thíp-bpà-dtai
democrat	ผู้นิยมประชาธิปไตย	phôo ní-yom bprà-chaa-típ-bpà-dtai
democratic (adj)	แบบประชาธิปไตย	bàep bprà-chaa-thíp-bpà-dtai
Democratic party	พรรคประชาธิปัตย์	phák bprà-chaa-tí-bpàt
liberal (n)	ผู้เอียงเสรีนิยม	phôo iang săy-ree ní-yom
liberal (adj)	แบบเสรีนิยม	bàep săy-ree ní-yom
conservative (n)	ผู้เอียงอนุรักษ์นิยม	phôo iang a-nú rák ní-yom
conservative (adj)	แบบอนุรักษ์นิยม	bàep a-nú rák ní-yom
republic (n)	สาธารณรัฐ	săa-thaa-rá-ná rát
republican (n)	รีพับลิกัน	ree pháp lí gan
Republican party	พรรครีพับลิกัน	phák ree-pháp-lí-gan
elections	การเลือกตั้ง	gaan lêuak dtâng
to elect (vt)	เลือก	lêuak
elector, voter	ผู้ออกเสียงลงคะแนน	phôo òrk sĭang long khá-naen
election campaign	การรณรงค์หาเสียง	gaan ron-ná-rorng hăa sĭang

voting (n)	การออกเสียง	gaan òrk sĭang
	ลงคะแนน	long khá-naen
to vote (vi)	ลงคะแนน	long khá-naen
suffrage, right to vote	สิทธิ์ใน	sìt-thí nai
	การเลือกตั้ง	gaan lêuak dtâng
candidate	ผู้สมัคร	phôo sà-màk
to be a candidate	ลงสมัคร	long sà-màk
campaign	การรณรงค์	gaan ron-ná-rorng
opposition (as adj)	ฝ่ายค้าน	fàai kháan
opposition (n)	ฝ่ายคาน	fàai kháan
visit	การเยือน	gaan yeuan
official visit	การเยือนอย่างเป็น	gaan yeuan yàang bpen
	ทางการ	thaang gaan
international (adj)	แบบสากล	bàep săa-gon
negotiations	การเจรจา	gaan jayn-rá-jaa
to negotiate (vi)	เจรจา	jayn-rá-jaa

244. Politics. Government. Part 2

society	สังคม	săng-khom
constitution	รัฐธรรมนูญ	rát-thà-tham-má-noon
power (political control)	อำนาจ	am-nâat
corruption	การทุจริต	gaan thút-jà-rìt
	คอรัปชัน	khor-ráp-chân
law (justice)	กฎหมาย	gòt măai
legal (legitimate)	ทางกฎหมาย	thaang gòt măai
justice (fairness)	ความยุติธรรม	khwaam yút-dtì-tham
just (fair)	เป็นธรรม	bpen tham
committee	คณะกรรมการ	khá-ná gam-má-gaan
bill (draft law)	ราง	râang
budget	งบประมาณ	ngóp bprà-maan
policy	นโยบาย	ná-yoh-baai
reform	ปฏิรูป	bpà-dtì rôop
radical (adj)	รุนแรง	run raeng
power (strength, force)	กำลัง	gam-lang
powerful (adj)	ทรงพลัง	song phá-lang
supporter	ผู้สนับสนุน	phôo sà-nàp-sà-nŭn
influence	อิทธิพล	ìt-thí pon
regime (e.g., military ~)	ระบอบการปกครอง	rá-bòrp gaan bpòk khrorng
conflict	ความขัดแย้ง	khwaam khàt yáeng
conspiracy (plot)	การคบคิด	gaan khóp khít

provocation	การยั่วยุ	gaan yûa yú
to overthrow (regime, etc.)	ลมล้าง	lóm láang
overthrow (of government)	การลม	gaan lóm
revolution	ปฏิวัติ	bpà-dtì-wát

coup d'état	รัฐประหาร	rát-thà-bprà-hăan
military coup	การยึดอำนาจ	gaan yéut am-nâat
	ด้วยกำลังทหาร	dûay gam-lang thá-hăan

crisis	วิกฤติ	wí-grìt
economic recession	ภาวะเศรษฐกิจ	phaa-wá sàyt-thà-gìt
	ถดถอย	thòt thŏi
demonstrator (protester)	ผู้ประท้วง	phôo bprà-thúang
demonstration	การประทวง	gaan bprà-thúang
martial law	กฎอัยการศึก	gòt ai-yá-gaan sèuk
military base	ฐานทัพ	thăan tháp

stability	ความมั่นคง	khwaam mân-khong
stable (adj)	มั่นคง	mân khong

exploitation	การขูดรีด	gaan khòot rêet
to exploit (workers)	ขูดรีด	khòot rêet

racism	คตินิยม	khá-dtì ní-yom
	เชื้อชาติ	chéua châat
racist	ผู้เหยียดผิว	phôo yìat phĭw
fascism	ลัทธิฟาสซิสต์	lát-thí fâat-sít
fascist	ผู้นิยมลัทธิฟาสซิสต์	phôo ní-yom lát-thí fâat-sít

245. Countries. Miscellaneous

foreigner	คนต่างชาติ	khon dtàang châat
foreign (adj)	ต่างชาติ	dtàang châat
abroad	ต่างประเทศ	dtàang bprà-thâyt
(in a foreign country)		

emigrant	ผู้อพยพ	phôo òp-phá-yóp
emigration	การอพยพ	gaan òp-phá-yóp
to emigrate (vi)	อพยพ	òp-phá-yóp

the West	ตะวันตก	dtà-wan dtòk
the East	ตะวันออก	dtà-wan òrk
the Far East	ตะวันออกไกล	dtà-wan òrk glai

civilization	อารยธรรม	aa-rá-yá-tham
humanity (mankind)	มนุษยชาติ	má-nút-sà-yá-châat
the world (earth)	โลก	lôhk
peace	ความสงบสุข	khwaam sà-ngòp-sùk
worldwide (adj)	ทั่วโลก	thûa lôhk
homeland	บ้านเกิด	bâan gèrt

people (population)	ประชาชน	bprà-chaa chon
population	ประชากร	bprà-chaa gon
people (a lot of ~)	ประชาชน	bprà-chaa chon
nation (people)	ชาติ	châat
generation	รุ่น	rûn

territory (area)	อาณาเขต	aa-naa khàyt
region	ภูมิภาค	phoo-mí-phâak
state (part of a country)	รัฐ	rát

tradition	ธรรมเนียม	tham-niam
custom (tradition)	ประเพณี	bprà-phay-nee
ecology	นิเวศวิทยา	ní-wâyt wít-thá-yaa

Indian (Native American)	อินเดียนแดง	in-dian daeng
Gypsy (masc.)	คนยิปซี	khon yíp-see
Gypsy (fem.)	คนยิปซี	khon yíp-see
Gypsy (adj)	ยิปซี	yíp see

empire	จักรวรรดิ	jàk-grà-wàt
colony	อาณานิคม	aa-naa ní-khom
slavery	การใช้แรงงานทาส	gaan chái raeng ngaan thâat
invasion	การบุกรุก	gaan bùk rúk
famine	ความอดอยาก	khwaam òt yàak

246. Major religious groups. Confessions

| religion | ศาสนา | sàat-sà-nǎa |
| religious (adj) | ศาสนา | sàat-sà-nǎa |

faith, belief	ศรัทธา	sàt-thaa
to believe (in God)	นับถือ	náp thěu
believer	ผู้ศรัทธา	phôo sàt-thaa

| atheism | อเทวนิยม | a-thay-wá ní-yom |
| atheist | ผู้เชื่อว่าไม่มีพระเจ้า | phôo chêua wâa mâi mee phrá jâo |

Christianity	ศาสนาคริสต์	sàat-sà-nǎa khrít
Christian (n)	ผู้นับถือศาสนาคริสต์	phôo náp thěu sàat-sà-nǎa khrít
Christian (adj)	ศาสนาคริสต์	sàat-sà-nǎa khrít

Catholicism	ศาสนาคาธอลิก	sàat-sà-nǎa khaa-thor-lík
Catholic (n)	ผู้นับถือศาสนาคาธอลิก	phôo náp thěu sàat-sà-nǎa khaa-thor-lík
Catholic (adj)	คาธอลิก	khaa-thor-lík
Protestantism	ศาสนาโปรแตสแตนท์	sàat-sà-nǎa bproh-dtàet-dtaen

Protestant Church	โบสถ์นิกาย โปรแตสแตนท์	bòht ní-gaai bproh-dtàet-dtaen
Protestant (n)	ผู้นับถือศาสนา โปรแตสแตนท์	phôo náp thĕu sàat-sà-nǎa bproh-dtàet-dtaen
Orthodoxy	ศาสนาออร์ทอดอกซ์	sàat-sà-nǎa or-thor-dòrk
Orthodox Church	โบสถ์ศาสนา ออรทอดอกซ์	bòht sàat-sà-nǎa or-thor-dòrk
Orthodox (n)	ผู้นับถือ ศาสนาออรทอดอกซ์	phôo náp thĕu sàat-sà-nǎa or-thor-dòrk
Presbyterianism	นิกายเพรสไบ ที่เรียน	ní-gaai phrayt-bai-thee-rian
Presbyterian Church	โบสถ์นิกาย เพรสไบที่เรียน	bòht ní-gaai phrayt-bai-thee-rian
Presbyterian (n)	ผู้นับถือนิกาย เพรสไบที่เรียน	phôo náp thĕu ní-gaai phrayt bai thee rian
Lutheranism	นิกายลูเทอแรน	ní-gaai loo-thay-a-rǎen
Lutheran (n)	ผู้นับถือนิกาย ลูเทอแรน	phôo náp thĕu ní-gaai loo-thay-a-rǎen
Baptist Church	นิกายแบ๊บติสท์	ní-gaai báep-dtìt
Baptist (n)	ผู้นับถือนิกาย แบบติสท	phôo náp thĕu ní-gaai báep-dtìt
Anglican Church	โบสถ์นิกาย แองกลิกัน	bòht ní-gaai ae-ngók-lí-gan
Anglican (n)	ผู้นับถือนิกาย แองกลิกัน	phôo náp thĕu ní-gaai ae ngók lí gan
Mormonism	นิกายมอร์มอน	ní-gaai mor-mon
Mormon (n)	ผู้นับถือนิกาย มอรมอน	phôo náp thĕu ní-gaai mor-mon
Judaism	ศาสนายิว	sàat-sà-nǎa yiw
Jew (n)	คนยิว	khon yiw
Buddhism	ศาสนาพุธ	sàat-sà-nǎa phút
Buddhist (n)	ผู้นับถือ ศาสนาพุธ	phôo náp thĕu sàat-sà-nǎa phút
Hinduism	ศาสนาฮินดู	sàat-sà-nǎa hin-doo
Hindu (n)	ผู้นับถือ ศาสนาฮินดู	phôo náp thĕu sàat-sà-nǎa hin-doo
Islam	ศาสนาอิสลาม	sàat-sà-nǎa ìt-sà-laam
Muslim (n)	ผู้นับถือ ศาสนาอิสลาม	phôo náp thĕu sàat-sà-nǎa ìt-sà-laam
Muslim (adj)	มุสลิม	mút-sà-lim
Shiah Islam	ศาสนา อิสลามนิกายชีอะฮ์	sàat-sà-nǎa ìt-sà-laam ní-gaai shi-à

Shiite (n)	ผู้นับถือนิกาย ชีอะฮ	phôo náp thĕu ní-gaai shi-à
Sunni Islam	ศาสนาอิสลามนิ กายซุนนี	sàat-sà-nǎa ìt-sà-laam ní-gaai sun-nee
Sunnite (n)	ผู้นับถือนิกาย ซุนนี	phôo náp thĕu ní-gaai sun-nee

247. Religions. Priests

priest	นักบวช	nák bùat
the Pope	พระสันตะปาปา	phrá sǎn-dtà-bpaa-bpaa
monk, friar	พระ	phrá
nun	แม่ชี	mâe chee
pastor	ศาสนาจารย์	sàat-sà-nǎa-jaan
abbot	เจ้าอาวาส	jâo aa-wâat
vicar (parish priest)	เจ้าอาวาส	jâo aa-wâat
bishop	มุขนายก	múk naa-yók
cardinal	พระคาร์ดินัล	phrá khaa-dì-nan
preacher	นักเทศน์	nák thâyt
preaching	การเทศนา	gaan thâyt-sà-nǎa
parishioners	ลูกวัด	lôok wát
believer	ผู้ศรัทธา	phôo sàt-thaa
atheist	ผู้เชื่อวา ไม่มีพระเจ้า	phôo chêua wâa mâi mee phrá jâo

248. Faith. Christianity. Islam

Adam	อาดัม	aa-dam
Eve	เอวา	ay-waa
God	พระเจ้า	phrá jâo
the Lord	พระเจ้า	phrá jâo
the Almighty	พระผู้เป็นเจ้า	phrá phôo bpen jâo
sin	บาป	bàap
to sin (vi)	ทำบาป	tham bàap
sinner (masc.)	คนบาป	khon bàap
sinner (fem.)	คนบาป	khon bàap
hell	นรก	ná-rók
paradise	สวรรค์	sà-wǎn
Jesus	พระเยซู	phrá yay-soo
Jesus Christ	พระเยซูคริสต์	phrá yay-soo khrít
the Holy Spirit	พระจิต	phrá jìt

the Savior	พระผู้ไถ่	phrá phôo thài
the Virgin Mary	พระนางมารีย์	phrá naang maa ree
	พรหมจารี	phrom-má-jaa-ree
the Devil	มาร	maan
devil's (adj)	ของมาร	khŏrng maan
Satan	ซาตาน	saa-dtaan
satanic (adj)	ซาตาน	saa-dtaan
angel	เทวทูต	thay-wá-thôot
guardian angel	เทวดาผู้	thay-wá-daa phôo
	คุมครอง	khúm khrorng
angelic (adj)	ของเทวดา	khŏrng thay-wá-daa
apostle	สาวก	săa-wók
archangel	หัวหน้าทูตสวรรค์	hŭa nâa thôot sà-wăn
the Antichrist	ศัตรูของพระคริสต์	sàt-dtroo khŏrng phrá khrít
Church	โบสถ์	bòht
Bible	คัมภีร์ไบเบิ้ล	kham-phee bai-bêrn
biblical (adj)	ไบเบิ้ล	bai-bêrn
Old Testament	พันธสัญญาเดิม	phan-thá-săn-yaa derm
New Testament	พันธสัญญาใหม่	phan-thá-săn-yaa mài
Gospel	พระวรสาร	phrá won săan
Holy Scripture	พระคัมภีร์ไบเบิล	phrá kham-phee bai-bern
Heaven	สวรรค์	sà-wăn
Commandment	บัญญัติ	ban-yàt
prophet	ผู้เผยพระวจนะ	phôo phŏie phrá wá-jà-ná
prophecy	คำพยากรณ์	kham phá-yaa-gon
Allah	อัลลอฮ์	an-lor
Mohammed	พระมุฮัมหมัด	phrá moo ham màt
the Koran	อัลกุรอาน	an gù-rá-aan
mosque	สุเหร่า	sù-rào
mullah	มุลละ	mun lá
prayer	บทสวดมนต์	bòt sùat mon
to pray (vi, vt)	สวด	sùat
pilgrimage	การจาริกแสวงบุญ	gaan jaa-rík sà-wăeng bun
pilgrim	ผู้แสวงบุญ	phôo sà-wăeng bun
Mecca	มักกะฮ	mák-gà
church	โบสถ์	bòht
temple	วิหาร	wí-hăan
cathedral	มหาวิหาร	má-hăa wí-hăan
Gothic (adj)	แบบโกธิก	bàep goh-thík
synagogue	โบสถ์ของ	bòht khŏrng
	ศาสนายิว	sàat-sà-năa yiw
mosque	สุเหร่า	sù-rào

chapel	ห้องสวดมนต์	hôrng sùat mon
abbey	วัด	wát
convent	สำนักแม่ชี	săm-nák mâe chee
monastery	อาราม	aa raam
bell (church ~s)	ระฆัง	rá-khang
bell tower	หอระฆัง	hŏr rá-khang
to ring (ab. bells)	ตีระฆัง	dtee rá-khang
cross	ไม้กางเขน	mái gaang khăyn
cupola (roof)	หลังคาทรงโดม	lăng kaa song dohm
icon	รูปเคารพ	rôop kpao-róp
soul	วิญญาณ	win-yaan
fate (destiny)	ชะตากรรม	chá-dtaa gam
evil (n)	ความชั่วร้าย	khwaam chûa ráai
good (n)	ความดี	khwaam dee
vampire	ผีดูดเลือด	phĕe dòot lêuat
witch (evil ~)	แมมด	mâe mót
demon	ปีศาจ	bpee-sàat
spirit	ผี	phĕe
redemption (giving us ~)	การไถ่ถอน	gaan thài thŏrn
to redeem (vt)	ไถ่ถอน	thài thŏrn
church service, mass	พิธีมิสซา	phí-tee mít-saa
to say mass	ประกอบพิธี	bprà-gòp phí-thee
	ศีลมหาสนิท	sĕen má-hăa sà-nìt
confession	การสารภาพ	gaan săa-rá-phâap
to confess (vi)	สารภาพ	săa-rá-phâap
saint (n)	นักบุญ	nák bun
sacred (holy)	ศักดิ์สิทธิ์	sàk-gà-dì sìt
holy water	น้ำมนต์	nám mon
ritual (n)	พิธีกรรม	phí-thee gam
ritual (adj)	แบบพิธีกรรม	bpaep phí-thee gam
sacrifice	การบูชายัญ	gaan boo-chaa yan
superstition	ความเชื่อ	khwaam chêua
	งมงาย	ngom-ngaai
superstitious (adj)	เชื่องมงาย	chêua ngom-ngaai
afterlife	ชีวิตหลัง	chee-wít lăng
	ความตาย	khwaam dtaai
eternal life	ชีวิตอันเป็นนิรันดร์	chee-wít an bpen ní-ran

MISCELLANEOUS

249. Various useful words

background (green ~)	ฉากหลัง	chàak lăng
balance (of situation)	สมดุล	sà-má-dun
barrier (obstacle)	สิ่งกีดขวาง	sìng gèet-khwăang
base (basis)	ฐาน	thăan
beginning	จุดเริ่มต้น	jùt rêrm-dtôn
category	หมวดหมู่	mùat mòo
cause (reason)	สาเหตุ	săa-hàyt
choice	ตัวเลือก	dtua lêuak
coincidence	ความบังเอิญ	khwaam bang-ern
comfortable (~ chair)	สะดวกสบาย	sà-dùak sà-baai
comparison	การเปรียบเทียบ	gaan bprìap thîap
compensation	การชดเชย	gaan chót-choie
degree (extent, amount)	ระดับ	rá-dàp
development	การพัฒนา	gaan phát-thá-naa
difference	ความแตกต่าง	khwaam dtàek dtàang
effect (e.g., of drugs)	ผลกระทบ	phŏn grà-thóp
effort (exertion)	ความพยายาม	khwaam phá-yaa-yaam
element	องค์ประกอบ	ong bprà-gòrp
end (finish)	จบ	jòp
example (illustration)	ตัวอย่าง	dtua yàang
fact	ข้อเท็จจริง	khôr thét jing
frequent (adj)	ถี่	thèe
growth (development)	การเติบโต	gaan dtèrp dtoh
help	ความช่วยเหลือ	khwaam chûay lĕua
ideal	อุดมคติ	u-dom khá-dtì
kind (sort, type)	ประเภท	bprà-phâyt
labyrinth	เขาวงกต	khăo-wong-gòt
mistake, error	ขอผิดพลาด	khôr phìt phlâat
moment	ช่วงเวลา	chûang way-laa
object (thing)	สิ่งของ	sìng khŏrng
obstacle	อุปสรรค	u-bpà-sàk
original (original copy)	ต้นฉบับ	dtôn chà-bàp
part (~ of sth)	ส่วน	sùan
particle, small part	อนุภาค	a-nú phâak
pause (break)	การหยุดพัก	gaan yùt phák

253

position	ตำแหน่ง	dtam-nàeng
principle	หลักการ	làk gaan
problem	ปัญหา	bpan-hăa
process	กระบวนการ	grà-buan gaan
progress	ความก้าวหน้า	khwaam gâao nâa
property (quality)	คุณสมบัติ	khun-ná-sŏm-bàt
reaction	ปฏิกิริยา	bpà-dtì gì-rí-yaa
risk	ความเสี่ยง	khwaam sìang
secret	ความลับ	khwaam láp
series	ลำดับ	lam-dàp
shape (outer form)	รูปร่าง	rôop râang
situation	สถานการณ์	sà-thăan gaan
solution	ทางแก้	thaang gâe
standard (adj)	เป็นมาตรฐาน	bpen mâat-dtrà-thăan
standard (level of quality)	มาตรฐาน	mâat-dtrà-thăan
stop (pause)	การหยุด	gaan yùt
style	สไตล์	sà-dtai
system	ระบบ	rá-bòp
table (chart)	ตาราง	dtaa-raang
tempo, rate	จังหวะ	jang wà
term (word, expression)	คำ	kham
thing (object, item)	สิ่ง	sìng
truth (e.g., moment of ~)	ความจริง	khwaam jing
turn (please wait your ~)	ตา	dtaa
type (sort, kind)	ประเภท	bprà-phâyt
urgent (adj)	เร่งด่วน	râyng dùan
urgently (adv)	อย่างเร่งด่วน	yàang râyng dùan
utility (usefulness)	ความมีประโยชน์	khwaam mee bprà-yòht
variant (alternative)	ขอ	khôr
way (means, method)	วิธีทาง	wí-thĕe thaang
zone	โซน	sohn

250. Modifiers. Adjectives. Part 1

additional (adj)	เพิ่มเติม	phêrm dterm
ancient (~ civilization)	โบราณ	boh-raan
artificial (adj)	เทียม	thiam
back, rear (adj)	หลัง	lăng
bad (adj)	แย่	yâe
beautiful (~ palace)	สวย	sŭay
beautiful (person)	สวย	sŭay
big (in size)	ใหญ่	yài

bitter (taste)	ขม	khŏm
blind (sightless)	ตาบอด	dtaa bòrt
calm, quiet (adj)	สงบ	sà-ngòp
careless (negligent)	ประมาท	bprà-màat
caring (~ father)	ที่หวงใย	thêe hùang yai
central (adj)	กลาง	glaang
cheap (low-priced)	ถูก	thòok
cheerful (adj)	รื่นเริง	rêun rerng
children's (adj)	ของเด็ก	khŏrng dèk
civil (~ law)	พลเรือน	phon-lá-reuan
clandestine (secret)	ลับ	láp
clean (free from dirt)	สะอาด	sà-àat
clear (explanation, etc.)	ชัดเจน	chát jayn
clever (smart)	ฉลาด	chà-làat
close (near in space)	ใกล้	glâi
closed (adj)	ปิด	bpìt
cloudless (sky)	ไร้เมฆ	rái mâyk
cold (drink, weather)	เย็น	yen
compatible (adj)	เข้ากันได้	khâo gan dâai
contented (satisfied)	มีความสุข	mee khwaam sùk
continuous (uninterrupted)	ต่อเนื่อง	dtòr nêuang
cool (weather)	เย็น	yen
dangerous (adj)	อันตราย	an-dtà-raai
dark (room)	มืด	mêut
dead (not alive)	ตาย	dtaai
dense (fog, smoke)	หนาแน่น	nǎa nâen
destitute (extremely poor)	ยากจน	yâak jon
different (not the same)	ต่างกัน	dtàang gan
difficult (decision)	ยาก	yâak
difficult (problem, task)	ยาก	yâak
dim, faint (light)	สลัว	sà-lǔa
dirty (not clean)	สกปรก	sòk-gà-bpròk
distant (in space)	ห่างไกล	hàang glai
dry (clothes, etc.)	แห้ง	hâeng
easy (not difficult)	ง่าย	ngâai
empty (glass, room)	ว่าง	wâang
even (e.g., ~ surface)	เรียบ	rîap
exact (amount)	ถูกต้อง	thòok dtôrng
excellent (adj)	ยอดเยี่ยม	yôrt yîam
excessive (adj)	เกินขีด	gern khèet
expensive (adj)	แพง	phaeng
exterior (adj)	ภายนอก	phaai nôrk
far (the ~ East)	ไกล	glai

fast (quick)	เร็ว	reo
fatty (food)	มันๆ	man man
fertile (land, soil)	อุดมสมบูรณ์	ù-dom sŏm-boon
flat (~ panel display)	แบน	baen
foreign (adj)	ต่างชาติ	dtàang châat
fragile (china, glass)	เปราะบาง	bpròr baang
free (at no cost)	ฟรี	free
free (unrestricted)	ไม่จำกัด	mâi jam-gàt
fresh (~ water)	จืด	jèut
fresh (e.g., ~ bread)	สด	sòt
frozen (food)	แช่แข็ง	châe khăeng
full (completely filled)	เต็ม	dtem
gloomy (house, forecast)	มืดมัว	mêut mua
good (book, etc.)	ดี	dee
good, kind (kindhearted)	ดี	dee
grateful (adj)	สำนึกในบุญคุณ	sǎm-néuk nai bun khun
happy (adj)	มีความสุข	mee khwaam sùk
hard (not soft)	แข็ง	khăeng
heavy (in weight)	หนัก	nàk
hostile (adj)	เป็นศัตรู	bpen sàt-dtroo
hot (adj)	ร้อน	rórn
huge (adj)	ใหญ่	yài
humid (adj)	ชื้น	chéun
hungry (adj)	หิว	hĭw
ill (sick, unwell)	ป่วย	bpùay
immobile (adj)	ไม่ขยับ	mâi khà-yàp
important (adj)	สำคัญ	sǎm-khan
impossible (adj)	เป็นไปไม่ได้	bpen bpai mâi dâai
incomprehensible	เข้าใจไม่ได้	khâo jai mâi dâai
indispensable (adj)	จำเป็น	jam bpen
inexperienced (adj)	ขาดประสบการณ์	khàat bprà-sòp gaan
insignificant (adj)	ไม่สำคัญ	mâi sǎm-khan
interior (adj)	ภายใน	phaai nai
joint (~ decision)	รวมกัน	rûam gan
last (e.g., ~ week)	กลาย	glaai
last (final)	ท้ายสุด	tháai sùt
left (e.g., ~ side)	ซ้าย	sáai
legal (legitimate)	ทางกฎหมาย	thaang gòt mǎai
light (in weight)	เบา	bao
light (pale color)	ออน	òrn
limited (adj)	จำกัด	jam-gàt
liquid (fluid)	เหลว	lĕo
long (e.g., ~ hair)	ยาว	yaao

| loud (voice, etc.) | ดัง | dang |
| low (voice) | ต่ำ | dtàm |

251. Modifiers. Adjectives. Part 2

main (principal)	หลัก	làk
matt, matte	ด้าน	dâan
meticulous (job)	พิถีพิถัน	phí-thěe-phí-thǎn
mysterious (adj)	ลึกลับ	léuk láp
narrow (street, etc.)	แคบ	khâep

native (~ country)	ดั้งเดิม	dâng derm
nearby (adj)	ใกล้	glâi
nearsighted (adj)	สายตาสั้น	sǎai dtaa sân
needed (necessary)	จำเป็น	jam bpen
negative (~ response)	แง่ลบ	ngâe lóp

neighboring (adj)	เพื่อนบ้าน	phêuan bâan
nervous (adj)	กระวนกระวาย	grà won grà waai
new (adj)	ใหม่	mài
next (e.g., ~ week)	ถัดไป	thàt bpai

nice (agreeable)	ดี	dee
pleasant (voice)	ดี	dee
normal (adj)	ปกติ	bpòk-gà-dtì
not big (adj)	ไม่ใหญ่	mâi yài
not difficult (adj)	ไม่ยาก	mâi yâak

obligatory (adj)	จำเป็น	jam bpen
old (house)	เก่า	gào
open (adj)	เปิด	bpèrt
opposite (adj)	ตรงข้าม	dtrorng khâam

ordinary (usual)	ปกติ	bpòk-gà-dtì
original (unusual)	ดั้งเดิม	dâng derm
past (recent)	ที่ผ่านมา	thêe phàan maa
permanent (adj)	ถาวร	thǎa-won
personal (adj)	ส่วนตัว	sùan dtua

polite (adj)	สุภาพ	sù-phâap
poor (not rich)	จน	jon
possible (adj)	เป็นไปได้	bpen bpai dâai
present (current)	ปัจจุบัน	bpàt-jù-ban
previous (adj)	ก่อนหน้า	gòrn nâa

principal (main)	หลัก	làk
private (~ jet)	ส่วนบุคคล	sùan bùk-khon
probable (adj)	เป็นไปได้	bpen bpai dâai
prolonged (e.g., ~ applause)	ยาวนาน	yaao naan

public (open to all)	สาธารณะ	săa-thaa-rá-ná
punctual (person)	ตรงเวลา	dtrorng way-laa
quiet (tranquil)	เงียบ	ngîap
rare (adj)	หายาก	hăa yâak
raw (uncooked)	ดิบ	dìp
right (not left)	ขวา	khwăa
right, correct (adj)	ถูก	thòok
ripe (fruit)	สุก	sùk
risky (adj)	เสี่ยง	sìang
sad (~ look)	เศร้า	sâo
sad (depressing)	เศร้า	sâo
safe (not dangerous)	ปลอดภัย	bplòrt phai
salty (food)	เค็ม	khem
satisfied (customer)	พอใจ	phor jai
second hand (adj)	มือสอง	meu sŏrng
shallow (water)	ตื้น	dtêun
sharp (blade, etc.)	คม	khom
short (in length)	สั้น	sân
short, short-lived (adj)	มีอายุสั้น	mee aa-yú sân
significant (notable)	สำคัญ	săm-khan
similar (adj)	คล้ายคลึง	khláai khleung
simple (easy)	ง่าย	ngâai
skinny	ผอม	phŏrm
small (in size)	เล็ก	lék
smooth (surface)	เนียน	nian
soft (~ toys)	นิ่ม	nîm
solid (~ wall)	แข็ง	khăeng
sour (flavor, taste)	เปรี้ยว	bprîeow
spacious (house, etc.)	กว้างขวาง	gwâang khwăang
special (adj)	พิเศษ	phí-sàyt
straight (line, road)	ตรง	dtrorng
strong (person)	แข็งแกร่ง	khăeng gràeng
stupid (foolish)	โง่	ngôh
suitable (e.g., ~ for drinking)	ที่เหมาะสม	thêe mòr sŏm
sunny (day)	แดดแรง	dàet raeng
superb, perfect (adj)	ยอดเยี่ยม	yôrt yîam
swarthy (adj)	คล้ำ	khlám
sweet (sugary)	หวาน	wăan
tan (adj)	ผิวดำแดง	phĭw dam daeng
tasty (delicious)	อร่อย	à-ròi
tender (affectionate)	อ่อนโยน	òn yohn
the highest (adj)	สูงสุด	sŏong sùt
the most important	ที่สำคัญที่สุด	thêe săm-khan thêe sùt

the nearest	ใกล้ที่สุด	glâi thêe sùt
the same, equal (adj)	เหมือนกัน	měuan gan
thick (e.g., ~ fog)	หนา	năa
thick (wall, slice)	หนา	năa
thin (person)	ผอม	phǒrm
tight (~ shoes)	คับ	kháp
tired (exhausted)	เหนื่อย	nèuay
tiring (adj)	น่าเหนื่อยหน่าย	nâa nèuay nàai
transparent (adj)	ใส	sǎi
unclear (adj)	ไม่ชัดเจน	mâi chát jayn
unique (exceptional)	อย่างเดียว	yàang dieow
various (adj)	หลาย	lǎai
warm (moderately hot)	อุ่น	ùn
wet (e.g., ~ clothes)	เปียก	bpìak
whole (entire, complete)	ทั้งหมด	tháng mòt
wide (e.g., ~ road)	กว้าง	gwâang
young (adj)	หนุ่ม	nùm

MAIN 500 VERBS

252. Verbs A-C

to accompany (vt)	ร่วมไปด้วย	rûam bpai dûay
to accuse (vt)	กล่าวหา	glàao hǎa
to acknowledge (admit)	ยอมรับ	yorm ráp
to act (take action)	ปฏิบัติ	bpà-dtì-bàt
to add (supplement)	เพิ่ม	phêrm
to address (speak to)	พูดกับ	phôot gàp
to admire (vi)	ชมเชย	chom choie
to advertise (vt)	โฆษณา	khôht-sà-naa
to advise (vt)	แนะนำ	náe nam
to affirm (assert)	ยืนยัน	yeun yan
to agree (say yes)	เห็นด้วย	hěn dûay
to aim (to point a weapon)	เล็ง	leng
to allow (sb to do sth)	อนุญาตให้	a-nú-yâat hâi
to amputate (vt)	ตัดอวัยวะ	dtàt a-wai-wá
to answer (vi, vt)	ตอบ	dtòrp
to apologize (vi)	ขอโทษ	khǒr thôht
to appear (come into view)	ปรากฏ	bpraa-gòt
to applaud (vi, vt)	ปรบมือ	bpròp meu
to appoint (assign)	มอบหมาย	môrp mǎai
to approach (come closer)	เขาใกล	khâo glâi
to arrive (ab. train)	มาถึง	maa thěung
to ask (~ sb to do sth)	ขอ	khǒr
to aspire to ...	ปรารถนา	bpràat-thà-nǎa
to assist (help)	ช่วย	chûay
to attack (mil.)	โจมตี	johm dtee
to attain (objectives)	บรรลุ	ban-lú
to avenge (get revenge)	แก้แค้น	gâe kháen
to avoid (danger, task)	หลีกเลี่ยง	lèek lîang
to award (give medal to)	มอบรางวัล	môrp raang-wan
to battle (vi)	สู้รบ	sôo róp
to be (vi)	เป็น	bpen
to be a cause of ...	เป็นสาเหตุ...	bpen sǎa-hàyt...
to be afraid	กลัว	glua
to be angry (with ...)	โกรธ	gròht

to be at war	ทำสงคราม	tham sŏng-khraam
to be based (on …)	อิง	ing
to be bored	เบื่อ	bèua
to be convinced	ถูกโน้มน้าว	thook nóhm náao
to be enough	พอเพียง	phor phiang
to be envious	อิจฉา	ìt-chăa
to be indignant	ขุ่นเคือง	khùn kheuang
to be interested in …	สนใจ	sŏn jai
to be lost in thought	มัวแต่ครุ่นคิด	mua dtàe khrûn-khít
to be lying (~ on the table)	อยู่	yŏo
to be needed	เป็นที่ต้องการ	bpen thêe dtôrng gaan
to be perplexed (puzzled)	สับสน	sàp sŏn
to be preserved	ได้รับการรักษา	dâai ráp gaan rák-săa
to be required	มีความจำเป็น	mee khwaam jam bpen
to be surprised	ประหลาดใจ	bprà-làat jai
to be worried	กังวล	gang-won
to beat (to hit)	ตี	dtee
to become (e.g., ~ old)	กลายเป็น	glaai bpen
to behave (vi)	ประพฤติตัว	bprà-phréut dtua
to believe (think)	คิด	khít
to belong to …	เป็นของของ...	bpen khŏrng khŏrng...
to berth (moor)	จอดเรือ	jòrt reua
to blind (other drivers)	ทำให้มองไม่เห็น	tham hâi morng mâi hĕn
to blow (wind)	เป่า	bpào
to blush (vi)	หน้าแดง	nâa daeng
to boast (vi)	อวด	ùat
to borrow (money)	ขอยืม	khŏr yeum
to break (branch, toy, etc.)	ทำพัง	tham phang
to breathe (vi)	หายใจ	hăai jai
to bring (sth)	นำมา	nam maa
to burn (paper, logs)	เผา	phăo
to buy (purchase)	ซื้อ	séu
to call (~ for help)	เรียก	rîak
to call (yell for sb)	เรียก	rîak
to calm down (vt)	ทำให้...สงบ	tham hâi...sà-ngòp
can (v aux)	สามารถ	săa-mâat
to cancel (call off)	ยกเลิก	yók lêrk
to cast off (of a boat or ship)	ถอดออก	thòrt òrk
to catch (e.g., ~ a ball)	รับ	ráp
to change (~ one's opinion)	เปลี่ยน	bplìan
to change (exchange)	แลกเปลี่ยน	lâek bplìan
to charm (vt)	หวานเสน่ห์	wàan sà-này
to choose (select)	เลือก	lêuak

to chop off (with an ax)	ตัดออก	dtàt òrk
to clean (e.g., kettle from scale)	ทำความสะอาด	tham khwaam sà-àat
to clean (shoes, etc.)	ทำความสะอาด	tham khwaam sà-àat
to clean up (tidy)	จัดระเบียบ	jàt rá-bìap
to close (vt)	ปิด	bpìt
to comb one's hair	หวีผม	wěe phǒm
to come down (the stairs)	ลง	long
to come out (book)	ออกวางจำหน่าย	òrk waang jam-nàai
to compare (vt)	เปรียบเทียบ	bprìap thîap
to compensate (vt)	ชดเชย	chót-choie
to compete (vi)	แข่งขัน	khàeng khǎn
to compile (~ a list)	รวบรวม	rûap ruam
to complain (vi, vt)	บ่น	bòn
to complicate (vt)	ทำให้...ซับซ้อน	tham hâi...sáp són
to compose (music, etc.)	แต่ง	dtàeng
to compromise (reputation)	ทำให้...เสียเกียรติ	tham hâi...sǐa gìat
to concentrate (vi)	ตั้งสมาธิ	dtâng sà-maa-thí
to confess (criminal)	สารภาพ	sǎa-rá-phâap
to confuse (mix up)	สับสน	sàp sǒn
to congratulate (vt)	แสดงความยินดี	sà-daeng khwaam yin dee
to consult (doctor, expert)	ปรึกษา	bprèuk-sǎa
to continue (~ to do sth)	ดำเนินการต่อ	dam-nern gaan dtòr
to control (vt)	ควบคุม	khûap khum
to convince (vt)	โน้มน้าว	nóhm náao
to cooperate (vi)	รวมมือ	rûam meu
to coordinate (vt)	ประสานงาน	bprà-sǎan ngaan
to correct (an error)	แก้ไข	gâe khǎi
to cost (vt)	มีราคา	mee raa-khaa
to count (money, etc.)	นับ	náp
to count on ...	พึ่งพา	phêung phaa
to crack (ceiling, wall)	แตก	dtàek
to create (vt)	สร้าง	sâang
to crush, to squash (~ a bug)	บี้	bêe
to cry (weep)	ร้องไห้	rórng hâi
to cut off (with a knife)	ตัดออก	dtàt òrk

253. Verbs D-G

to dare (~ to do sth)	กล้า	glâa
to date from ...	มาตั้งแต่...	maa dtâng dtàe...

to deceive (vi, vt)	หลอก	lòrk
to decide (~ to do sth)	ตัดสินใจ	dtàt sǐn jai
to decorate (tree, street)	ตกแต่ง	dtòk dtàeng
to dedicate (book, etc.)	อุทิศ	u thít
to defend (a country, etc.)	ปกป้อง	bpòk bpôrng
to defend oneself	ปกป้อง	bpòk bpôrng
to demand (request firmly)	เรียกร้อง	rîak rórng
to denounce (vt)	ประณาม	bprà-naam
to deny (vt)	ปฏิเสธ	bpà-dtì-sàyt
to depend on …	พึ่งพา…	phêung phaa…
to deprive (vt)	ตัด	dtàt
to deserve (vt)	สมควรได้รับ	sǒm khuan dâai ráp
to design (machine, etc.)	ออกแบบ	òrk bàep
to desire (want, wish)	ปรารถนา	bpràat-thà-nǎa
to despise (vt)	รังเกียจ	rang gìat
to destroy (documents, etc.)	ทำลาย	tham laai
to differ (from sth)	แตกต่าง	dtàek dtàang
to dig (tunnel, etc.)	ขุด	khùt
to direct (point the way)	บอกทาง	bòrk thaang
to disappear (vi)	หายไป	hǎai bpai
to discover (new land, etc.)	คนพบ	khón phóp
to discuss (vt)	หารือ	hǎa-reu
to distribute (leaflets, etc.)	แจกจ่าย	jàek jàai
to disturb (vt)	รบกวน	róp guan
to dive (vi)	ดำ	dam
to divide (math)	หาร	hǎan
to do (vt)	ทำ	tham
to do the laundry	ซักผ้า	sák phâa
to double (increase)	เพิ่มเป็นสองเท่า	phêrm bpen sǒrng thâo
to doubt (have doubts)	สงสัย	sǒng-sǎi
to draw a conclusion	สรุป	sà-rùp
to dream (daydream)	ฝัน	fǎn
to dream (in sleep)	ฝัน	fǎn
to drink (vi, vt)	ดื่ม	dèum
to drive a car	ขับรถ	khàp rót
to drive away (scare away)	ไล่ไป	lâi bpai
to drop (let fall)	ทำให้…ตก	tham hâi…dtòk
to drown (ab. person)	จมน้ำ	jom náam
to dry (clothes, hair)	ทำให้…แห้ง	tham hâi…hâeng
to eat (vi, vt)	กิน	gin
to eavesdrop (vi)	ลอบฟัง	lôrp fang

to emit (diffuse - odor, etc.)	ปล่อย	bplòi
to enjoy oneself	มีความสุข	mee khwaam sùk
to enter (on the list)	เขียน...ใส่	khĭan...sài
to enter (room, house, etc.)	เขา	khâo
to entertain (amuse)	ทำให้รื่นเริง	thám hâi rêun rerng
to equip (fit out)	ติด	dtìt
to examine (proposal)	ตรวจสอบ	dtrùat sòrp
to exchange (sth)	แลกเปลี่ยน	lâek bplìan
to excuse (forgive)	ให้อภัย	hâi a-phai
to exist (vi)	มีอยู่	mee yòo
to expect (anticipate)	คาดหวัง	khâat wăng
to expect (foresee)	คาดหวัง	khâat wăng
to expel (from school, etc.)	ไล่ออก	lâi òrk
to explain (vt)	อธิบาย	à-thí-baai
to express (vt)	แสดงออก	sà-daeng òrk
to extinguish (a fire)	ดับ	dàp
to fall in love (with …)	ตกหลุมรัก	dtòk lŭm rák
to feed (provide food)	ให้อาหาร	hâi aa-hăan
to fight (against the enemy)	สู้	sôo
to fight (vi)	สู้	sôo
to fill (glass, bottle)	เติมให้เต็ม	dterm hâi dtem
to find (~ lost items)	คนหา	khón hăa
to finish (vt)	จบ	jòp
to fish (angle)	จับปลา	jàp bplaa
to fit (ab. dress, etc.)	เหมาะ	mò
to flatter (vt)	ชม	chom
to fly (bird, plane)	บิน	bin
to follow … (come after)	ไปตาม...	bpai dtaam...
to forbid (vt)	ห้าม	hâam
to force (compel)	บังคับ	bang-kháp
to forget (vi, vt)	ลืม	leum
to forgive (pardon)	ยกโทษให้	yók thôht hâi
to form (constitute)	ก่อตั้ง	gòr dtâng
to get dirty (vi)	สกปรก	sòk-gà-bpròk
to get infected (with …)	ติดเชื้อ	dtìt chéua
to get irritated	หงุดหงิด	ngùt-ngìt
to get married	แต่งงาน	dtàeng ngaan
to get rid of …	กำจัด...	gam-jàt...
to get tired	เหนื่อย	nèuay
to get up (arise from bed)	ลุกขึ้น	lúk khêun

| to give (vt) | ให้ | hâi |
| to give a bath (to bath) | อาบน้ำให้ | àap náam hâi |

to give a hug, to hug (vt)	กอด	gòrt
to give in (yield to)	ยอม	yorm
to glimpse (vt)	เหลือบมอง	lèuap morng
to go (by car, etc.)	ไป	bpai

to go (on foot)	ไป	bpai
to go for a swim	ว่ายน้ำ	wâai náam
to go out (for dinner, etc.)	ออกไป	òrk bpai
to go to bed (go to sleep)	ไปนอน	bpai norn

to greet (vt)	ทักทาย	thák thaai
to grow (plants)	ปลูก	bplòok
to guarantee (vt)	รับประกัน	ráp bprà-gan
to guess (the answer)	คาดเดา	khâat dao

254. Verbs H-M

to hand out (distribute)	แจกจ่าย	jàek jàai
to hang (curtains, etc.)	แขวน	khwǎen
to have (vt)	มี	mee
to have a try	ลอง	lorng
to have breakfast	ทานอาหารเช้า	thaan aa-hǎan cháo

to have dinner	ทานอาหารเย็น	thaan aa-hǎan yen
to have lunch	ทานอาหารเที่ยง	thaan aa-hǎan thîang
to head (group, etc.)	นำ	nam
to hear (vt)	ได้ยิน	dâai yin
to heat (vt)	อุ่นให้ร้อน	ùn hâi rórn

to help (vt)	ช่วย	chûay
to hide (vt)	ซ่อน	sôrn
to hire (e.g., ~ a boat)	จ้าง	jâang
to hire (staff)	จ้าง	jâang
to hope (vi, vt)	หวัง	wǎng

to hunt (for food, sport)	ล่าหา	lâa hǎa
to hurry (vi)	รีบ	rêep
to imagine (to picture)	มีจินตนาการ	mee jin-dtà-naa gaan
to imitate (vt)	เลียนแบบ	lian bàep
to implore (vt)	ขอร้อง	khǒr rórng
to import (vt)	นำเข้า	nam khâo
to increase (vi)	เพิ่ม	phêrm
to increase (vt)	เพิ่ม	phêrm
to infect (vt)	ทำให้ติดเชื้อ	tham hâi dtìt chéua
to influence (vt)	มีอิทธิพล	mee ìt-thí phon
to inform (e.g., ~ the police about)	แจ้ง	jâeng

to inform (vt)	แจ้ง	jâeng
to inherit (vt)	รับมรดก	ráp mor-rá-dòrk
to inquire (about …)	สอบถาม	sòrp thǎam
to insert (put in)	สอดใส่	sòrt sài
to insinuate (imply)	พูดเป็นนัย	phôot bpen nai
to insist (vi, vt)	ยืนยัน	yeun yan
to inspire (vt)	บันดาลใจ	ban-daan jai
to instruct (teach)	สอน	sǒrn
to insult (offend)	ดูถูก	doo thòok
to interest (vt)	ทำให้...สนใจ	tham hâi...sǒn jai
to intervene (vi)	แทรกแซง	sâek saeng
to introduce (sb to sb)	แนะนำ	náe nam
to invent (machine, etc.)	ประดิษฐ์	bprà-dìt
to invite (vt)	เชิญ	chern
to iron (clothes)	รีด	rêet
to irritate (annoy)	ทำให้...รำคาญ	tham hâi...ram-khaan
to isolate (vt)	แยก
แยก	yâek
to join (political party, etc.)	เขารวมใน	khâo rûam nai
to joke (be kidding)	ล้อเล่น	lór lên
to keep (old letters, etc.)	เก็บ	gèp
to keep silent, to hush	นิ่งเงียบ	nîng ngîap
to kill (vt)	ฆ่า	khâa
to knock (on the door)	เคาะ	khór
to know (sb)	รู้จัก	róo jàk
to know (sth)	รู้	róo
to laugh (vi)	หัวเราะ	hǔa rór
to launch (start up)	เปิด	bpèrt
to leave (~ for Mexico)	ออกเดินทาง	òrk dern thaang
to leave (forget sth)	ลืมฺ	leum
to leave (spouse)	หยา	yàa
to liberate (city, etc.)	ปลดปล่อย	bplòt bplòi
to lie (~ on the floor)	นอน	norn
to lie (tell untruth)	โกหก	goh-hòk
to light (campfire, etc.)	จุดไฟ	jùt fai
to light up (illuminate)	ทำให้สว่าง	tham hâi sà-wàang
to like (I like …)	ชอบ	chôrp
to limit (vt)	จำกัด	jam-gàt
to listen (vi)	ฟัง	fang
to live (~ in France)	อยู่อาศัย	yòo aa-sǎi
to live (exist)	มีชีวิต	mee chee-wít
to load (gun)	ใส่กระสุน	sài grà-sǔn
to load (vehicle, etc.)	ขนของ	khǒn khǒrng
to look (I'm just ~ing)	มองดู	morng doo
to look for … (search)	หา	hǎa

to look like (resemble)	เหมือน	mĕuan
to lose (umbrella, etc.)	ทำหาย	tham hăai
to love (e.g., ~ dancing)	ชอบ	chôrp

to love (sb)	รัก	rák
to lower (blind, head)	ลด	lót
to make (~ dinner)	ทำ	tham
to make a mistake	ทำผิดพลาด	tham phìt phlâat
to make angry	ทำให้...โกรธ	tham hâi...gròht

to make easier	ทำให้...ง่ายขึ้น	tham hâi...ngâai khêun
to make multiple copies	ถ่ายสำเนา หลายฉบับ	thàai săm-nao lăai chà-bàp
to make the acquaintance	ทำความรู้จัก	tham khwaam róo jàk
to make use (of ...)	ใช้	chái
to manage, to run	จัดการ	jàt gaan

to mark (make a mark)	ทำเครื่องหมาย	tham khrêuang măai
to mean (signify)	บงบอก	bòng bòrk
to memorize (vt)	จดจำ	jòt jam
to mention (talk about)	กล่าวถึง	glàao thĕung
to miss (school, etc.)	พลาด	phlâat

to mix (combine, blend)	ผสม	phà-sŏm
to mock (make fun of)	เยาะเย้ย	yór-yóie
to move (to shift)	ยาย	yáai
to multiply (math)	คูณ	khoon
must (v aux)	ต้อง	dtôrng

255. Verbs N-R

to name, to call (vt)	เรียก	rîak
to negotiate (vi)	เจรจา	jayn-rá-jaa
to note (write down)	จดโน้ต	jòt nóht
to notice (see)	สังเกต	săng-gàyt

to obey (vi, vt)	เชื่อฟัง	chêua fang
to object (vi, vt)	คาน	kháan
to observe (see)	สังเกตการณ์	săng-gàyt gaan
to offend (vt)	ลวงเกิน	lûang gern
to omit (word, phrase)	เว้น	wén

to open (vt)	เปิด	bpèrt
to order (in restaurant)	สั่งอาหาร	sàng aa-hăan
to order (mil.)	สั่งการ	sàng gaan
to organize (concert, party)	จัด	jàt
to overestimate (vt)	ตีค่าสูงเกิน	dtee khâa sŏong gern

| to own (possess) | เป็นเจ้าของ | bpen jâo khŏrng |
| to participate (vi) | มีส่วนรวม | mee sùan rûam |

to pass through (by car, etc.)	ผ่าน	phàan
to pay (vi, vt)	จ่าย	jàai
to peep, spy on	แอบดู	àep doo
to penetrate (vt)	แทรกซึม	sâek seum
to permit (vt)	อนุญาต	a-nú-yâat
to pick (flowers)	เก็บ	gèp
to place (put, set)	วาง	waang
to plan (~ to do sth)	วางแผน	waang phǎen
to play (actor)	เล่นบท	lên bòt
to play (children)	เล่น	lên
to point (~ the way)	ชี้	chée
to pour (liquid)	ริน	rin
to pray (vi, vt)	ภาวนา	phaa-wá-naa
to prefer (vt)	ชอบ	chôrp
to prepare (~ a plan)	เตรียม	dtriam
to present (sb to sb)	แนะนำ	náe nam
to preserve (peace, life)	รักษา	rák-sǎa
to prevail (vt)	ชนะ	chá-ná
to progress (move forward)	คืบหน้า	khêup nâa
to promise (vt)	สัญญา	sǎn-yaa
to pronounce (vt)	ออกเสียง	òrk sǐang
to propose (vt)	เสนอ	sà-něr
to protect (e.g., ~ nature)	ปกป้อง	bpòk bpôrng
to protest (vi)	ประท้วง	bprà-thúang
to prove (vt)	พิสูจน์	phí-sòot
to provoke (vt)	ยั่วยุ	yûa yú
to pull (~ the rope)	ดึง	deung
to punish (vt)	ลงโทษ	long thôht
to push (~ the door)	ผลัก	phlàk
to put away (vt)	เก็บที่	gèp thêe
to put in order	จัดเรียง	jàt riang
to put, to place	วาง	waang
to quote (cite)	อ้างอิง	âang ing
to reach (arrive at)	ไปถึง	bpai thěung
to read (vi, vt)	อ่าน	àan
to realize (a dream)	ทำให้...เป็นจริง	tham hâi...bpen jing
to recognize (identify sb)	จดจำ	jòt jam
to recommend (vt)	แนะนำ	náe nam
to recover (~ from flu)	ฟื้นตัว	féun dtua
to redo (do again)	ทำซ้ำ	tham sám
to reduce (speed, etc.)	ลด	lót

to refuse (~ sb)	ปฏิเสธ	bpà-dtì-sàyt
to regret (be sorry)	เสียใจ	sĭa jai
to reinforce (vt)	เสริม	sĕrm
to remember (Do you ~ me?)	จำ	jam
to remember (I can't ~ her name)	จำ	jam
to remind of ...	นึกถึง	néuk thĕung
to remove (~ a stain)	ล้างออก	láang òrk
to remove (~ an obstacle)	กำจัด	gam-jàt
to rent (sth from sb)	เช่า	châo
to repair (mend)	ซ่อม	sôrm
to repeat (say again)	พูดซ้ำ	phôot sám
to report (make a report)	รายงาน	raai ngaan
to reproach (vt)	ตำหนิ	dtam-nì
to reserve, to book	จอง	jorng
to restrain (hold back)	ยับยั้ง	yáp yáng
to return (come back)	กลับ	glàp
to risk, to take a risk	เสี่ยง	sìang
to rub out (erase)	ขัดออก	khàt òrk
to run (move fast)	วิ่ง	wîng
to rush (hurry sb)	รีบ	rêep

256. Verbs S-W

to satisfy (please)	ทำให้...พอใจ	tham hâi...phor jai
to save (rescue)	ช่วยชีวิต	chûay chee-wít
to say (~ thank you)	พูด	phôot
to scold (vt)	ดุว่า	dù wâa
to scratch (with claws)	ข่วน	khùan
to select (to pick)	เลือก	lêuak
to sell (goods)	ขาย	khăai
to send (a letter)	ส่ง	sòng
to send back (vt)	ส่งคืน	sòng kheun
to sense (~ danger)	รับรู้	ráp róo
to sentence (vt)	พิพากษา	phí-phâak-săa
to serve (in restaurant)	เซิร์ฟ	sêrf
to settle (a conflict)	ยุติ	yút-dtì
to shake (vt)	เขย่า	khà-yào
to shave (vi)	โกน	gohn
to shine (gleam)	ส่องแสง	sòrng săeng
to shiver (with cold)	หนาวสั่น	năao sàn
to shoot (vi)	ยิง	ying

269

to shout (vi)	ตะโกน	dtà-gohn
to show (to display)	แสดง	sà-daeng
to shudder (vi)	สั่น	sàn
to sigh (vi)	ถอนหายใจ	thŏrn hăai-jai
to sign (document)	ลงนาม	long naam
to signify (mean)	บงบอก	bòng bòrk
to simplify (vt)	ทำให้ง่ายขึ้น,	tham hâi ngâai khêun
to sin (vi)	ทำบาป	tham bàap
to sit (be sitting)	นั่ง	nâng
to sit down (vi)	นั่ง	nâng
to smell (emit an odor)	มีกลิ่น	mee glìn
to smell (inhale the odor)	ดมกลิ่น	dom glìn
to smile (vi)	ยิ้ม	yím
to snap (vi, ab. rope)	ขาด	khàat
to solve (problem)	แก้ไข	gâe khǎi
to sow (seed, crop)	หว่าน	wàan
to spill (liquid)	ทำให้...หก	tham hâi...hòk
to spill out, scatter (flour, etc.)	หก	hòk
to spit (vi)	ถุย	thǔi
to stand (toothache, cold)	ทน	thon
to start (begin)	เริ่ม	rêrm
to steal (money, etc.)	ขโมย	khà-moi
to stop (for pause, etc.)	หยุด	yùt
to stop (please ~ calling me)	หยุด	yùt
to stop talking	หยุดพูด	yùt phôot
to stroke (caress)	ลูบ	lôop
to study (vt)	เรียน	rian
to suffer (feel pain)	ทรมาน	thor-rá-maan
to support (cause, idea)	สนับสนุน	sà-nàp-sà-nǔn
to suppose (assume)	สมมติ	sǒm mút
to surface (ab. submarine)	ขึ้นมาที่ผิวน้ำ	khêun maa thêe phĭw náam
to surprise (amaze)	ทำให้...ประหลาดใจ	tham hâi...bprà-làat jai
to suspect (vt)	สงสัย	sǒng-sǎi
to swim (vi)	ว่ายน้ำ	wâai náam
to take (get hold of)	เอา	ao
to take a bath	อาบน้ำ	àap náam
to take a rest	พัก	phák
to take away (e.g., about waiter)	เอาไป	ao bpai
to take off (airplane)	บินขึ้น	bin khêun

to take off (painting, curtains, etc.)	เอาออก	ao òrk
to take pictures	ถ่ายภาพ	thàai phâap
to talk to …	คุยกับ	khui gàp
to teach (give lessons)	สอน	sǒrn
to tear off, to rip off (vt)	ฉีก	chèek
to tell (story, joke)	เล่า	lâo
to thank (vt)	แสดงความขอบคุณ	sà-daeng khwaam khòrp kun
to think (believe)	เชื่อ	chêua
to think (vi, vt)	คิด	khít
to threaten (vt)	ขู่	khòo
to throw (stone, etc.)	ขว้าง	khwâang
to tie to …	ผูกกับ...	phòok gàp...
to tie up (prisoner)	มัด	mát
to tire (make tired)	ทำให้...เหนื่อย	tham hâi...nèuay
to touch (one's arm, etc.)	สัมผัส	sǎm-phàt
to tower (over …)	ทำให้...สูงเหนือ	tham hâi...sǒong nĕua
to train (animals)	ฝึก	fèuk
to train (sb)	ฝึก	fèuk
to train (vi)	ฝึก	fèuk
to transform (vt)	เปลี่ยนแปลง	bplìan bplaeng
to translate (vt)	แปล	bplae
to treat (illness)	รักษา	rák-sǎa
to trust (vt)	เชื่อ	chêua
to try (attempt)	พยายาม	phá-yaa-yaam
to turn (e.g., ~ left)	เลี้ยว	líeow
to turn away (vi)	มวนหน้า	múan nâa
to turn off (the light)	ปิด	bpìt
to turn on (computer, etc.)	เปิด	bpèrt
to turn over (stone, etc.)	พลิก	phlík
to underestimate (vt)	ดูถูก	doo thòok
to underline (vt)	ขีดเส้นใต้	khèt sên dtâi
to understand (vt)	เข้าใจ	khâo jai
to undertake (vt)	ดำเนินการ	dam-nern gaan
to unite (vt)	ทำให้...รวมกัน	tham hâi...ruam gan
to untie (vt)	แก้มัด	gâe mát
to use (phrase, word)	ใช้	chái
to vaccinate (vt)	ฉีดวัคซีน	chèet wák-seen
to vote (vi)	ลงคะแนน	long khá-naen
to wait (vt)	รอ	ror
to wake (sb)	ปลุกให้ตื่น	bplùk hâi dtèun
to want (wish, desire)	ต้องการ	dtôrng gaan

271

to warn (of the danger)	เตือน	dteuan
to wash (clean)	ล้าง	láang
to water (plants)	รดน้ำ	rót náam
to wave (the hand)	โบกมือ	bòhk meu
to weigh (have weight)	มีน้ำหนัก	mee nám nàk
to work (vi)	ทำงาน	tham ngaan
to worry (make anxious)	ทำให้...เป็นห่วง	tham hâi...bpen hùang
to worry (vi)	เป็นห่วง	bpen hùang
to wrap (parcel, etc.)	ห่อ	hòr
to wrestle (sport)	มวยปล้ำ	muay bplâm
to write (vt)	เขียน	khǐan
to write down	จด	jòt

www.ingramcontent.com/pod-product-compliance
Lightning Source LLC
Chambersburg PA
CBHW071318090426
42738CB00012B/2722